School Violence in Context

Culture, Neighborhood, Family, School, and Gender

Rami Benbenishty and Ron Avi Astor

OXFORD
UNIVERSITY PRESS

2005

OXFORD
UNIVERSITY PRESS

Oxford   New York
Auckland   Bangkok   Buenos Aires   Cape Town   Chennai
Dar es Salaam   Delhi   Hong Kong   Istanbul   Karachi   Kolkata
Kuala Lumpur   Madrid   Melbourne   Mexico City   Mumbai   Nairobi
São Paulo   Shanghai   Taipei   Tokyo   Toronto

Published by Oxford University Press, Inc.
198 Madison Avenue, New York, New York 10016

www.oup.com

Oxford is a registered trademark of Oxford University Press

Library of Congress Cataloging-in-Publication Data
Benbenishty, Rami.
School violence in context : culture, neighborhood, family, school, and gender / Rami
Benbenishty & Ron Avi Astor.
p. cm.
Summary: "Draws on surveys comparing Jewish and Arab-Israeli students with students in
the United States. Presents an empirically-based model for understanding school violence,
highlighting both universal and culturally specific patterns of school violence"—Provided
by publisher.
Includes bibliographical references.
ISBN-13 978-0-19-515780-2
ISBN 0-19-515780-X (hardcover : alk. paper)
1. School violence—Social aspects—Israel—Case studies.   2. School violence—Social
aspects—United States—Case studies.   3. School violence—Cross-cultural studies.   I.
Asòtor, Ron.   II. Title.
LB3013.34.I75B465 2005
371.7'82—dc22   2004023054

9 8 7 6 5 4 3 2 1

Printed in the United States of America
on acid-free paper

This book is dedicated to all schoolchildren and educators in the world.
May peace be with you.

Foreword

We have all witnessed the consequences of missed signals or indications of trouble, the reaction of disbelief, and the damaging, often tragic consequences of school violence. Dr. Rami Benbenishty and Dr. Ron Astor's *School Violence in Context: Culture, Neighborhood, Family, School, and Gender* offers an in-depth, intellectual look at how violence presents in a school setting, factors that contribute to violence, and how the information presented may be transferable across cultures and national boundaries.

In the United States, it seemed for a time as if school violence were the only topic on the national news. Americans were shocked but fascinated. Due in part to the media attention and the sheer magnitude of some of the episodes, the American public was no longer lulled into thinking that violence took place only in inner-city schools, in a drug deal gone wrong, or among rival gang members. Suddenly, rage had no color, no location, no community, no socioeconomic ties. Fear knew no boundaries. Bullying had an effect more serious than the loss of some lunch money. The country woke up to the seriousness of violence among its youth in their schools.

Sensationalistic media coverage of high-profile acts soon gave way to a sort of acceptance, perhaps even apathy. However, just because there are no images of children flooding out of a school building to escape the horrors inside doesn't mean that school violence has been eliminated. School violence is not just a picture of shooting victims on the 6 o'clock news, it is also real-life assault, sexual harassment, rape, and intimidation. Continuing incidents across the nation attest to the fact that this is a critical issue facing our children, their parents, our teachers, and our society.

The violence among youth that we experience in the United States tends to be a consequence of alienation. Youth who are disenfranchised, discounted, frustrated, or fearful strike back against those whom they perceive to be the oppressors. Conversely, Americans, unlike citizens in many countries, are rarely exposed to daily incidents of violence as a consequence of war. The same media outlets that looped continuous coverage of school shootings sanitize or guard us against the horrific images other nations are exposed to firsthand, war being an unavoidable part of their everyday life.

One such nation experiencing ongoing unrest is Israel. Arab and Jewish communities in Israel each have their own culture, their own identity, and their own schools, all in a comparatively small geographic area. The continuing turmoil often heightens the sensitivity to their differences rather than magnifying their similarities. It is the commonalties and uniquenesses of these cultures that provided Drs. Astor and Benbenishty an unprecedented opportunity to study the effects of school violence on Israeli youth, who exist together in one nation yet are apart in belief and culture.

Drs. Astor and Benbenishty forged new research territory when they responded to the call from the Israeli government to more closely investigate violence in the nation's schools. Although organizationally dedicated to both preventing and confronting incidents, the government did not truly have the up-to-date and accurate data needed to inform and advise about the state of violent incidents and interventions in the schools or what issues needed to be addressed. In response to this call, Astor and Benbenishty conceived of a large-scale, comprehensive, cross-cultural study of Israel's schools, in which they would examine the experiences and attitudes of the three distinct cultures of Israel: Arabs, secular Jews, and Orthodox Jews—the first national study to include these groups.

Astor and Benbenishty approached the study with a distinct insight and a well-designed and thoughtful methodology: Using a "contextual nesting" approach to examine violence where it occurs, teachers, students, and administrators were all surveyed, all forms of school violence were assessed, and a hypothesis was rendered and subsequently tested against empirical evidence. Benbenishty and Astor asked vital questions: To what extent does culture factor into school violence? Does gender, either of the offender or the victim, matter? What role does the social hierarchy inherent in all schools play? What effect does parenting have on offenders and victims? Does the school context perpetuate or shield students from violence? They subsequently offer conclusions rich in theory and epidemiology and firmly based on solid and credible data on the determinants of school violence.

Do not make the mistake of thinking this book is only about the Arab-Jewish conflict, or that the research does not translate to other countries or cultures. Astor and Benbenishty refer to the "transferability of theory," the identification of universal variables that can apply equally to schools in Colorado, Michigan, and Japan. This research, in fact, has the potential to have a far-reaching effect on future exploration into the areas of culture, victimization, and acts of violence, whether by serving as a model or as a comparison.

Presented in a way that is accessible to anyone who is in the position to understand or prevent school violence, the information contained in this book is essential for social workers, educators, psychologists, sociologists, and those in the field of public health as they approach the considerable task of defining, identifying, and dealing with violence in an educational system. In addition to practitioners, researchers and policymakers should take note of the authors' conclusions as they approach new and more effective solutions to the threat of school violence. In their thorough treatment of the subject, the authors have built a solid foundation on which educators, parents, students, and other professionals can base their discussion and plans to address the problems and together work toward a meaningful educational experience for all involved.

Paula Allen-Mears, PhD
Dean and Norma Radin Collegiate Professor of Social Work
University of Michigan School of Social Work
Ann Arbor, Michigan

Acknowledgments

First, we want to thank the students, teachers, principals, superintendents, and the Israeli Ministry of Education for their active participation in this project. Analyses and sections of this book have been published in numerous academic journals and as scholarly chapters, foundation reports, grants, and national Israeli reports. Our co-authors on these other publications have been Anat Zeira, Amiram Vinokur, Mona Khoury-Kassabari, Ronald O. Pitner, Muhammad Haj-Yahia, Roxana Marachi, Heather Ann Meyer, Ilan Roziner, Mark Weisman, and Suzanne Perkins-Hart. We have learned from each of our collaborators and thank them for their contributions. We also thank Anat Zeira, Michelle Rosemond, Susan Stone, Jikang Chen, Giovanni Arteaga, and Dianne Shammas for reading drafts of this manuscript and providing valuable feedback.

We'd like to acknowledge the countless committee reviewers in the Israeli Ministry of Education and at the University of Michigan, the anonymous reviewers of all our peer-reviewed manuscripts, and the countless graduate students and colleagues not mentioned who gave us advice throughout the project. For support of this project, we thank the Israeli Ministry of Education, the Office of the Chief Scientist (especially Nora Cohen and Zmira Mevarech), the Hebrew University, the University of Michigan, the University of Southern California, the W. K. Kellogg Foundation, the Spencer Foundation, the National Academy of Education, the Fulbright Foundation, the city of Herzliya, and the William T. Grant Foundation.

Thanks to our many friends and academic peers who have been patient with us during the countless hours we engaged in deep deliberations conducting this study and writing the book. Special thanks go to Peter K. Smith, whose work has influenced our thinking. Professor Smith has taught us so much about school violence in Europe and globally. Special thanks to Mike Furlong, who not only generously shared with us his ideas, instruments, and insights but also allowed us to use his

U.S. database, which helped illuminate some of the more important issues in the book. It is on this kind of sharing that scientific progress is based.

Most important, we'd like to thank our wonderful family members, who endured the many years, hours, days, and minutes that this project consumed. In Israel, Ruthy, Inbar, Rowee, Amit, Yaara, and Mocca deserve our gratitude and thanks; in the United States, Gina, Sheva, Maya, Roee, Shachar, and Carmi. The thoughts, support, feedback, love, ideas, pride, enthusiasm, and company of family and friends were the key ingredients in allowing us to pursue this work.

We wish to note that the order of authorship does not signify the level of contribution to this book. We contributed equally to the intellectual development of ideas presented and in all other aspects of the book. We have been good friends and close colleagues for many years. It is through our friendship and continual collaboration that the ideas in this book emerged.

Preface:
Exploring the Meaning of School Violence
in Geopolitical Conflict

It is virtually impossible to live in the Middle East and be unaffected by geopolitical violence. This morning CNN, the *New York Times*, and most other international media outlets reported the capture of yet another terror cell that was planning to commit another tragedy against innocents. For the past few years there have been almost weekly, if not daily, tragic losses of innocent Jewish and Arab children's lives due to political violence. Adding to the existing stress, while this book was being written, the United States was conducting a massive war in Iraq. Early in the war, the Israeli Jewish and Arab public were concerned about possible use of biological or chemical weapons by Iraq; every family in Israel was issued gas masks and biological weapon kits, and each house prepared a special room in the event of a chemical weapon attack. The continual painful images of victims portrayed by the media following a terror attack permeate the daily emotional and psychological lives of all children who are potential targets of political violence. Suffice it to say that in Israel, terrorism and war are constant variables in the psyche of each individual.

Now, this societal concern about terrorism and random political violence extends beyond Israel. It seems as though most of the Western world is living in a post-9/11 awareness that peace and safety are intermittent and fleeting qualities—that politically motivated terrorism can impinge on the day-to-day lives of people anywhere and everywhere. Clearly, we live in a globally dangerous era, and there is heightened awareness that the terror threats are real.

Nevertheless, coexisting with this heightened awareness and almost paradoxically, the day-to-day lives of most children and the interpersonal transactions in families and schools (at least at the most proximal levels) do not always mirror the horrid images seen in the media, even in the most threatening and seemingly dire geopolitical climates, such as the Middle East. For example, today, after hearing the lachrymose CNN report about potential chemical attacks from Arab countries on

Israel, I (Astor) went on a long neighborhood walk (in Reut, Israel, less than one mile from the border with the West Bank) and observed hundreds of ordinary-looking students walking to school, taking buses, and discussing their personal events of the day concerning family, friends, and teachers. I have also observed this in schools in Israel during high-tension political periods.

In many ways, Israeli schools and the students in them continue to function with day-to-day routines and transactions similar to those in California or Michigan. The students' behaviors are connected to their relationships with other students and with life in the school itself. The images of student interactions with teachers and other students are strikingly similar to those I observed in Los Angeles and Ann Arbor a few weeks and months earlier.

Even in our (Astor's and Benbenishty's) respective families, our school-age children are keenly aware of political events, yet they are emotionally and socially heavily involved with the life and interactions in their schools and associated peer groups and school-oriented events. For example, this past weekend, both our teenage daughters (one in the United States and the other in Israel) spent the vast majority of their time at friends' houses, at sleepovers, talking to friends on the phone, attending informal youth gatherings and formal youth groups, participating in sports events, doing homework, complaining vociferously about specific teachers or classes at school, and talking—in great detail—about their relationships with other students.

Coming from the United States and given the tragic images of the political crisis in the Middle East, I was struck by the extent to which Israeli teenagers are socially interwoven, active, and involved when compared to their U.S. counterparts. I expected a more concerned and constrained peer social environment similar to the one I experienced in the United States shortly after 9/11. Instead, on Friday night, I observed scores of students out in the streets, socializing with their friends and hanging out until the early hours of the next day.

Ironically, although the threat of terrorism-related violence is real in Israel, the threat of random violence due to crime is relatively low. Thus, at face value, the students in Israel appeared socially freer, in many respects, than their U.S. counterparts. In any case, it seems possible that in both cultures the dominating influences revolve around the proximal relationships students have in the contexts of family, school, and peer group.

This does not imply that children and youth don't have concerns or stresses about geopolitical violence. Clearly, we know they are worried and stressed about potential violence directed at them or their group. We know that there are children in high-violence war zones whose lives are thrown into turmoil by geopolitical conflict. However, the vast majority of students in the United States and Israel (Jewish and Arab) are not going to school in these environments. Many, if not all, of the images seen on Western television occur in specific locations in the West Bank and Gaza. A comparable U.S. situation was the Washington, D.C., sniper shootings. We are certain that the sniper shootings affected thousands of students who attended schools in the targeted areas. How did these widely publicized acts of terror, shown continually on CNN and other news channels, affect the school behavior in Kansas City, Philadelphia, Los Angeles, Boston, Seattle, Tampa, New Haven, Ann Arbor, and Phoenix? How did the bombing of the World Trade Center or the Murra Federal Building in Oklahoma affect students' school behaviors in areas not immediately targeted by the terror acts?

As researchers, we are not entirely clear if or how school violence rates were influenced by any of these U.S. events. From an empirical perspective, it is not directly obvious how geopolitical events impact students' daily transactions with peers, teachers, and family members. Perhaps fears are most evident in settings that have a higher likelihood of violence (on the bus or other forms of public transportation, in malls or shopping centers, driving though dangerous areas, in restaurants, and with air travel). But do children have these same worries, and do they act them out through violent behavior in the classroom or at school? The answer is not clear. Are incidence levels of bullying, school fights, weapon use, sexual harassment, and other forms of interpersonal school violence influenced directly by these terror events? If so, how are they influenced? More international studies on school violence and geopolitical violence need to be conducted before we can make strong assertions about the relationships between political and interpersonal violence. However, preliminary evidence from multiple sources provides indirect support that more proximal and context-oriented relational violence (e.g., school violence, community violence, family violence) is a somewhat different phenomenon that is not causally or directly affected by geopolitical terrorism.

Data collected in scores of studies over two decades suggest that varying rates of interpersonal violence in schools, families, and communities in Israel are influenced primarily by socioeconomic and socially hierarchical relationships in these social contexts. Furthermore, the wide variance in school violence among schools in Israel (which share the same sociopolitical environment) is a strong testimony to the operation of these other important factors. Our three waves of national data provide evidence that school violence in Israel, as is the case in Western countries, is influenced largely by student individual characteristics and by proximal issues such as the sociodemographic composition of the student body, poverty and crime in the community, school climate, effective school leadership, and other such factors reported in the literature.

Other evidence that questions the link between geopolitical violence and school violence is that in the midst of Israel's greatest escalations of terror (between 1999 and 2002), national school violence rates across many categories actually showed significant reductions for students; some school violence rates stayed stable. This reduction is evident in the face of huge unemployment rates and a growing number of families struggling with poverty. Given current conceptions, escalations in political violence and criminal violence along with deteriorating economic conditions should increase rates in interpersonal violence, yet we find that the data refute these assumptions. We believe it is possible that reductions in school violence are responsive to regional interventions and policies implemented at school or community levels. Because Israel has been very active in creating antiviolence policy in schools during the same period, the reductions may be due in part to these changes in norms, training, policy, and interventions.

One way to think of this issue is that the social dynamics of schools behave somewhat like a semi-permeable membrane against more macro and geopolitical types of violence. That is, distal events can occasionally filter through and influence feelings, thoughts, and behaviors at the proximal levels. However, we suspect that the dynamics of the proximal context dominate the majority of transactions that later become the sources for different types of school victimization. In essence, we suspect that it is the climate, policies, and interactions in the students' school environments that are mediating the outside influences and creating the greatest opportunities for school violence, as well as barriers against it. Looking at school violence from this perspective, it is not surprising that there are many cross-cultural commonalties. We explore this issue in depth in Chapter 4.

THEORETICAL APPLICABILITY: CROSS-CULTURAL IMPLICATIONS

There are many commonalties among cultures, and each culture has unique aspects as well. In our research, we use the phrase *transferability of theory* rather than *generalizability*, which connotes a very specific epidemiological relationship between the data collected and the population for which these findings can be generalized. Even within a single country or culture the word *generalizable* is often misused at the local or regional level. For example, a careful reading of the U.S. Centers for Disease Control and Prevention (CDC) publications on school violence in the United States provides ample evidence of high variance *among* states as well as *within* them. Thus, one cannot generalize from the findings regarding prevalence of guns in schools in rural North Dakota to rural Washington State. Even within the state of California, San Francisco has a unique set of circumstances that lead to prevalence rates that are not generalizable to Fresno or Los Angeles. Thus, researchers ought to be very careful when generalizing epidemiological prevalence rates from one region to another, even when they appear to be similar cultures and political contexts. We think it would be inappropriate to generalize the prevalence of violent acts and the levels of teachers' support and school policies from any one culture to another (although comparisons are potentially informative and interesting).

Given this caveat, our study does not focus only on epidemiological rates (which are important in and of themselves), but instead focuses mainly on the relationships among theoretical concepts that we believe are functioning in many countries. We describe the theoretical underlying structures and mechanisms that reflect community and school organizational issues that impact or lower rates of school violence. We examine these in three diverse cultures in Israel and hope to find a common core of variables that cut across the three. The relationships among these variables are likely to be common to many other cultures and contexts as well.

The bully/victim literature (which is quite extensive and includes studies that were conducted across many countries over the past 30 years) shows strong similarities between forms of school violence and dynamics in schools across seemingly diverse educational systems and cultures, such as Norway, Japan, Ireland, the United States, Scotland, Israel, Sweden, Australia, New Zealand, Spain, and Denmark. Moreover, interventions that were developed originally in Norway appear to have strong effects in reducing bully/victim rates and other forms of aggression in these other countries.

Our current work, presented in this book, is another testimony to common cross-cultural patterns. Our findings on the prevalence of violent acts describe the Israeli context and are slightly different from findings in the United States and Europe. However, the structure of the findings and relationships among variables are quite similar. Thus, the relative rankings of the various violent acts in Israel replicate almost exactly the reports by Furlong and associates (1998) on school violence in California. That is, if we sort the violent acts that occur in California schools by their frequency, the order is approximately replicated. We explore this issue in depth in Chapter 4.

SCHOOL VIOLENCE AS A TOPIC OF RESEARCH— IN ISRAEL? HOW THIS STUDY CAME INTO BEING

In Israel there is a long-standing national interest in dealing with school violence, and it has been a topic of research in Israeli academia for over 30 years. Scholars such as Tamar Horowitz, Yossi Harel, Tom Gumple, Mirta Forman, Salman Elbedour, Gad Yair, Avi Assor, and Amos Rolidor are some of the early pioneers and current researchers exploring aspects of school violence in Israeli society. Similarly, since the late 1970s the Ministry of Education and the Knesset subcommittee on education have been discussing issues of school safety and creating educational code surrounding the problem. At least three major divisions in the Ministry of Education deal with certain aspects of school violence on a national level. A special office in the Ministry devoted entirely to school violence and safety has been in existence for close to two decades.

Nevertheless, even with this kind of infrastructure, there was strong consensus in the field and in Israeli educational policy circles that the topic of school violence was only being given lip service by the Ministry of Education. In large part, this view was perpetuated by the fact that the Ministry did not have accurate national epidemiological or outcome intervention data on school violence. Many in Israeli society were not entirely sure that school violence was in fact a serious national problem. Some felt that Israeli schools were much safer than their European or U.S. counterparts and that the interest in school violence was conjured up mainly by distorted media coverage on sensational cases. Until the late 1990s there were no national data that could be relied on to help define the problem. During this period, whenever a tragic violent event occurred, the Ministry would rely mainly on police youth crime statistics as estimates of school violence (this is common practice in many countries). Thus, Knesset members, municipal policymakers, and school safety advocates really had no direct estimate of the kinds of school violence problems Israel was facing and subsequently what kinds of interventions or laws would work best to address the problems. This kind of situation persisted with waxing and waning public interest from the late 1970s to the late 1990s.

During the mid- to late 1990s a series of national and international events co-occurred that increased the interest in the issue of school violence in Israeli society. First, and perhaps most important, the Israeli mass media began reporting more frequently and more intensely on an array of interpersonal forms of violence, including family violence, sexual harassment, child abuse, gangs, and sexual abuse and incest. This process is very similar to the role the media played in raising awareness of these issues in most Western countries a decade earlier (see Olweus, 1993; Smith, 2003; Smith, Morita, Junger-Tas, Olweus, Catalano, & Slee, 1999, for the role of the media in heightening awareness of bullying issues in Europe, Japan, Australia, and other countries). The intense coverage of these forms of interpersonal violence raised the awareness of the general public and politicians and created political pressure to deal with the perceived problem.

The second important event that occurred involved an international health behavior survey sponsored by the World Health Organization (WHO) that included issues of youth violence. During the early 1990s, WHO invited Israel to participate in this survey, Israel's first opportunity to have internationally comparative information on school safety issues. Yossi Harel and the Brookdale Institute led this study (Harel, Kenny, & Rahav, 1997). Released in 1997, the results shocked the Israeli public. The findings showed that Israel had a measurable school violence problem that was comparable to and in some respects greater than the problem in many other industrialized countries. The amplified coverage of results created a national environment wherein school violence issues were discussed in many sectors of Israeli society. The Ministry of Education was in the position of needing to answer to the Knesset, the media, and the general public on issues of school safety. Specifically, the office of the chief scientist (at the time, Nora Cohen and Zmira Mevarech) and the office of psychological services (Bilha Noy and Rachel Ehrhard) of the Ministry began asking detailed policy and training questions.

Unfortunately, because of the parameters imposed by the WHO survey, the Harel study had several limitations impeding its use for the creation of new policy on school violence. The WHO study was a broad-spectrum survey that explored many public health issues; there were only five questions related to youth violence. Moreover, those questions were not worded to highlight the context of the school, so the violence reported could have occurred outside the jurisdiction of the school and spread over an array of social contexts. Furthermore, Arab students were not included in the first Harel/WHO survey; hence, no inferences could be made about Arab schools. The study also did not examine primary schools.

In the midst of the national heightened awareness and public pressure created by the media surrounding the WHO study, key Israeli policymakers were frustrated by the lack of national data on this issue. Yet, despite the public pressure, many researchers believed that given the overall political problems Israel faced, the government would not allocate funds to conduct a large-scale national survey on school violence.

During the 1997–1998 academic year, I (Astor) was visiting Hebrew University on a Fulbright Fellowship and U.S. National Academy of Education/Spencer Fellowship designed to study school violence in different cultures. I was working with professors Muhammad Haj-Yahia, Rami Benbenishty, and Anat Zeira to adapt an existing U.S. survey instrument on school violence (the research version of the California School Climate and Safety Survey [CSCSS], developed by Furlong and associates) to the Israeli context. This included translating the CSCSS from English to Hebrew and Arabic in two versions (primary and secondary). The survey was then piloted on a large Jewish and Arab sample of close to 7,000 primary and secondary students.

This large-scale pilot study caught the attention of Ministry officials because the overall survey had 105 questions (compared to WHO's five). Furthermore, the survey instrument could provide the Ministry with policy and practice direction. During his year in Israel, I presented multiple workshops and lectures at the Ministry, highlighting the need for a comprehensive national survey on school violence. Among senior staff in the Ministry's chief scientist office there was a growing consensus that a national monitoring survey was the best direction for the Israeli educational system. Still, there was a feeling that there was not enough political interest by the Israeli superintendent of schools and by the Knesset subcommittee on education to move forward.

Nevertheless, early in 1998, a series of attempted murders (with knives) on school grounds in Israel coincided with unprecedented intense international media coverage on the rash of school shootings in the United States and Europe. These events, along with international concern, elevated school safety/violence to the top concern in the Israeli Ministry of Education (as it did in the United States and in many countries in Europe). I was invited to the Knesset subcommittee on education (along with other academicians from Israel) to propose next steps in the effort to stem school violence. In that meeting I suggested that Israel take the international lead in creating a comprehensive, national monitoring system that included surveys of students, teachers, and principals from the same schools. The committee was very receptive to this idea. The Israeli public and many politicians were primed to address school violence in a serious way that would put Israel at the forefront of scientific inquiry on this issue.

The last important factor that moved Israel to address this issue was a very supportive minister of education, Yitzchak Levy, who earlier in his career was a school principal and whose wife was a social worker dealing with violence. He made it very clear that dealing with school violence from a scientific and accurate national monitoring perspective was his top priority. He was also clear that he wanted such a system developed quickly.

During the spring of 1998, the Ministry of Education put out a call for the national monitoring system. Benbenishty, an expert on child welfare monitoring systems and childhood victimization, collaborated with Zeira and me to develop a proposal for an ambitious study. Compared with prior studies of school violence, this inquiry was unique in several respects. First, rather than measure the national prevalence of school violence only once in an academic year, the survey was conducted twice with the same students, teachers, and principals. This had never been done in any national survey for any country. Second, the inquiry was the first national study for both Jewish and Arab students in primary, junior high, and high school settings. Third, the study used a nationally representative design that was contextually nested rather than a simple national random sample of students (the way it had been done in most other national studies). Along these lines, teachers, principals, and students were surveyed in the same schools in order to examine further the context effects and multiple perspectives. Finally, the inquiry linked census data on families and communities around the schools to study the influence of these nested contexts on the school. Wave 1 was conducted in the 1998 fall academic year and included a sample of over 15,000 students. Wave 2 surveyed the same students and their teachers and principals in the spring of 1999. The results were remarkably similar. We believe this attests to the reliability of the instrument and our overall data that serve as the backbone of this book (see Chapter 2 for details about the study).

The results made headlines in the Israeli electronic and print news media. Benbenishty participated actively in the national debate on school violence surrounding the results of the survey. A blue ribbon government committee headed by Mattan Vilnaee was exploring the issue of school violence and in the end adopted the findings of the study. In fact, many Israelis equate the study with the recommendations of the Vilnaee committee, even though that committee did not commission the study. The Vilnaee report amplified the meaning of the findings. Vilnaee later become a Knesset member and the minister of science.

The findings have had an ongoing impact on educational establishments, including mandatory safety plans, teacher training, changes in approaches to psychological services, new guidelines against corporal punishment in schools, and other school violence policies. The findings have also impacted national norms concerning the definition of school violence. The superintendent of Israeli schools (Ronit Tirosh) has been active in creating a national response to these findings; schools throughout Israel have created policies and programs to address the problem.

During spring 2002 the third wave of the national monitoring study was conducted on over 21,500 students, teachers, and principals in 440 schools. As of the writing of this book, the results have not been released to the Israeli national media and public. However, by the time the book is published, the Israeli public and policymakers will have heard this data.

This latest wave offers an interesting and theoretically important twist to the story of school violence in Israel. The findings reflect a sizable reduction in school violence rates for both Jews and Arabs since 1998–1999. However, the reduction of school violence in the midst of radically escalating political violence, terrorism, war, and rising crime rates is an important theoretical issue to explore. In the case of Israel, these macroevents occurred concurrently with the earnest efforts of school officials and teachers, massive media coverage on school violence, and the creation of national policy associated with school violence.

These studies are the empirical backbone of this book. The data allow us to answer many questions that have long been asked in the school violence and childhood violence literature. These questions have been difficult to answer because the appropriate databases have not existed. Together, these studies represent the largest empirical effort of any country on issues of school violence. The national studies are the only nested school-based samples devoted exclusively to issues of school safety for any country. These are the only comprehensive school violence studies that sample students, teachers, and principals from the same schools and are able to compare them.

Finally, following our quantitative national studies, we are conducting a national mixed-method study of school violence. For this study we used quantitative methods to identify nine schools in our national sample that showed extreme levels of violence (either very low or very high) that were atypical of what one would expect based on the characteristics of their neighborhood and student population. We then employed a range of qualitative and ethnographic methods to supplement our quantitative studies and obtain a richer understanding of these phenomena. In this study, we followed up these schools for a whole school year with a large team of well-trained graduate students. Although this mixed-method study is still in progress, many of the observations and insights gained through the investigation have enriched this book.

Contents

School Violence in Context

Chapter 1

School Victimization Embedded in Context:
A Heuristic Model

THE SOCIAL COMPLEXITY OF A SCHOOL FIGHT:
A CASE OF IMPOVERISHED THEORY

I recall, in detail, the circumstances that led to a fistfight between two fellow class-mates when I was in fourth grade.[1] On the playground during recess, several stu-dents, including myself, spread a false rumor that David had called Carl a girl because of the way he kicked the ball. Within a few minutes, Carl heard of the rumor from other boys in our class. He marched over to the basketball court and pushed David. Almost immediately, a group of excited boys gathered in anticipation of a fight and circled the two students. Carl barked, "Why did you call me a girl?" David vehe-mently denied it, and there was an awkward moment of indecision. Then, from the crowd, several voices rang out, mainly from other boys, encouraging Carl to fight David. One student, named Randy, egged Carl on, saying, "You are afraid to fight him, you are a girl—Carla." Carl appeared flustered, humiliated, and publicly pres-sured by the comment. At the time, being called a girl in front of a crowd of boys was indeed a challenge that required proof of machismo. In a somewhat contem-plative and delayed response, Carl called David a liar and punched him in the nose; it started to bleed. Clearly stunned by the baseless accusation and subsequent at-tack, David fought back and punched Carl several times in the gut. More than a dozen students silently watched with contorted expressions on their faces, while a handful of other boys gleefully cheered the fighters on. Students from all over the playground ran to the circle like a magnet once they heard the echo of "Fight, fight, fight." A group of younger girls ran in the opposite direction and alerted the teach-ers on yard duty. Soon the mainly female teachers and yard aides arrived and sepa-rated the boys, the energized crowd disbursed, and the two fighting students were escorted to the principal's office. There, a verbal debriefing of students was conducted by the yard teachers with the goal of determining who started the fight and, ultimately, who would have the greatest culpability.

The three instigators, myself included, were also called into the principal's office. All five of us were suspended for the fight and the instigation of the fight. However, the punishment of the three main instigators was more severe than the fighters'. Thus, we stood anxiously in line waiting to be paddled by the principal before being suspended. At the time, corporal punishment was allowed in California schools, and my elementary principal, who was a strong believer in "Spare the rod, spoil the child," had a foot-long paddle. She provided a detailed explanation of why the paddling was in our best educational interest and then paddled us only once (very hard) on the buttocks with the intent of deterring future inappropriate behaviors. This was the first time in a series of many times I was paddled as part of a socioeducational intervention at school. Most of my male friends were also paddled many times throughout their elementary school years. I do not recall ever hearing about a female student being paddled. I am certain, though, that my former principal had my best interests in mind and would most likely assert that the paddling contributed to my later academic success.

Certain aspects of this fight scenario may transcend time and space and might be familiar to many readers, while other aspects would seem foreign. For example, today it would be hard to find a principal who would endorse paddling as a formal educational policy to deter violence. By contrast, school fight scenarios were a regular part of my childhood development, and we suspect they are recognizable to students growing up in today's schools and across diverse cultures and countries. The predictable and familiar aspects of a school fight as public event are part of the social fabric and relationships generic to the school setting itself. These kinds of fight scenarios rarely happen in other contexts with groups of students. Most important, the social backdrop familiar to those attending school is absent from current theoretical formulations on school violence and, with a few exceptions, has gone virtually unexplored.

Why would this kind of detailed personal recollection of a researcher be an entry point for a scholarly book on school violence? First, we believe it is highly likely that most adults and children who have attended school also have personal experiences concerning different forms of school violence, including sexual harassment, the presence of weapons, and teacher-student violence. The descriptions of these events may include the location of dangerous areas (such as cafeterias, playgrounds, hallways, and routes to and from school), the response of the teachers and principal to violent events, and the response of the peer group. Personal familiarity with social phenomena related to school violence may explain why members of the general public, policymakers, and even researchers often put forth naïve theories based on their own experiences as to the causes of school violence and prescriptions for interventions.

These kinds of common experiences may impact theory development as well. From a theory development perspective, personal experiences with school violence can be seen in two contradictory ways. On one hand, personal experiences could become an obstacle to the development of school violence theory because the contextual social dynamics in schools appear so obvious that an intense study of them seems superfluous. On the other hand, familiarity can facilitate theory development. The richness of these encounters could suggest to us what components are missing from our theories. For example, personal experiences with violence that share a common cultural familiarity could be viewed as a repository of hypotheses or clues about the social environment in schools that facilitate or regulate violent behaviors. If articulated, these hypotheses could be tested by theory development and empirical study.

As exemplified by the scenario above, we suspect that awareness of social context details surrounding school violence surpasses the current status of school violence theory and empirical studies. In fact, many of the familiar social dynamics mentioned in the scenario (e.g., the circle around the fighters, the role of bystanders, the procedures used to discipline children, the gender differences in the response to violence, and the staff's response to the violent events) are not addressed in most school violence theories. Understanding the potential power of the peer circle, the staff's response, or gender difference on school grounds could result in better interventions and theories of school violence. There are many theories and questions raised by the scenario that could be examined by research. For example, why would calling a boy a girl during recess be interpreted as such an affront? Would the same peer group response transpire if it occurred in the classroom with a teacher present? If not, why? What are the gendered group dynamics surrounding a common school fight on a playground? Did ethnicity or socioeconomic factors contribute to fight-provoking social interactions? What happens in principals' offices that perpetuates or stems violence? Who is responsible for violence on school grounds when it occurs outside of the classroom? Why do most fights occur out of the classroom? Were the observing students held responsible for their role in witnessing and encouraging the fight? Do these dynamics occur in different countries and cultures?

MOVING SCHOOLS TO THE CENTER OF THE THEORETICAL MODEL: EXPLORING THE SCHOOL IN SCHOOL VIOLENCE

Our call for more detailed research on the influence of school social contexts on victimization is associated closely with a host of other literatures that explore specific social contexts surrounding violence and children's development. This call for more detailed explorations of contexts in theories of human interaction is not new. For example, during the 1930s, Lewin (1935) posited that behavior is equal to the function of the person in the environment (the classic $B = f(PE)$). In 1979, Brofenbrenner urged researchers to better conceptualize the meaning of context for developing children. Since then, researchers in the areas of youth violence, family violence, and community violence have made serious headway in documenting the influential role of the neighborhood, peer group, and family on children's aggression patterns (see, e.g., Allen-Meares & Fraser, 2004; Catalano & Hawkins, 1996; Fraser, 1996; Herrenkohl, Chung, & Catalano, 2004). Now, 20 years later, leading researchers are advocating for an even greater understanding of the contexts of children's development. Thus, Duncan and Raudenbush stated:

> This research [on context] is relevant to social policy aimed at improving settings such as neighborhoods and schools; for if certain settings are found to be especially helpful in promoting desired child and youth outcomes, policy might aim to recreate those settings on a broader scale. (1999, p. 29)

Over the past several decades, there has been a growing realization in the various violence literatures that specific social contexts influence the dynamics of victimization and thus warrant separate research literatures. Hence, there are now robust literatures in family violence (even this is broken down to spousal, parent-child, sibling), community violence, and school violence. These are just a few of the newer context-oriented violence literatures that have emerged out of a historical generic and virtually acontextual violence literature (see, e.g., Rapp-Paglicci, Roberts, & Wodarsky, 2002). The school violence literature has begun only recently to distinguish itself from other types of violence literatures. Despite tremendous public attention to school violence issues all through the late 1980s and 1990s (Astor & Meyer, 2001; Astor, Pitner, Benbenishty, & Meyer, 2002), it was only in 2002 that the words "school violence" first appeared in a research journal's title.

It may seem fairly obvious to most education practitioners that school social contexts (e.g., social organization, peer group dynamics, teachers' roles, perceived mission of education) impact student victimization differently in elementary, middle, and high school contexts (Meyer, Astor, & Behre, 2002, in press). However, this popular belief has not filtered into either theories or interventions. Empirical evidence that establishes the degree to which school social dynamics contribute to student victimization is extremely rare (for recent reviews and studies with similar conclusions, see Allen-Meares, 2004; Astor & Meyer, 2001; Bosworth, Espelage, & Simon 1999; Furlong & Morrison, 2000; Hyman & Perone, 1998; Morrison & Skiba, 2001; Mulvey & Cauffman, 2001).

Even though researchers across the globe have been involved in school violence research, most questions regarding within-school dynamics and their relationships to other social settings, such as the family or community, have not been explored. As researchers, we do not know the co-occurrence of different kinds of violence that constitute "school violence." We do not have strong empirical evidence of how social factors in schools encourage or quell violence. We don't know if the same school factors are at play in different cultures or in different school contexts (primary, junior high, and high schools). We do not know to what extent and in what ways the school, the community, or the family contribute to violence on school grounds.

THEORETICAL MODEL

Based on the above analysis and our work in this area, we developed a heuristic model that presents school violence in nested contexts. Our model is highly influenced by Bronfenbrenner's (1979) ecological developmental theory, which conceives of violence as interplay among several relevant subsystems. Goldstein (1994) describes this type of nested ecological theory as *interactionist*. This genre of theories considers human behavior a "duet" between the individual's personal traits and the contextual and environmental variables (social and physical). This environment might include other human beings who are involved in the situation in which the behavior occurs (such as other students, teachers), and also includes the physical environment (such as school and class size, school structure). In this book, we show how victimization in school is associated with the effects of several subsystems, such as factors in the school, students' families, communities, and the larger societal context. Figure 1.1 is a visual depiction of our heuristic theoretical model that places the school context in the center of the model. This model serves as a road map for the conceptualization of ideas and analyses presented in this book. The overarching goal of this model and the book are the same: *To address empirically theoretical questions regarding the intersections of context and school violence.* Our model differs from other ecological models because the school, rather than the individual, is in the center. Starting on the right side of Figure 1.1, the primary focus is on victimization that occurs on school grounds.

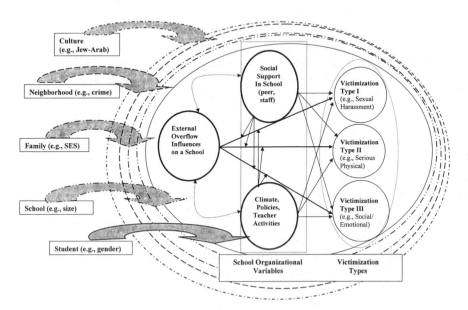

Figure 1.1.   A model of social-ecological and school influences on student victimization.

The Many Faces of School Violence

As depicted in Figure 1.1, there are many types of school victimization. Theoretically and empirically it is important to (1) describe the basic rates of different types of school victimization and (2) describe how each type of victimization is associated with the major independent variables included in our conceptual model.

From a theoretical point of view, this kind of differentiated description is essential because each type of school victimization may have different patterns: What are the descriptive distribution patterns for each form of victimization? Does victimization vary by gender, ethnicity, and school type? We believe that a theory of school violence must address the unique and common patterns of different types of victimization. Although there are many forms of victimization, in this book we examine physical violence, threatening behaviors, verbal-emotional victimization, sexual harassment, weapon-related victimization, and victimization by staff members. However, describing each type of victimization separately is not enough. The questions that emerge out of the heuristic model go a step further by suggesting that the grouping of various forms of victimization should be examined carefully using empirical approaches (as opposed to a conceptual/theoretical approach).

These guiding questions revolve around how different forms of victimization are associated with one another, or how they are grouped together in real life. Currently, victimization types are classified by conceptually driven domains (e.g., verbal, physical, or sexual). It is possible, however, that in real life, being a victim of one type of behavior in a domain (such as the physical, verbal, or sexual domain) increases or decreases the probability of being a victim of another type of violent act from this domain. For example, there may be certain types of sexual harassment behaviors that are more associated with verbal threats, and other forms of sexual harassment that are more associated with physical assault. This is important to know both theoretically and practically because it may suggest a different conceptual approach to understanding and intervening with the specific type of victimization.

This issue has analytical as well as theoretical importance. From a theory-building perspective, the association between different types of violent acts may provide clues to the various mechanisms and processes involved in being victimized in school settings. For example, in the current youth violence literature there is a tendency to distinguish between emotional-relational and physical types of victimization. In contrast to this assumption, we present analyses strongly suggesting that school-based victimization is organized more around mild and severe types of victimization. Differentiating school-related victimization by empirical methods may have theoretical, practical-clinical, and policy implications.

In Figure 1.1, school victimization is viewed as being related directly to practices within the school itself, as well as being influenced by factors that spill over from outside contexts into the school. Even so, in our model, the within-school factors have direct and indirect effects on levels of school violence. The school policies, procedures, and climate and the reactions of staff and peer group influence student victimization directly and indirectly.

Our model acknowledges that schools are embedded within socioecologically nested contexts (in Figure 1.1, the circles surrounding the school environment). Thus, victimization experienced by students is influenced by their personal characteristics (e.g., gender) and by these wider social contexts, such as the school-neighborhood characteristics (e.g., crime, poverty), students' family characteristics (e.g., education, socioeconomic status [SES]), and students' cultural context (e.g., ethnicity, religion). Yet, the influences of the external contexts are both mediated and directly affected by within-school contexts (the arrows pointing down toward the lines from all the external influences in Figure 1.1). For instance, consistent and appropriate school policies regarding violence may mediate the influences of a violent neighborhood. Therefore, we believe that a viable theory of school violence needs to explore detailed questions about the policies, practices, procedures, and social influences within the school setting as well as the impact of the variables external to the school.

A comprehensive theory of school violence must also include the views of all key school constituents around issues of victimization. Most theories of school violence rest mainly on student reports. Figure 1.1 may be seen through the lens of a student, teacher, principal, staff member, parents, or community member. At minimum, an understanding of the school's impact requires an exploration of perceptions surrounding violence, including multiple teacher, student, and principal perspectives. These reports should be compared to reveal any systematic differences between their perceptions.

The forms of victimization listed in Figure 1.1 are behavioral. We believe that a comprehensive theory of school violence should explore how victimization relates to the emotional, cognitive, and social domains. This is especially important when looking at cognitive interpretations or emotional reactions directly connected to victimization events at school. The relationship between students' victimization in school and fear of going to school is one example. How students perceive the overall safety or danger of their school is another area open for exploration. However, there are many kinds of subjective interpretations, emotional reactions, and social consequences surrounding victimization and the school social system that are ripe for inclusion in a viable theory of school violence.

Finally, we would like to differentiate explicitly our use of the terms *school violence* and *bullying*. Some researchers and practitioners use these terms interchangeably (see Astor, Benbenishty, Pitner, & Zeira, 2004, for a discussion). In this book we focus on a broader concept of school violence and do not limit ourselves to the concept of bullying. Bullying is most often defined as a subtype of aggressive behavior that is characterized by (1) the intention to harm another person, (2) the perpetration of harmful acts on the same or similar victim that occur repeatedly and over time, and (3) an imbalance of power between the bully and the victim, where the more powerful bully asserts physical or psychological power over the weaker victim (for discussions of definitions, see Nansel, Overpeck, Pilla, Ruan, Simons-Morton, & Scheidt, 2001; Olweus, 1993; Olweus, Limber, & Mihalic, 1999; Smith, et al., 1999; Smith & Sharp, 1994; Sullivan, 2000).

We concur with Olweus (1999), who suggests that the term bullying should not be used interchangeably with school violence. As he emphasizes, bullying is a form of aggression and violent behavior with specific characteristics that *only partially* overlap characteristics of other forms of violent behavior in school. We think, for example, that the component of the definition referring to an imbalance of power between the bully and the victim is fraught with potential conceptual problems. Using this component, researchers would not be allowed to define a younger or physically weaker child as a bully, even if that child continually perpetrates harmful psychological or physical acts on an older or stronger child. Another problematic example is a child who continually targets another child who is physically of the same strength or size; this child would not be defined as a bully even if the victim, other children, or teachers perceive him or her as one. Another problematic component in definitions of bullying is the idea that bullying is usually repetitive and occurs over time in an ongoing interpersonal relationship (Olweus, 1999). Hence, an incident in which a student violently attacks a group of students with whom he or she did not have direct interaction before the incident will not be called bullying.

The term bullying tends to assume different meanings in different cultures and countries. Peter Smith (2003; Smith et al., 1999) edited two books that brought together researchers on bullying from all over the world. These impressive collections show clearly that the definitions and meaning of the term vary across the globe. To illustrate, in Harel et al.'s (1997) study of youth health risk behavior, Israeli students were asked whether they were bullied; the question asked about *Hatrada* (harassment), *Hatzaka* (teasing), and *Biryonoot* (bullying). Each of these words has a quite different meaning and connotation in Hebrew. The word for bullying strongly implies physical force applied by a stronger student (a "thug" or a "goon"). The other two words are often used to describe a weaker student nagging, teasing, and getting on the nerves of another student, possibly stronger than the perpetrator. It is not clear, therefore, what students meant when they said they were bullied (Benbenishty & Astor, 2003). In fact, an international study of 14 countries coordinated by Smith and associates (Smith, Cowie, Olafsson, & Liefooghe, 2002) showed how the terms used to translate the English term bully influenced the responses of 8- and 14-year-old students.

Given such limitations of the term bullying, we prefer to use the much broader definition of school violence and victimization that we discussed earlier in this chapter (Benbenishty, Zeira, & Astor, 2000). We define school violence as any behavior intended to harm, physically or emotionally, persons in school and their property (as well as school property). We define victimization as a student's report that another student or staff member perpetrated school violence against him or her. This broad definition includes verbal and social violence (such as curses, humiliation, social exclusion); threatening behaviors (direct, indirect, extortion, scary behavior); physical violence (such as pushes, kicks, punches, beating); stealing and damaging property; weapon use (carrying, threatening, using); and sexual harassment.

BACKGROUND ON THE VARIABLES
PRESENTED IN THE MODEL

Types of Victimization

According to our heuristic model, school victimization is a very broad concept and encompasses many forms of harm, including but not limited to victimization from verbal harm, physical harm, sexual harassment, threats, and weapon-related threatening and violent behaviors. The model also posits that these separate and distinct types of victimization may interrelate and create meaningful groupings and clusters of victimization.

During the past 30 years, many physically and psychologically harmful behaviors have been subsumed under the term *school violence*. The concept of school violence has been expanded to include physical harm, psychological harm, and property damage. Currently, the term can include behaviors that vary in severity and frequency, such as bullying, verbal threats, and intimidation (Batsche & Knoff, 1994; Olweus, 1993; Olweus et al., 1999); relational victimization (Baldry & Winkel, 2003; Crick & Grotpeter, 1996); vandalism (Goldstein, 1996); school fighting (Boulton, 1993; Kingery, Coggeshall, & Alford, 1998; Schafer & Smith, 1996); corporal punishment by staff (Benbenishty, Zeira, & Astor, 2002; Benbenishty, Zeira, Astor, & Khoury-Kassabri, 2002; Youssef, Attia, & Kamel, 1998); sexual harassment (Stein, 1995; Stein, Marshall, & Tropp, 1993); gang violence (Kodluboy, 1997; Parks, 1995; Thompkins, 2000); the presence of weapons (Wilcox & Clayton, 2001); violence directed at school staff (Benbenishty et al., 2000); rape (Page, 1997); hate crimes geared at students from specific ethnic or religious groups or at gay, lesbian, bisexual, or transgender students (Berrill, 1990); dating violence (Burcky, Reuterman, & Kopsky, 1988; Cano, Avery-Leaf, Cascardi, & O'Leary, 1998); and murder (Anderson et al., 2001; Bragg, 1997; Hays, 1998).

The many forms of school victimization raise questions of how these different types are associated with each other and to what extent they have similar or different etiologies. Does physical victimization have the same developmental patterns as verbal victimization? Is sexual harassment a different form of victimization from being victimized by threats? An exploration of the unique and distinct patterns between victimization types could help researchers better understand school victimization as a phenomenon.

Our model raises another important set of questions of whether various types of victimization are influenced differently by diverse social contexts. For instance, would within-school context factors, such as teacher support and peer group behaviors, influence verbal teasing and bullying differently from severe violent acts, such as bringing guns to school? Such questions are extremely important for designing interventions that focus on a specific type of victimization. A school that attempts to address serious physical victimization may need to change a different aspect of the school's climate from a school that struggles with weapon threats.

Most studies have focused on a very limited set of victimization types. Therefore, many of the questions we raise about the interrelationships among forms of school violence could not be addressed well. In the present study, we examine a wide range of within-school violent acts; consequently, we are able to explore these issues.

School-level Factors

In Figure 1.1, the school context is at the center of the model. Some studies (see Olweus, 1993, for a review) have shown that the risk of being victimized or becoming a perpetrator is 4 to 5 times greater depending on the school. Many studies on school-based factors emerged from the bully/victim literature; discussion of school context issues has not been as strong for other forms of school victimization, except for more recent treatments of the effects of school context on weapon possession (Kodjo, Auinger, & Ryan, 2003). The following school context factors have been associated with school victimization.

AWARENESS.   Olweus (1991, 1993; Olweus et al., 1999; see also Sharp & Smith, 1994; Smith & Sharp, 1994, for a similar perspective) states that without schoolwide awareness of the problem of violence, many of the recommended intervention methods will not be effective. The lack of an overarching vision or ideology could put schools at risk for bullying behaviors. Creating an ongoing awareness of the problem is a key element to prevention. The attitudes and behaviors of the school staff, particularly the teachers and principal, play the most vital role in contributing to or decreasing bullying behaviors (Olweus et al., 1999).

RESPONSES TO VIOLENCE.   International studies suggest that what teachers and school staff do in response to a bullying event makes a big difference in outcomes for both the bully and the victim as well as other students in the class (Smith et al., 1999). Early bullying studies suggested that, on the whole, without specific training or an awareness of bullying patterns and their long-term effects, school staff tended to do nothing in response to persistent bullying (Olweus, 1993).

Olweus (1993) also found that students were critical of their teachers for their lack of response. For example, the vast majority of junior high and high school students reported that teachers almost never talked about bullying to individual students or their classes. Over 85% of secondary students said that their teachers did not respond or rarely responded to bullying events. Recent studies of school violence in the United States and Israel report similar findings regarding students and their views of teachers who do not respond to violent situations at school (Astor, Meyer, & Behre, 1999; Benbenishty et al., 2000).

Studies have shown that a negative response of the peer group to bullying behaviors and their support of victims is essential to reducing bullying levels (Olweus, 1993). A crowd of students encouraging and cheering acts of bullying can have a very different effect from when the bully is confronted by multiple peers or older students who respond negatively to the bully or attempt to intervene (Besag, 1989; Olweus, 1993). A lack of response in the peer group, by parents/caregivers, and school staff has been identified as a risk factor for the perpetuation of bullying behaviors.

SCHOOL CLIMATE.   Many researchers emphasize the importance of developing a positive school climate to reduce school violence (Colvin, Tobin, Beard, Hagan, & Sprague, 1998; Dwyer, Osher, & Hoffman, 2000; Flannery, 1997; Fraser, 1996; Stephens, 1994; Welsh, 2000). Astor, Benbenishty, Zeira, and Vinokur (2002) found that students' judgments of their school's overall violence problem were related directly to school climate characteristics. Further, school climate was associated indirectly with fear of attending school due to violence (these findings are reported later in this book).

Negative school climate has been implicated as a contributing risk factor for bullying. Schools that have a larger-than-average bullying problem tend to be characterized by an overall negative social climate (Rigby, 1996). In general, these schools tend to be less focused academically, students at these schools feel less satisfied with school life, and the teachers are less clear on what procedures to follow or their role surrounding bullying events (Olweus et al., 1999; Sullivan, 2000). The following are components that are part of school climate:

School Policy against Violence. Schools that have policies that include clear, consistent, and fair rules may be able to reduce violence (Adams, 2000; Astor, Vargas, Pitner, & Meyer, 1999; Limper, 2000; Olweus, 1991; Smith & Sharp, 1994).

Teacher Support of Students. Supportive relationships may reduce students' alienation toward their school and give them a chance to develop positive relationships with adults who support, counsel, and help them overcome their emotional and behavioral problems (Dwyer et al., 2000).

Students' Participation. School policies and teacher support of students may be most effective if they also include student participation in decision making and in the design of interventions to prevent school violence. This participation may enhance students' involvement in the school and increase their interest in a peaceful school, whereas students disengaged from school have little or no investment in acting appropriately at school (Flannery, 1997).

SCHOOL SIZE AND CLASS SIZE.   Other school-level aspects that are relevant to school violence are school and class size. One common view, popular especially among teachers, is that bully/victim problems increase in proportion to the size of the school and the class (Olweus, 1993). Bowen, Bowen, and Richman (2000) found that feelings of personal safety are lowest in the largest schools and highest in the smallest ones. According to Walker and Greshman (1997), large schools and classrooms pose a major challenge. Teachers in large schools and classes have difficulty developing and maintaining meaningful relationships with students, especially at-risk students who have more intense needs for attention and involvement. A high child-to-teacher ratio makes it practically impossible for teachers to monitor their students' behavior effectively, so discipline problems and crime increase (Hellman & Beaton, 1986). In contrast to these hypotheses, Olweus (1993) found that there were no positive relationships between level of bully/victim problems and school or class size.

LOCATION AND TIME.   As with other forms of school violence, studies show that bullying and victimization occur mainly in specific locations and times in each school (Astor & Meyer, 1999, 2001; Astor, Meyer, et al., 1999; Astor, Meyer, & Pitner, 2001). Most commonly, playgrounds during recess and before and after school have high rates of bullying. The cafeteria and territories immediately outside of school grounds also have high rates of bullying. Each school may have specific locations and times where occurrences of bullying vary by age, gender, ethnic group, or other variables. Primary, middle, and high schools tend to have different organizational structures and daily patterns that affect where, when, and with whom violent and bullying events occur (Astor et al., 2001). Lack of adult supervision in locations with many students tends to be highly associated with bullying behaviors, as it is with other forms of school violence such as fighting, sexual harassment, and verbal aggression.

PEER GROUPS.   There have been many studies exploring peer group dynamics and culture as they relate to victimization (Ahmad & Smith, 1994; American Association of University Women, 2001; Cairns & Cairns, 1991; Carnegie Council on Adolescent Development, 1993; Coie, Lochman, Terry, & Hyman, 1992; Farrington, 1993; Nansel et al, 2001; Olweus, 1993; Owens & MacMullin, 1995; Owens, Slee, & Shute, 2000; Pellegrini & Bartini, 2000; Sherer, 1991; Youssef et al., 1998). Review of these studies indicates that, on one hand, some researchers conducting developmental studies assume that there is a set of cross-cultural social elements common to peer-group development and victimization patterns

(Caplan, Weissburg, Grober, Sivo, Grady, & Jacoby, 1992; Farrington, 1993; Olweus, 1991). On the other hand, researchers conducting studies in anthropology and sociology predict that there will be qualitatively different peer dynamics and norms regarding the acceptability of risky peer group behaviors across Western and non-Western cultures (for a discussion of these different views, see Turiel, 1987, 1998). To date, most studies on peer group dynamics and victimization have been conducted in Anglo or European cultures.

Several studies in Israel have provided evidence suggesting that risky peer group behaviors (such as substance abuse, bullying, vandalism, and bringing weapons to school) on school grounds are strongly associated with both Arab and Jewish students' victimization (Astor, Benbenishty, Marachi, et al., 2002; Astor, Benbenishty, Haj-Yahia, et al., 2002; Astor, Benbenishty, Zeira, et al., 2002; Benbenishty, Astor, Zeira, and Vinokur, 2002). The schools' rules and policies, the teachers' responses to violent events, and the overall care and maintenance of the school have all been implicated as possible contributing variables to students' fear and their assessment of the school violence problem, both in Israel and internationally (Astor, Benbenishty, Zeira, et al., 2002; Benbenishty, Astor, Zeira, et al., 2002; Olweus, 1993; Smith & Sharp, 1994; Sullivan, 2000).

Individual Factors

Individual factors contributing to aggression have a long history of research in psychology. In Figure 1.1 we include the role of student characteristics. The following are some of the individual factors that have been emphasized in the literature relevant to school violence.

GENDER.   The international literature on school violence clearly indicates that boys are more violent than girls (Borg, 1999; Centers for Disease Control and Prevention [CDC], 1996, 1998, 2000; Everett & Price, 1995; Fizpatrick, 1997, Lowry, Sleet, Duncan, Powell, & Kolbe, 1995). For instance, the Youth Risk Behavior Surveillance Survey (YRBS; Kann et al., 1995) asked students if they had been in a physical fight at school in the previous year. Male students (23.5%) were almost three times as likely as female students (8.6%) to have fought. Boys are also more often victimized by others (Benbenishty et al., 2000; CDC, 2000).

The bullying literature has good examples of this gender trend. Overall, the international body of research suggests that compared with girls, boys are more frequently victims of bullies and engaged in bullying behaviors. Boys also tend to report higher rates of chronic victimization. In a recent national study in the United States, 25.9% of boys and 13.7% of girls in sixth through tenth grades reported being frequent victims of bullying (Nansel et al., 2001).

Overall, boys tend to be victimized more often by direct forms of bullying (e.g., hitting, slapping), and girls are victimized more often by indirect and relational forms of bullying (e.g., rumors, exclusion from groups; e.g., Nansel et al., 2001; Olweus et al., 1999; Pellegrini & Long, 2002; Smith & Sharp, 1994; Sullivan, 2000). However, recent U.S. data show that both boys and girls report similar rates of indirect bullying, but boys have much higher rates of direct bullying (Nansel et al., 2001). Some theories point to the differences in the friendship patterns of boys and girls as the underlying reason for these distinctive forms of bullying (e.g., Owens & MacMullin, 1995; Owens et al., 2000). Because girls tend to have closer-knit groups of friends based on intimacy and belonging, bullying based on exclusion and/or social isolation would have the most significant impact on girls. During the teenage years, boys tend to form bigger and more amorphous friendship groups, where indirect forms of bullying are not as effective as direct methods of aggression (Owens & MacMullin, 1995).

Direct forms of aggression (hitting, punching, physical intimidation) are much more overt and easy to identify and punish than the more indirect forms of victimization, which girls appear to use more often than boys. Olweus (1993) reported that in his research studies, female bullies "typically use less visible, and sneakier means of harassment" (p. 59). This brings up interesting questions regarding the reporting of indirect forms of aggression by other classmates and teachers. The nature of indirect aggression often allows it to be missed by teachers, parents, and even other students (Owens & MacMullin, 1995). Victims may not report these behaviors either because they feel ashamed or fear retaliation (Baldry & Winkel, 2003). However, despite being a more covert form of aggression, indirect forms of aggression can have a lasting negative impact on victims (Owens et al., 2000; Owens & MacMullin, 1995; Rigby & Slee, 1999). In fact, Baldry and Winkel (2003) found that suicidal ideation was associated more strongly with relational victimization in school than with direct victimization. Some of the negative psychological effects reported by girls who were victims included "embarrassment, anger, worry, fear, humiliation, loneliness, self-consciousness, betrayal, and sadness" (Owens & MacMullin, 1995, p. 367). In addition, Owens et al. (2000) found that victims did not receive the support they needed from teachers, parents, and school staff, often because these acts of aggression were invisible. Overall, these findings suggest that boys and girls are vulnerable to different kinds of victimization.

AGE.   There is a consistent tendency for younger students to report greater victimization than older students (Benbenishty et al., 2000; Borg, 1999; Boulton & Underwood, 1992; Whitney & Smith, 1993). Indeed, research from the United States and international studies suggest that there is a strong inverse relationship between age and specific types of victimization (Olweus et al., 1999; Smith et al., 1999; Sullivan, 2000). The chances of becoming a victim of bullying are much higher in the early elementary school grades and then drop significantly every year as a child grows older (Olweus, 1993), with a possible slight increase in the early stages of middle school (Pellegrini & Long, 2002). Internationally, bullying victimization seems to be lower in high schools than in middle or elementary schools, and middle schools have lower rates than elementary schools (e.g., Smith, Madsen, & Moody, 1999). In the United States and some other countries (Sullivan, 2000), there is a slight increase in bullying behaviors in sixth through eighth grades and a slight decrease in high school. Furlong, Chung, Bates, and Morrison (1995) compared students who reported no victimization experiences with students reporting 12 or more types of victimization in the previous month. They found that in junior high schools (seventh through eighth grades), there are many more students with high victimization levels than in high schools (eleventh and twelfth grades).

PHYSICAL CHARACTERISTICS AND STEREOTYPES.   Research from Europe suggests that some popular notions associated with victimization may be more myth than reality (Olweus et al., 1999). For example, it is commonly assumed that children who differ physically from other children along several dimensions (e.g., obesity, hair color, unusual dialect or foreign language, unusual clothing/glasses) may be picked on and bullied more by other schoolchildren. Research in Scandinavian countries, however, suggests that these kinds of factors do not distinguish between those who are chronic victims and those who are not (Olweus, 1991, 1993). Also, although visible physical disability is mentioned as a risk factor for victimization (e.g., Gofin, Palti, & Gordon, 2002), the empirical findings do not support this association (Dawkins, 1996).

The only common physical factor shown to make a difference in the bullying literature so far is the child's size and physical strength. Victims tended to be physically smaller, shorter, and weaker than average children their age (e.g., Voss & Mulligan, 2000). Bullies, on the other hand, tended to be physically larger and stronger than other children their age (see Olweus, 1993, for a detailed description of these studies). In fact, Olweus contends that what characterizes victims of bullying is a combination of anxious behavior and physical weakness. Bullies, on the other hand, are characterized by a combination of aggressive behavior and physical strength.

In the United States, some researchers have noted that gender, racial background, ethnic affiliation, and sexual orientation may be risk factors for bully victimization (see Berrill, 1990; Klipp, 2001, for a review of this issue). The literature on lesbian, gay, bisexual, or transsexual (LGBT) youth suggests that bullying in schools is a serious problem for students who are openly LGBT. Moreover, this literature suggests that bully victimization is a serious problem for any student who is viewed as LGBT (Klipp, 2001). Often, these students are teased, bullied, and harassed because of stereotypes based on their physical appearance, speech or motor patterns, or gendered social preferences. Students may be harassed only because they are deemed by the peer group to be LGBT. Anti-LGBT comments are heard commonly in the hallways and playgrounds of many U.S. schools (see Klipp, 2001). For boys, harassment focuses on the appearance of physical weakness or stereotypical "feminine" characteristics. For girls, these stereotypes are based on so-called masculine characteristics (looking male, talking like a boy; Klipp, 2001). Problems of LGBT youth have not been addressed directly in bullying studies. Future studies should rectify this and explore bullying that targets other vulnerable groups, such as those based on gender, race, ethnic affiliation, religious practice, and physical disabilities.

Factors Outside the School

PARENTING OF BULLIES AND VICTIMS.   Researchers suggest that certain parenting styles increase the chances of a child's becoming a bully. For instance, Garbarino (1995; see also Catalano & Hawkins, 1996; McEvoy & Welker, 2000) suggests that parents in socially toxic neighborhoods try to protect their children in ways that condition the children to behave in an aggressive, defiant, and distrustful manner that generalizes to school. Other researchers argue that a lack of emotional support for the child, lack of supervision and monitoring, and a lack of overall parental involvement with the child tend to increase bullying behaviors (Batsche & Knoff, 1994; Bowers, Smith, & Binney, 1994; Olweus, 1993; Orpinas, Murray, & Kelder, 1999; Sullivan, 2000).

Summarizing the research literature on parenting and bullying, Olweus (1993) suggests that there are several parenting factors that contribute to bullying behavior. Foremost among these is that parenting not characterized by warmth or direct involvement in the child's daily life increases the risk that the child will act out, often aggressively. Second, parents who do not set clear ground rules about what behavior is acceptable and unacceptable or who tolerate their child's aggressive behavior increase the risk that the child will become a bully. This includes parents who use "power assertive" methods such as physical punishment on a frequent basis. Third, parents who model aggressive behavior in their daily interactions with others will likely increase the risk that the child will become a bully. This is the typical "violence begets violence" argument, which suggests that children learn violence through their exposure to it. Many other researchers support this perspective (e.g., Batsche & Knoff, 1994; Farrington, 1993; see a review in Fraser, 1996).

Research suggests that victims of bullies tend to come from overprotective families. These children tend not to develop the assertive skills that make them less vulnerable (Bowers et al., 1994: Sullivan, 2000). An important research finding regarding parenting practices of both victims and bullies is that such parents have poor and deteriorating relationships with the school over time. These parents are rarely aware of the bullying and victimization on a day-to-day basis (Olweus, 1993). Furthermore, parents rarely respond in any concrete way when they find out about bullying at school. Schools, on the other hand, tend not to contact parents of either victims or bullies unless the bullying results in severe physical injury (Olweus, 1991, 1993). Finally, over time, parents of victims and bullies develop negative views toward the school and the school toward these parents, which tends to create an atmosphere of noncooperation and a lack of contact between home and school. Several researchers speculate that this dynamic prevents the problem of victimization and bullying from being addressed at home or school.

FAMILY POVERTY.   Many researchers found a link between student or youth violence and family poverty (e.g., Attar, Guerra, & Tolan, 1994; Comer, 1980; Dwyer et al., 2000; Earls, 1991; Farrington, 1989; Haapasalo & Tremblay, 1994; Kupersmidt, Griesler, DeRosier, Patterson, & Davis, 1995; Patterson, Kupersmidt, & Vaden, 1990; Soriano, Soriano, & Jimenez, 1994). Brownfield (1987) found that male students (both White and Black) whose fathers had a history of unemployment were more likely to engage in violent behavior than sons of fully employed fathers (see also Guerra, Huesmann, Tolan, Van Acker, & Eron, 1995). In contrast to these findings, Borg (1999) investigated the relationship between a father's SES and his child's being a bully or a victim in 50 primary and secondary schools in Malta. Borg found that bullies and victims may belong to any social background. Similarly, the study found no association between bullies or victims and their mother's employment status.

COMMUNITY CONTEXT.   The neighborhoods in which children and adolescents grow and develop play very influential roles in young people's relationship with violence. Poverty, discrimination, and lack of opportunities for education and employment have all been identified as important community risk factors for interpersonal violence (Attar et al., 1994; Catalano & Hawkins, 1996; Garbarino & Kostelny, 1997; Hamburg, 1998; Herrenkohl et al., 2004; Tolan, Guerra, & Kendall, 1995). The relationship between community factors and school victimization is not direct. Even within the same communities there appears to be sizable variation in victimization rates between different schools; this is another indication that schools may be mediating community and family effects.

Another important aspect of the community that may impact school violence is crime rates. Crime and violence in the schools do not occur in isolation from crime in the rest of the society (Wilson, 1980). In a sample of schools in Boston, Hellman and Beaton (1986) found positive relationships between school violence (measured by suspension rates) and community crime rates (see also Attar et al., 1994; Dodge, Pettit, & Bates, 1994; Lowry et al., 1995). Furthermore, Everett and Price (1995) found that children from communities with higher crime rates were significantly more likely to be victims of an act of violence in and around school than other children.

ETHNICITY AND CULTURE.   Ethnicity and culture have been important variables in the study of school violence. It appears that school violence rates differ by ethnicity and culture. A recent volume on school violence reported great variation among European cultures (Smith, 2003). In the United States, victimization and perpetration rates vary by ethnic background. For example, Hispanic youth report marginally higher involvement in moderate (12%) and frequent (10.4%) bullying compared with African American youth (10.2% and 8.3%, respectively) and White youth (10.5% and 8.5%, respectively; Nansel et al., 2001). However, it should be noted that across the globe, ethnic and cultural variables often covary with SES. This is especially relevant to this book because we compare Jewish and Arab students. As a group, the Arab population is more disadvantaged than the Jewish population on every socioeconomic indicator (e.g., Hareven, 1998; Kop, 1999). These circumstances may strongly impact school victimization, because neighborhood poverty and high crime rates influence the schools and the social dynamics that impact victimization and its consequences (Lorion, 1998; see Soriano et al., 1994, for similar points on the United States). Furthermore, in many societies there may be a confound between ethnicity/culture and socioeconomic issues. Often, cultural differences are attributed to a group when it is entirely possible that differences stem mainly from economic disparities rather than from cultural differences. These distinctions need to be examined carefully in all studies that compare cultural groups.

Given the model depicted in Figure 1.1, we ask and answer questions using empirical data from several large-scale studies conducted in Israel. We present the methods and sample in the following chapter.

NOTE

1. Sections of this chapter are written in the voice of Ron Astor.

Chapter 2

Context and Methods

The model we presented in the previous chapter served as our road map in a series of empirical studies in which we examined parts of the model and replicated many of the findings that we report here. In each of the following chapters we present a set of findings that addresses aspects of our model. Much of our empirical work in this area has been published in journal articles and book chapters. In this book we present a more comprehensive view of this body of work and try to avoid technical details as much as possible. When appropriate, we refer interested readers to technical notes and appendixes and to journal articles that present methodological and statistical procedures in more detail.

OVERVIEW OF THE ISRAELI EDUCATION SYSTEM

The findings reported in this book are from studies we conducted in Israel. It is important, therefore, to describe the Israeli education system that is the context of this book. This is mainly a public system that is divided into three school types: primary schools for grades 1 to 6, junior high schools for grades 7 to 9, and high schools for grades 10 to 12. In 1999 there were about 1.9 million students in 3,540 schools in Israel.

Israel's population is multicultural, with many religious and ethnic groups; the education system reflects this diversity. To preserve cultural identities, the system is divided into cultural subsystems (*streams*, in the Israeli jargon) supervised by the Ministry of Education: Jewish secular (*Mamlachti*), Jewish Orthodox (*Mamlachti-Dati*), and Arab. The Israeli system includes only Israeli citizens. Arabs in the West Bank and Gaza are not Israeli citizens; they have separate, independent education systems and are not included in the present study.

Israeli Arab families almost never send their children to Jewish schools and vice versa. Most of the religious Jewish parents send their children to religious schools; secular Jewish parents rarely do so. This de facto segregation allows each cultural group to maintain its cultural identity.

Ninety percent of the Jewish population is either secular or practices a modern Orthodox Judaism that identifies strongly with Western values and culture and tends to be more liberal about gender roles, dress codes dealing with modesty, and sexual issues in general. At the same time, 10% of the Jewish Israeli population is Ultra-Orthodox. This latter group resists Western values, does not adhere to the same liberal Western values and gender roles, and has its own private education system that is not supervised by the Israeli Ministry of Education. In this study we included Jewish schools that are supervised by the Ministry and excluded schools that belong to the independent Ultra-Orthodox group.

Jewish schools supervised by the Ministry of Education are divided into two subsystems that share much in common but still differ in curricula and structure: secular and religious schools. Jewish religious schools have regular curricula that include social sciences, language, and sciences, but they also emphasize studies of the Bible and religious practices. Starting in junior high, there are separate schools for male and female students in the religious stream and in some Arab schools. Some primary schools separate male and female students as early as fourth grade.

Almost a fifth of Israel's population is Arab (19.6%; Israel Central Bureau of Statistics, 2001). This Arab population is highly diverse in religion (Muslim, Christian, and Druze) and ethnic background. Even so, Arab groups in Israel share a similar history, language, and culture. Despite variation in liberal and conservative attitudes within the Arab groups, many polls, articles, and surveys suggest that Israeli Arabs as a group are generally conservative, traditional, and hierarchical with regard to sex roles, the centrality of the family, and sociocultural hierarchy (Haj-Yahia, 1997). Overall, the Arab minority in Israel is characterized by high rates of poverty and unemployment and receipt of much lower expenditures of public funds for social services such as education than the Jewish majority (Hareven, 1998; Kop, 1999).

OVERVIEW OF THE STUDY

We conducted a series of national studies of school violence in Israel. The first two waves were carried out in collaboration with Zeira in fall 1998 and spring 1999. The third and most recent wave was conducted in spring 2002, while the work on this book was already under way. Simultaneously, we conducted a longitudinal study in the city of Herzliya and monitored school violence in 25 schools with 7,000 students for four years. Most of the analyses presented in this book are based on the second wave of our national study. It should be noted, however, that many of the findings reported here were replicated in the other studies that we conducted.

PROCEDURE

Data collection was carried out under a standardized protocol by a professional survey team and supervised closely by the investigators. Each professional surveyor received training before going out to the field and provided a protocol fidelity report for each class and school surveyed. The implementation across schools was highly controlled and similar across schools. The vast majority of students completed the questionnaire in 15 to 30 minutes (depending largely on the student's reading level and age). The entire data collection process spanned three weeks.

Students were given a structured questionnaire in classrooms under the guidance of professionally trained survey monitors. Principals and homeroom teachers were given questionnaires to complete individually. The questionnaires, procedures, and informed consent forms and instructions were reviewed extensively through the Israeli Ministry of Education Human Subjects Protection protocol and were also implemented in accordance with the ethical and human subject review guidelines at Hebrew University in Jerusalem. Participants were free to withdraw from the study at any time and for any reason. Confidentiality was ensured to all participants.

Sample

In our theoretical model, students and staff are nested in the context of their schools. Thus, the sample was designed to represent schools and the students (and staff) in these schools. The sample was designed to represent all students in grades 4–11 in the official public school system supervised by the Israeli Ministry of Education.[1] The probability sampling method was a two-stage stratified cluster sample. We used two independent sets of strata. One was a school-level dimension with three strata: primary school, junior high school, and high school; the second was a cultural dimension, also with three strata: Jewish, Arab, and, within the Jewish schools, religious or secular.

In the first stage, schools were selected randomly from the sampling frame according to their strata. In the second stage, one class was selected randomly from each grade level in each of the randomly selected schools. The school-level response rate was 95%. Almost all students present in their classes during the survey agreed to participate. The sample was weighted to represent the entire Israeli student population (see Table 2.1). All analyses were conducted with these weights (Nirel & Saltzman, 1999).

Principals

We targeted all principals of the schools included in our sample, and we mailed the questionnaires to the principals. Half of the respondents handed in the completed questionnaires to the survey team that visited their school and the other half sent their questionnaires in the mail, often after reminder calls. We received 197 questionnaires, a response rate of about 85% (see Table 2.2).

Table 2.1.   Summary of Students' Sample

School Level	Ethnic Group	Schools	Classes	Students
Primary	Jewish	47	135	3,283
	Arab	24	71	2,189
	Total	71	206	5,472
Junior High	Jewish	58	172	4,655
	Arab	25	75	2,271
	Total	83	247	6,926
High School	Jewish	57	110	2,503
	Arab	21	40	1,015
	Total	78	150	3,518
TOTAL		232	603	15,916

Homeroom Teachers

We targeted all homeroom teachers in the schools and grade levels from which we sampled the students. We sent questionnaires to these homeroom teachers ahead of the arrival of the survey team. A third of the homeroom teachers handed in the completed questionnaires to the team that visited their school and the rest mailed back the questionnaires to the authors, in most cases after reminder calls. Overall, 1,509 homeroom teachers participated in the study (response rate of 61%). The range of respondents in each school was between 1 and 26 teachers, with a median of 6 respondents and a mean of 6.82 (sd = 4.8; see Table 2.3).

Student Instrument

The questionnaire used in this study is an adaptation of the research version of the California School Climate and Safety Survey (CSCSS; Furlong, 1996; Furlong, Morrison, Bates, & Chung, 1998; Rosenblatt & Furlong, 1997; for a recent short form, see Furlong, Greif, Bates, Whipple, Jimenez, & Morrison, 2004). The survey was modified to fit the Israeli context and to address issues of interest to the

Table 2.2.   Summary of Principals' Sample

	Overall		Gender		Jewish		
	N	%	Female (%)	Male (%)	Nonreligious (%)	Religious (%)	Arab (%)
Primary	70	35.5	56.1	43.9	34.3	32.9	32.9
Junior High	68	34.5	28.8	71.2	36.8	32.4	30.9
High School	59	29.9	32.7	67.3	28.8	37.3	33.9
Total	197	100	40.1	59.9	33.5	34.0	32.5

Table 2.3. Summary of Homeroom Teachers' Sample

	Overall		Gender		Jewish		
	N	%	Female (%)	Male (%)	Nonreligious (%)	Religious (%)	Arab (%)
Primary	407	27.0	81.5	18.5	29.2	34.9	35.1
Junior High	631	41.8	63.2	36.8	25.2	36.1	38.7
High School	471	31.2	55.7	44.3	18.5	36.7	36.0
Total*	1509	100	65.8	34.2	39.6	24.2	34.2

*12 teachers did not provide any background information.

researchers. The research instrument contained more than 100 questions pertaining to several areas:

1. Personal victimization by peers (over a range of low-level behaviors, such as pinching and shoving, to severe, such as extortion, serious beating, and gun threats, and sexual harassment in secondary schools).
2. Weapons in school (carrying, seeing others carrying a weapon, being threatened with weapons).
3. Personal victimization by staff (emotional, physical, sexual).
4. Risky behaviors in school (by peers and staff).
5. Feelings and assessments regarding school violence (severity of the problem, fear of attending school, feeling safe or unsafe at school).
6. School climate (teacher support, policies against violence, student participation).

The original items were translated from English to Hebrew and Arabic. Some items were adapted to the Jewish Israeli and Arab Israeli culture and jargon. To ensure translation accuracy, items were retranslated into English; multiple translations and retranslations were made and then compared. We piloted the translated questionnaires in a pretest on approximately 7,000 Jewish and Arab students. The instrument was also used in a first wave of data collection in fall 1998. A few changes were introduced on the basis of the pilot study and the first wave of data collection. In Appendix 1 we present the parts of the student questionnaire used in our study.

Principals' Instrument

The principals' questionnaire included the following sections (see Appendix 1 for the translated questions):

1. School policies and coping with violence.
2. School climate relevant to violence.

3. Report on violent acts in the past month and assessment of the seriousness of the problem.
4. Interventions and projects implemented to deal with school violence in
the past two years.
5. Training needs.
6. Relationships with and support from others in the school (e.g., PTA)
and out of the school (e.g., the police, the central district office).
7. Background information on the school and its staff (such as turnover
rates)

Homeroom Teachers' Questionnaire

The teachers responded to a questionnaire that was very similar to the one used with
the principals (see Appendix 1 for exact questions). In the teachers' questionnaire
we omitted the section about relationships with others and background information on the school. We also added a section on the teachers' feelings and behaviors
regarding personal safety in the school.

School Context Information

We used several information sources to gather data on various aspects of the school
context:

Ministry of Education School Database. This database provided aggregated
information on school characteristics such as number of classes and
number of students. It also provided aggregated data on the families of the
students, such as percentages of low-income families, low education (fewer
than eight years of school), large families, and an aggregated SES score for
the students' families.

Census Information. We extracted census data for each school's census
tracts, including a range of school neighborhood characteristics such as
income, education, employment, family size, ethnic/religious heterogeneity, and heterogeneity in terms of new immigrants versus native Israelis.

Police Data. The police database was used to obtain rates and types of
crimes in the school's neighborhood.

NOTE

1. The sample did not include schools that belong to the (very small) Ultra-Orthodox
educational streams (El-Hamayan and Chinooch Azmay) and a small number of schools
that are designated for special education students only (students in special education classes
within regular schools were included in the sampling framework).

Chapter 3

Victimization Types

In this chapter, we explore three types of school-based victimization: physical victimization, victimization by threats, and verbal-social forms of victimization (such as exclusion). Sexual harassment is presented in Chapter 5. The conceptualization of sexual harassment has differed from other forms of school violence; empirically, however, it was not clear whether this difference actually exists. When we explored this question empirically, we found that sexual harassment indeed does have very different patterns from the forms of violence presented in this chapter. Consequently, to address fully the complexity of sexual harassment, those results are presented separately.

Most international surveys report events occurring during the prior 12 months. We believe that some of these events are so common that children cannot recall an entire year's worth of events; therefore, in an effort to increase both the meaning and the interpretability of the findings, we asked students to recall only events that happened in the prior month. We also present data from a large-scale study conducted in several central and southern counties in California by Furlong and associates (1998) during a similar period. This study was chosen because of the similarity in items used to describe victimization, allowing us to compare findings from both studies and to situate the findings from Israel.

First, we describe the frequency of the various victimization types. We examine how each of these types is associated with context factors such as gender, ethnic/cultural group, age/grade, and school level. This initial exploration prepares the groundwork for examinations of more complex issues, such as the interplay of several context variables (e.g., gender and ethnicity) in each type of school victimization. Our aim is to identify what are common and what are unique aspects of each type of victimization.

PHYSICAL VICTIMIZATION

We start by asking, How many Israeli students have been victimized by their peers? and How do these Israeli rates compare with rates in the United States? Overall, the rate of school victimization in Israel is high. The majority of Israeli students (64%) were victimized physically in the month preceding the survey.

Tables 3.1 and 3.2 represent the frequencies of victimization. Table 3.1 shows that close to half of the students were seized and shoved by another student in the prior month (48.9%: 36% plus 12.9% with one or more events). Involvement in fistfights and getting kicked or punched are also quite common experiences, involving almost a third of the students. Students report much less victimization by severe physically violent acts, such as being cut with a sharp object. We asked students if they had received a serious beating. In Hebrew, the question uses an idiom: "killing or murderous" beating; this conveys being overwhelmed by a stronger force and being severely beaten, but not necessarily being in a fight. It is interesting to note that the frequency of this behavior was closer to the rate of being cut with a sharp object than of requiring medical attention as a consequence of a fight.

Table 3.3 presents physical victimization reported in the California sample. When we compare Tables 3.2 and 3.3, it becomes apparent that Israel has approximately twice as many students reporting most kinds of physical victimization as their Californian counterparts during the same period. For instance, whereas 48.9% of the Israeli students reported being grabbed and shoved, 25.6% of the California students were victimized in this way. This kind of international comparison helps situate the Israeli data.

As Table 3.2 shows, in Israel male students are victimized more frequently than are female students. For most of the questions, the victimization rates of boys are at least double that of girls. Only the item "taking things by force" is reported in similar frequencies. Inspection of the table reveals a clear pattern: the more serious the

Table 3.1. Frequency of Physical Victimization (in percentages)

	Never	Once or Twice	More
A student seized and shoved you on purpose.	51.1	36.0	12.9
You were involved in a fistfight.	67.9	23.1	9.0
You were kicked or punched by a student who wanted to hurt you.	68.4	23.0	8.6
A student used a rock or another instrument in order to hurt you.	75.2	19.7	5.1
Another student took your things from you by force.	80.5	15.2	4.3
You were involved in a fight, were hurt, and required medical attention.	88.7	8.5	2.8
A student gave you a serious beating.	89.8	6.9	3.3
A student cut you with a knife or a sharp instrument on purpose.	94.3	4.3	1.4

Table 3.2. Frequency of Physical Victimization (by gender, grade level, and ethnic group, in percentages)

	Total	Gender		Ethnic Group		School Level		
		Male	Female	Jewish	Arab	Primary	Junior	High
A student seized and shoved you on purpose.	48.9	61.4	36.9	50.9	41.9	57.1	50.5	32.2
You were involved in a fistfight.	32.1	45.9	19.0	31.1	35.4	42.4	28.9	19.9
You were kicked or punched by a student who wanted to hurt you.	31.6	42.5	21.1	33.2	25.8	42.5	29.4	16.7
A student used a rock or another instrument in order to hurt you.	13.3	19.0	7.8	13.8	11.4	0.6	24.4	16.4
Another student took your things from you by force.	19.5	22.3	17.0	19.1	21.3	26.8	17.9	10.3
You were involved in a fight, were hurt, and required medical attention.	11.3	17.1	5.9	9.8	16.6	13.9	10.9	7.5
A student gave you a serious beating.	10.2	14.4	6.1	9.3	13.1	15.2	7.9	5.4
A student cut you with a knife or a sharp instrument on purpose.	5.7	9.5	2.0	5.2	7.5	*	6.0	5.0
At least one of the above.	64.0	76.5	52.3	64.1	63.6	75.0	63.6	45.7

*Not asked.

Table 3.3. Frequency of Physical Victimization in the California Sample
(by gender, in percentages)

	Total	Male	Female
Grabbed or shoved by someone being mean.	25.6	34.9	18.5
Punched or kicked by someone trying to hurt you.	16.0	25.9	8.3
Hit by rock or other object by someone trying to hurt you.	11.5	16.5	7.6
Something taken by force or threat of force.	7.8	11.4	5.0
Went to doctor or nurse because you were hurt in attack or fight.	5.7	8.5	3.5
Cut with knife, something sharp by someone trying to hurt you.	3.4	5.8	1.6

victimization, the larger the gap between boys and girls. Although the rate of victimization by the less serious behavior of being grabbed and shoved is higher among girls, reports on needing medical attention following a fight are almost three times more frequent among male students, and being cut by a sharp object is reported five times more by boys. To a large extent, the gender differences in the California sample parallel those in the Israeli sample.

On the Israeli sample, comparison of items between Arab and Jewish students is far less consistent. Table 3.2 suggests that Arab and Jewish students are equally likely to have experienced at least one act of victimization (63% and 64%, respectively). Certain types of physical victimization are more frequent among Jewish students, whereas others are reported slightly more by Arab students. On an item-by-item basis, a weak trend seems to emerge: The Arab students tend to be victimized by serious physical violence more than the Jewish students; specifically, more Arab students report being injured in a fight, getting a serious beating, and being cut by a knife or sharp object.

Gender, Age, Culture, and Physical Victimization Considered Together

Important trends are evident when age, gender, culture, and physical victimization are viewed together. So far, we have looked at gender, age, and ethnicity separately. We now ask whether the interplay of all these factors affects physical victimization. In other words, are gender differences across the age range similar for the different cultures, suggesting a developmental trend less influenced by culture? Or perhaps genders differ in their victimization levels over the age span according to their cultural group? Figure 3.1 combines all the victimization patterns shown in Table 3.2 and presents age trends by gender and ethnic group.

From our perspective, Figure 3.1 shows a remarkable set of trends. The figure illustrates clearly that developmental trajectories for male and female students are astoundingly similar for both Jewish and Arab students. Both Jewish and Arab girls show a steep decline in physical victimization starting between sixth and seventh grades that continues to decline as they mature. Boys, both Jews and Arabs, also show a slight decline beginning in seventh grade, with another decline in physical victimization

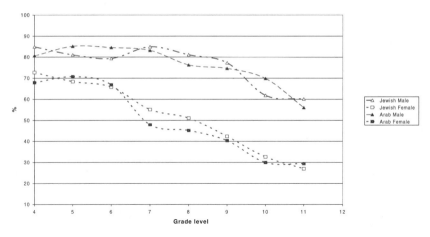

Figure 3.1. Percentage of students physically victimized (by gender, grade level, and ethnic group).

between ninth and tenth grades. Overall, in both cultures the declines for boys over time are not as steady and pronounced as the declines reported by girls. Figure 3.1 sets the stage for a theoretical argument that views gender and age rather than culture as the most important variables in understanding overall school victimization.

Figure 3.2 shows that these trends are similar in the California sample, with a few differences. Boys in the California sample have a sharper decline in victimization starting in middle school (seventh grade). By the end of high school the differential between boys' and girls' rates are much lower in the California sample than in Israel. Nevertheless, the dominant trend suggests that the victimization rates in California are also influenced mainly by age and gender.

Religious and Nonreligious Jewish Schools

Culture spans more than ethnic categories. How would these same trends look if we compared religious and nonreligious groups? In most religious communities, boys and girls attend the same primary schools but go to single-sex schools starting in junior high. Are rates of violence similar in religious and secular primary schools when schools are composed of mixed genders? Are rates of violence in junior high and high school different for religious boys and girls due to the single-sex schools? We suspect that an all-girl setting will result in less overall physical victimization given that boys are more often physical perpetrators.

Continuing our exploration of the effects of culture, we examined two groups in the Jewish student population: students in secular schools and students in religious schools. From a research perspective this comparison made the most sense because Israeli Jewish schools are organized by levels of religious practice. Arab

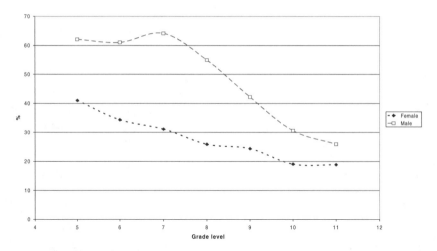

Figure 3.2. Percentage of physical victimization in the California sample (by gender and grade level).

schools are not organized in this way, so it is not possible to compare students based on religious practice.

Within the Jewish student population, the overall comparisons did not reveal any major consistent differences between the religious and nonreligious groups in victimization levels. However, when we explore gender trends, an interesting pattern becomes clear. Victimization rates among boys were quite similar between the two cultural groups. For instance, 76% of the boys in nonreligious schools reported being victimized physically at least once during the prior month, compared with 77% of the boys in religious schools. The differences between girls in these two cultural contexts were larger. For instance, 54% of the female students in nonreligious schools reported being victimized physically at least once, compared with only 45% of the female students in religious schools (similar trends were observed with regard to other types of victimization).

This is an interesting finding, but before we can interpret it, we should put it in context and examine it from several vantage points. Our first question is whether these differences between two groups are consistent across different school levels and age. Figure 3.3 shows that in primary schools, the levels of victimization reported by female students are similar in religious and nonreligious schools. However, starting in junior high school, female students in religious schools report considerably less victimization than female students in nonreligious schools. When we looked at levels of victimization across the grade levels we could see that the significant drop in physical victimization rates among female students in religious schools was between grades 6 and 7 (transition from primary to junior high): from 65% in grade 6 to 36% in grade 7. The drop among girls in nonreligious schools was only from 66% to 60%.

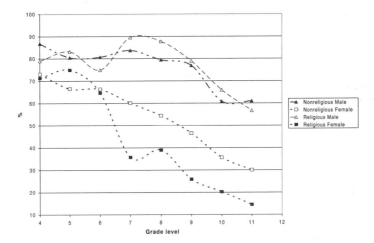

Figure 3.3.   Percentage of students verbally victimized (by gender, grade level, and ethnic group).

Although we cannot know for certain, we believe this trend is due primarily to the fact that female students who go to junior high school are moving to an all-girl setting. Such a setting may reduce victimization because boys, who tend to be the perpetrators, are not on the school grounds. Single-sex schools for girls should be explored in other cultures as well. It has great significance for our theoretical understanding of the role of mixed- versus single-gender schools.

Another potential explanation for this finding is that cultural values instilled in religious schools help reduce victimization by school violence. However, this explanation works only for religious girls, as we found that boys report similar victimization rates in the religious and nonreligious school systems. This finding seems to speak against the interpretation that religious values reduce violence in school. It is possible, however, that there are cultural influences that expect, demand, and perhaps support nonviolent behavior, specifically among female students in religious schools.

VICTIMIZATION BY THREATS

We next move to an explanation of victimization by threats, which differs from physical victimization as no violent transaction has yet transpired. Are patterns of threats at school similar to or different from patterns of physical victimization? Some theories categorize threats as verbal aggression; others see threats as part and parcel of the cycle of physical violence. If threats have trends similar to those for physical violence but different from verbal-social aggression, this could suggest that the dynamics surrounding threats should be seen as part of physical violence and not purely as verbiage.

Table 3.4. Frequency of Threatening Behaviors (in percentages)

	Never	Once or Twice	More
A student threatened to harm or hit you.	62.0	25.8	12.3
A student tried to intimidate you by the way he or she was looking at you.	75.6	18.9	5.5
Students threatened you on your way to or from school.	81.8	13.1	5.1
Gang members at school threatened, harassed, and pressured you.	91.7	5.6	2.8
You were blackmailed under threats by another student (for money, valuables, or food).	92.0	5.6	2.4

Tables 3.4 and 3.5 represent the percentage of students who report being threatened by another student. Being threatened by another student is a common experience in Israeli schools: Close to half of all the students reported at least one form of intimidation by another student during the prior month (58% and 39% for males and females, respectively); over a third of the students report being threatened and almost a quarter report that another student tried to intimidate them; the threat of extortion is reported by about 8% of the students. Many student experience victimization once or twice. A smaller percentage experienced more than two threats in the last month. Most of these figures are much higher than those reported in California (Table 3.6). Interestingly, only the prevalence of reports of being the victim of intimidating stares is higher in the California sample.

Our observations in schools indicate that threats represent an integral part of many conflicts among students during their stay in school. Some of these conflicts end up in physical contact, but many others do not. Students use threats that range from general warnings ("You will see what I/my friends will do to you when the teacher is gone") to more concrete ("I will beat you up"). Being threatened on the way to and from school seems to be associated either with a more severe conflict or with confrontation with more serious bullies who may victimize students as part of their pattern of behavior rather than due to an interpersonal conflict with a specific victim.

One of the reasons we examine threats separately from physical victimization is our desire to see whether victimization types are influenced by different contextual factors. Table 3.5 suggests, however, that victimization by threats follows very similar patterns to victimization by physical aggression.

In summary, male students report more victimization than female students, students are progressively less likely to experience threats as they advance from primary to junior high school and from junior high school to high school, and Arab and Jewish students are equally likely to have been threatened at least once during the past month.

Gender, Age, Culture, and Threats Looked at Together

Earlier we examined the interplay between gender, age, and ethnicity with regard to physical victimization (Figure 3.1). When we replicate this analysis for threats (as

Table 3.5. Frequency of Victimization by Threats (by gender, grade level, and ethnic group, in percentages)

	Total	Gender		Ethnic Group		School Level		
		Male	Female	Jewish	Arab	Primary	Junior	High
A student threatened to harm or hit you.	38.1	48.2	28.4	39.4	33.0	48.4	35.2	25.2
A student tried to intimidate you by the way he or she was looking at you.	24.4	28.5	20.6	23.6	27.1	28.4	23.1	19.8
Students threatened you on your way to or from school.	18.2	24.0	12.5	16.9	22.8	28.0	13.6	9.1
Gang members at school threatened, harassed, and pressured you.	8.4	13.0	3.7	7.9	9.8	*	8.6	7.7
You were blackmailed under threats by another student (for money, valuables, or food).	8.0	10.9	5.2	6.4	13.5	9.0	8.5	5.4
At least one type of threat.	48.1	57.6	39.3	47.6	49.8	58.4	45.2	35.1

*Not asked.

Table 3.6. Frequency of Threats in the California Sample (by gender, in percentages)

	Total	Male	Female
Someone threatened to hurt you.	21.8	28.5	16.6
Someone tried to scare you by the way he looked at you.	31.6	33.2	30.4
Threatened going to school or on the way home after school.	7.6	10.7	5.2
Bullied, threatened, or pushed by gang members.	6.7	11.1	3.4

presented in Figure 3.4), we can see identical patterns: both Arab and Jewish girls show a steady and steep decline in victimization by threats starting in fifth and sixth grade.

For Arab and Jewish boys, the decline in victimization by threats begins in the seventh and eighth grades. Similar to Figure 3.1, we can see that the decline in victimization with age is much steeper for girls than it is for boys. This remarkable similarity between physical victimization and threats suggests that the two kinds of victimization are influenced by similar mechanisms. Future research should explore the interconnectedness between these two types of victimization.

VERBAL-SOCIAL VICTIMIZATION

Tables 3.7 and 3.8 show verbal-social victimization. As can been seen in Table 3.7, verbal-social victimization is very common. More than 75% of students reported being cursed in the prior month. In Israel, approximately 45% of the students reported being cursed more than twice during the prior month. Similarly, about 60%

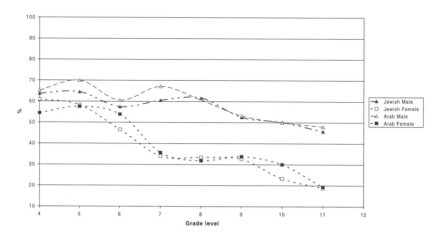

Figure 3.4. Percentage of students reporting threat victimization (by gender, grade level, and ethnic group).

Table 3.7. Frequency of Verbal-Social Victimization (in percentages)

	Never	Once or Twice	More
A student cursed you.	23.4	32.1	44.5
A student mocked, insulted, or humiliated you.	39.7	36.9	23.3
A group of students boycotted you and did not want to play or talk with you.	76.9	20.9	2.2

of students reported being insulted or humiliated by another student at least once during the prior month, and of these, about 23% reported being victimized in this manner more than twice during the prior month. These figures are considerably lower in the California sample. For instance, 58.2% of the California students reported being cursed in the prior month.

Indeed, our observations in schools showed that using foul language and cursing are very common phenomena. We observed that, in many cases, this language is part of the common talk among friends and is not only used during verbal fights. The use of words like *Ben-Zona* (literally, "whore's son") and *Koos Emack* or *Koos Ochtook* (literally in Arabic, "your mother's/sister's vagina") is quite common and usually does not prompt an emotional or physical response by the victim.

In Israel, social isolation by fellow students (a question not asked in the U.S. sample) has been experienced at least once by 23% of students. When all these social-verbal victimization types are taken together, 82% of Israeli children reported verbal-social victimization in the prior month.

The gender differences in this area are much less pronounced than in the areas of physical victimization and threats (see Table 3.8). For instance, 83% of the male students report that another student cursed them, compared with 70% of the female students, and 64% report being mocked, insulted, or humiliated, compared with 57% of the female students. Once again, similar gender patters are observed in the U.S. sample. Frequency of social isolation is similar across genders, which corresponds with recent data collected in the United States on nonphysical/emotional forms of bullying. Nansel and her associates (2001) report that both boys and girls describe high rates of indirect bullying, which corresponds to most of the behaviors mentioned in this section.

The patterns for verbal-social victimization appear to differ from patterns of threats and physical victimization. Social-verbal victimization seems to be more strongly dependent on a student's cultural group. For instance, social isolation is much more common among Arab than among Jewish students (35% compared with 20%). In contrast, cursing is much more common among Jewish students (83%, compared with 53% among Arab students).

In contrast to the age-related pattern seen with regard to physical victimization and threat, the differences between primary and junior high school students with regard to cursing and humiliation are very small. High school students, on the other hand, report the lowest levels of verbal-social victimization, as they do with most other forms of victimization we have explored so far.

Table 3.8. Frequency of Verbal-Social Victimization (by gender, grade level, and ethnic group, in percentages)

| | Total | Gender | | Ethnic Group | | School Level | | |
		Male	Female	Jewish	Arab	Primary	Junior	High
A student cursed you.	76.6	83.2	70.2	83.1	53.4	81.1	78.7	65.5
A student mocked, insulted, or humiliated you.	60.2	63.7	57.0	65.5	41.7	62.3	64.7	49.4
A group of students boycotted you and did not want to play or talk with you.	23.1	24.4	21.8	19.9	34.5	38.2	15.4	10.2
At least one type of threat.	82.3	87.8	77.3	86.1	68.8	88.2	83.2	70.7

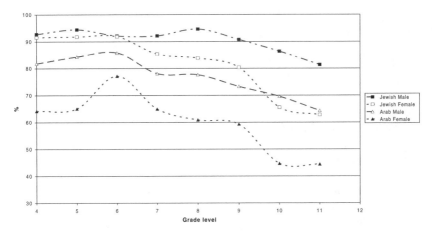

Figure 3.5. Percentage of students reporting verbal-social victimization (by gender, grade level, and ethnic group).

Figure 3.5 shows the percentage of students who had at least one experience of behaviors listed in Table 3.8 by grade level, gender, and ethnic group. Here we see a different pattern from that of physical and threat victimization. In terms of verbal victimization, Jewish boys and girls are more similar to each other during the primary school years. However, between grades 6 and 7, the Jewish girls begin a steep decline that mirrors a similar decline for Arab girls. The difference between the Arab boys and girls is significant from primary school, with a slight increase in differences over time.

LOOKING AT PHYSICAL AGGRESSION, THREATS, AND VERBAL-SOCIAL VICTIMIZATION TYPES TOGETHER

Our examination of the three different sets of victimization behaviors clearly suggests that victimization by physically aggressive acts is similar to victimization by threats and quite different from verbal-social victimization. Researchers and school professionals should be aware of these patterns. For example, physical victimization and threats are similar in their patterns and, most likely, their dynamics. The factors influencing threats are most likely the same ones influencing physical behaviors. By contrast, name-calling and social and emotional forms of victimization appear to be affected by different dynamics that may require different strategies to stem those behaviors.

School Level

The comparisons across school levels show a clear and consistent trend: primary school students report more victimization than junior high students, who report more victimization than high school students. In general, the differences between the three settings are more pronounced with regard to threats and physical victimization than verbal-social types of victimization. It is interesting to note, however, that social isolation is the behavior that differentiates the most between the reports of primary and junior high students: 38% of the primary school students reported being subjected to such a behavior, compared with 15% in junior high (and 10% in high school).

The decline in victimization as children grow older has been reported in the bullying literature and other youth violence research studies. Israeli data mirror these (e.g., Smith, Madsen, et al., 1999). This is important because the general public (and researchers) may not be aware that school victimization patterns consistently decrease as children progress through the education system. It calls for violence prevention and intervention programs at much younger ages and in primary systems, where the rates of victimization are much higher than junior high and high school settings. This goes against the trend of perceiving elementary schools only as places of prevention. Our data and other international data suggest that elementary schools are in dire need of interventions to lower their victimization rates.

Gender

When we examine the role of gender across the various types of victimization, some interesting patterns emerge. Mainly boys report the most severe and rare victimization types. For instance, boys are being threatened and harassed by gangs four times more than girls, and report being cut by a knife or a sharp object five times more. The types of victimization in which male and female students are most similar are related to the verbal-social domain: social isolation, humiliation, and being cursed by others.

To look into the gender differences in more detail, Figure 3.6 presents the ratio between boys' and girls' victimization rates by grade level with regard to the three different types of victimization we described above. This allows us to see in what age groups the differences between boys and girls are larger for each victimization type. In this figure we can see clearly that the ratio between boys' and girls' verbal victimization rates is less than 1.25; only in high school does the gap grow, but it does not reach a ratio of 1.5. In contrast, the ratio between boys' and girls' reporting of physical victimization and threats increases dramatically between sixth and seventh grades (i.e., between primary school and junior high) and then again beginning in the eighth and ninth grades.

Overall, the theoretical and empirical literatures on school violence have suggested that boys tend to be victimized more often by direct forms of physical victimization (e.g., hitting, slapping), and girls are victimized more often by indirect forms of bullying (e.g., rumors, exclusion from groups; Nansel et al., 2001; Olweus et al., 1999; Smith & Sharp, 1994; Sullivan, 2000). Similar findings were reported in studies that addressed gender differences in aggression across many other contexts

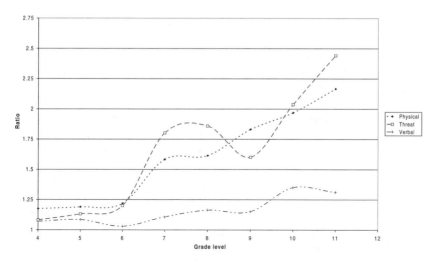

Figure 3.6.   The ratio between males' and females' reports of victimization (by grade level).

and behaviors. For instance, a comprehensive meta-analytic study concluded that there are gender differences in aggression and that the magnitude of difference was smaller for verbal and relational aggression, compared with physical aggression (Knight, Guthrie, Page, & Fabes, 2002). However, although our data strongly support gender differences with regard to physical and threat victimization, they also strongly indicate that boys and girls report similar rates of verbal-social victimization (see Nansel et al., 2001, for similar U.S. conclusions).

Some theories point to the differences in the friendship patterns of boys and girls as the underlying reason for these different rates of victimization (e.g., Owens & MacMullin, 1995; Owens et al., 2000). We think these differences may exist, but we also think that there is mounting evidence that boys have a problem with emotional/social violence similar to girls that has been largely overlooked or discounted because of boys' high rates of physical victimization. Nevertheless, based on the data, we encourage other researchers to consider that boys and girls may be suffering from similar social dynamics in verbal and social victimization. It appears that the arguments surrounding gender and victimization have a political-theoretical preference and are not always based on national data addressing the issue. For example, if boys have higher forms of both verbal-social and physical violence, we have heard some researchers state concerns that girls' victimization might be ignored. This does not have to be the case. We agree that victimization of girls has long been ignored and that verbal-social victimization is a primary form of victimization of girls. Having said this, it should not diminish the importance of addressing major issues for boys, who are suffering in the same emotional and verbal domains.

That adults lack awareness concerning both boys' and girls' verbal and social victimization brings up important questions surrounding the reporting of indirect forms of aggression by classmates and teachers. Figure 3.5 shows that the gender ratio grows with age; that is, among older students, the gap between victimization levels suffered by boys and girls is much larger than in younger students. This trend was also observed in a large study we conducted in the central and northern regions of Israel (Astor, Benbenishty, Haj-Yahia, et al., 2002). It seems that, whereas in primary schools violence and victimization are more defused and involve many male and female students, in later grades the group involved in violence and victimization is smaller, with many more boys than girls.

This finding may reflect a developmental trend in which, as children grow, a crystallization process takes place, and a small group of students emerges as consistently more prone to violence. Similar findings are evident in the literature on the development of juvenile aggression and delinquency, showing that there are overt and covert developmental pathways of disruptive behaviors (e.g., Loeber & Stouthamer-Loeber, 1998). Although many children are involved in the first step of the overt pathway, relatively few children progress along the full pathway. One of the implications of this interpretation of our findings is that although fewer boys are involved in school violence in higher grades, the select few may be involved in more serious violence. Consequently, interventions in junior high and high schools need to include components that differ qualitatively from those used with young students.

Cultural Groups

One of the questions raised by our model is how ethnic and cultural groups differ in their victimization patterns. When all types of victimization are seen together, a pattern emerges of very strong similarities between Arab, Jewish, and religious/nonreligious groups in Israel. Having said this, it should be noted that cultures and groups do differ on base rates. In our study, we focus on patterns showing that Arabs and Jews and religious and nonreligious groups tend not to differ on overall patterns of violence. Age and gender appeared to be much stronger variables regarding overall trends of different forms of violence; this was true with U.S. and Israeli comparisons. Although the rates of all these forms of violence were higher in Israel, the *patterns* were similar in each country.

KEY FINDINGS AND IMPLICATIONS

A. Victimization types on school grounds include verbal-social, threats, and physical. (Sexual harassment, weapons, and victimization by staff are completely different forms of victimization and are dealt with in separate subsequent chapters.)

B. Victimization by physical violence and by threats present similarly regarding gender, age, and culture. Verbal-social victimization has very different age, culture, and gender patterns.

C. With physical violence and threats, age and gender are the two most important variables. Culture does not seem to have much of an impact. These patterns appear to be the same in the California sample.

D. Israel has about twice as much physical victimization as in the California sample, but the overall patterns are the same.
   1. Boys are at least twice as likely as girls to be victimized physically in Israel and California.
   2. Children in primary schools have higher rates of physical victimization than junior high students, and junior high students have higher rates than high school students for Israel and the United States. Arab and Jewish children show similar patterns.
   3. Religious girls show a sharp decline in physical victimization in junior high, when they begin to attend all-girl schools.
   4. Although threats are often considered verbal victimization, the category really presents more like physical victimization.

E. With verbal-social victimization, culture and gender are the most important variables and age makes less of an impact.
   1. These patterns are the same in the California sample.
   2. Boys in each group are victimized more than girls, and rates for Jews tend to be higher than rates for Arabs.

Chapter 4

Patterns of Victimization

One problem with the development of a school violence theory stems from the literature's current narrow focus on exploring *base rates* of specific behaviors. We believe this has hampered a theoretical progression to understand basic patterns that drive school violence across different cultures and regions. As we discussed in the preface and Chapter 3, researchers have long known that base rates of victimization differ by culture, city, region, gender, and ethnic group. We propose that future research examine the many faces of victimization *simultaneously*. When looking at many different types of victimization together, researchers can ask questions about the relationships of the different forms of victimization to each other. For example, do all groups experience the same types of victimization in the same or different rank orders? Are the basic structures underlying the various victimization types similar or dissimilar across groups? These fairly simple yet potentially important questions have not yet been explored in school violence studies.

We devote this chapter to exploring the rank order and structure of victimization in our data. Most cultural theories would assume that different cultures experience types of violence in different rank orders based on differing values and circumstances unique to each culture, ethnicity, and country. If rank orders of the various types of violence are very different, researchers could see this as a sign that there are different mechanisms impacting violence in each culture. If rank orders are extremely similar or the same, it could mean that even though base rates differ (e.g., the rate could be twice as high for one group vs. another), the underlying forces creating victimization in each culture are similar or the same. This line of inquiry could have tremendous theoretical, empirical, and practice implications. If there was similarity or uniformity in ranking, policymakers and researchers might have more empirical evidence to justify using similar types of interventions for different cultures and groups. As far as we know, this is the first empirical examination of this question in the school violence literature.

RANK ORDERING SCHOOL VIOLENCE BEHAVIORS
WITHIN AND BETWEEN CULTURES

One of the most striking aspects in the comparisons made in the tables presented in Chapter 3 is that although groups differ in their levels of victimization, the frequency *patterns* appear to be almost identical. That is, the behaviors that are most frequent for one group are also the most frequent for all other groups. Similarly, certain types of victimization have the lowest frequency in all groups. From a theoretical perspective, this finding surprised us. Most theories of aggression and culture predict different normative experiences when it comes to victimization. We thought this would be true especially for diverse cultures, such as those described in Chapter 3. Given our reading of the literatures on violence, we expected that each group would have a different pattern of victimization. However, when we realized that the data looked similar across groups, we formally examined the rank order of the frequency of all the various types of victimization. Table 4.1 represents this ranking of each of the items separately by gender, culture, and school setting. We placed the rank order of each of the groups side by side so that the reader can see whether the rank order are similar across groups.

As we suspected, Table 4.1 shows that the rank orders of the frequencies of these victimization types are almost identical. In fact, the rank order correlations among the various groups is higher than r = 0.90. In this quite consistent picture, one type of victimization stands out: being boycotted, socially isolated/excluded, by a group of students. This behavior has a higher ranking among female and Arab students, which may serve as an indication that it has a special meaning in certain contexts and cultures. As mentioned in Chapter 2, research on aggression and gender suggests that girls may experience more of these kinds of socially isolating activities. To our knowledge there is no literature that predicts why Arab students would have higher levels of this kind of behavior; future research should explore this question.

The overall similarities are remarkably consistent and stable across all groups. As mentioned, this contrasts with most theories of culture and aggression. Our data suggest that victimization may share many characteristics between cultures that go beyond particular cultural norms and influences.

Table 4.1 indicates that victimization levels of all groups are aligned along a shared combined dimension of severity and frequency. The most frequently occurring and least severe types of victimization are the verbal-emotional (being cursed and humiliated) and the mild and moderately aggressive behaviors of being seized and shoved and being threatened by another student. The least frequent and most severe types of victimization are related to serious fights that result in students requiring medical attention, receiving a serious beating, and being cut by a knife or a sharp object. Serious threatening by gang members and being blackmailed by another student are included in the least frequent and most severe violent acts perpetrated against students in school.

Table 4.1. Rank Order of Frequency of Victimization Types in Israel

	Total	Gender		Ethnic Group		School Level		
		Male	Female	Jewish	Arab	Primary	Junior	High
A student cursed you.	1	1	1	1	1	1	1	1
A student mocked, insulted, or humiliated you.	2	2	2	2	2	2	2	2
A student seized and shoved you on purpose.	3	3	3	3	3	3	3	3
A student threatened to harm or hit you.	4	4	4	4	6	4	4	4
You were involved in a fistfight.	5	5	8	6	4	5	5	5
You were kicked or punched by a student.	6	6	6	5	8	6	6	7
A student used a rock or another instrument in order to hurt you.	7	7	9	7	9	8	7	8
A student tried to intimidate you by the way he or she was looking at you.	8	8	7	8	7	9	8	6
A group of students boycotted you and did not want to play or talk with you.	9	9	5	9	5	7	10	10
A student took your things from you by force.	10	11	10	10	11	11	9	9
Student threatened you on your way to or from school.	11	10	11	11	10	10	11	11
You were involved in a fight, were hurt, and required medical attention.	12	12	12	12	12	13	12	12
A student gave you a serious beating.	13	13	13	13	14	12	15	15
You were blackmailed under threats by another student (for money, valuables, or food).	14	14	14	14	13	14	13	14
Gang members at school threatened, harassed, and pressured you.	15	15	15	15	15	15	14	13
A student cut you with a knife or a sharp instrument on purpose.	16	16	16	16	16	16	16	16

We believe this severity/frequency dimension holds clues to what experiences are common and what is unique in different cultures. For example, one might suspect that raw frequency is affected greatly by culture and context. Indeed, our study shows that Arab students experience many victimization types more frequently than Jewish students. Nevertheless, the fact that scores are ranked similarly points to universality in the relative order of victimization, independent of culture.

Patterns Across Cultures

These findings raise the question: Would the same patterns emerge in a different context altogether? That is, will this similarity appear for boys and girls in a different culture? Furthermore, is it possible that the rank order we found in Israel will be similar to the rank order in another culture? To examine this question, we analyzed a data set provided by Furlong. Using an instrument similar to ours, Furlong collected data from about 8,750 students in more than 40 schools in various southern and central counties in California. The first issue we explored is whether the patterns between boys and girls and among Latina/o, African American, White/European, Native American, and Asian students in the California sample were similar to each other (within-culture).

Table 4.2 presents a more complex picture than in the Israeli sample. Here, too, the patterns are very similar across the groups: The most frequent behaviors are between boys and girls and Latinos and non-Latinos, and the least frequent have very low frequencies in all groups. Still, certain behaviors stand out. It is clear in this table that sexual victimization is a much more salient experience for female students. The frequency of sexual harassment was ranked 6th for girls and 14th for boys, and the frequency of unwanted physical sexual advances was ranked 10th for girls and 15th for boys. Additionally, for boys, the frequency of being punched and kicked was ranked higher than for girls.

The patterns of reports made by the different ethnic groups were very similar. The only difference was that unwanted physical sexual advances were ranked higher by Latino groups. Given that the California data showed consistent patterns across groups in the United States, we asked whether the rank order might be similar between the United States and Israel. Table 4.3 shows the similarity in ranking patterns between the two countries. Although there are significant differences in the raw frequencies of the various types of victimization, the rank orders are very similar. The only noticeable difference is the higher salience of intimidation by staring in the California sample. The similarities suggest that severity (and possibly pain) serves as an organizing mechanism for ranking the various behaviors in similar orders within and between societies that at face value appear quite diverse on victimization issues. It also suggests that culture has its greatest influence on the raw scores and not necessarily on the way different acts of victimization are experienced. Here, severity and frequency seem to go hand in hand and to be universal.

Table 4.2. Rank Order of Frequency of Victimization Types in the California Sample

	Total	Gender		Ethnic Group				
		Female	Male	White	Latina/o	Asian American	African American	Native American
Someone yelled bad words or cursed at you.	1	2	1	1	1	1	1	1
Someone made fun of you, put you down.	2	1	2	2	2	2	2	2
Your personal property was stolen.	3	3	4	3	3	3	3	3
Someone tried to scare you by the way he or she looked at you.	4	4	6	4	5	4	5	4
You saw a student on campus with a knife or razor.	5	5	3	6	4	6	4	5
You were grabbed or shoved by someone being mean.	6	7	5	5	6	5	7	6
Someone threatened to hurt you.	7	8	7	7	7	7	8	7
Your personal property was smashed or damaged on purpose.	8	10	9	8	9	8	11	8
Someone sexually harassed you.	9	6	13	10	10	12	9	10
You were punched or kicked by someone trying to hurt you.	10	12	8	9	12	10	13	9
Someone made unwanted physical sexual advances toward you.	11	9	14	11	13	13	10	11
You were involved in ethnic or racial conflict among students.	12	11	10	12	8	9	6	13
You were hit by a rock or other object by someone trying to hurt you.	13	14	11	13	14	11	14	12
You personally saw another student with a gun on campus.	14	13	12	17	11	14	12	15
Something of yours was taken by force or threat of force.	15	15	15	14	16	15	17	14
You were threatened on your way to or from school.	16	16	17	16	15	17	15	17
You were bullied, threatened, or pushed by gang members.	17	18	16	15	18	16	19	16
You went to a doctor or nurse because you were hurt in an attack or fight.	18	17	18	18	17	18	16	18
You were cut with a knife or something sharp by someone trying to hurt you.	19	19	19	19	21	19	18	21
You were threatened by a student with a knife and you saw the knife.	20	20	20	20	19	20	21	20
You were threatened by a student with a gun and you saw the gun.	21	21	21	21	20	21	20	19

Table 4.3. Rank Order of Frequency of Victimization Types in Israel and in the California Sample

	Israel				California			
			Rankings				Rankings	
	%	Total	Male	Female	%	Total	Male	Female
A student cursed you.	76.6	1	1	1	58.2	1	1	2
A student mocked, insulted, or humiliated you.	60.2	2	2	2	54.4	2	2	1
A student seized and shoved you on purpose.	48.9	3	3	3	25.6	5	4	5
You saw a student with a knife in school.	46.4	4	4	4	30.7	4	3	4
A student threatened to harm or hit you.	38.1	5	5	5	21.8	6	6	6
You were kicked or punched by a student who wanted to hurt you.	31.6	6	6	6	16.0	7	7	7
A student used a rock or another instrument in order to hurt you.	24.8	7	7	8	11.5	8	8	8
A student tried to intimidate you by the way he or she was looking at you.	24.4	8	8	7	31.6	3	5	3
A student took your things from you by force.	19.5	9	10	9	7.8	9	9	9
Students threatened you on your way to or from school.	18.2	10	9	10	7.6	10	10	10
You were involved in a fight, were hurt, and required medical attention.	11.3	11	11	11	5.7	12	12	12
Gang members at school threatened, harassed, and pressured you.	8.4	12	13	13	6.7	11	11	11
You were threatened by a student with a knife and you saw knife.	6.3	13	12	12	3.3	14	14	14
You saw a student in school with a gun.	4.4	14	14	14	2.9	15	15	15
You were threatened by a student with a gun and you saw the gun.	3.5	15	15	15	2.9	16	16	16
A student cut you with a knife or a sharp instrument on purpose.	3.5	16	16	16	3.4	13	13	13

This finding has great theoretical and pragmatic implications that we continue to discuss in this chapter. First, we wanted to examine if the dimensions of severity and frequency could also be confirmed empirically by a factor analysis strategy, so that we could speak more confidently about severity as a universal dimension.

FACTOR STRUCTURE OF VIOLENT BEHAVIOR

Current conceptualizations of violence victimization are classified by conceptually driven content-related domains of behavior (e.g., verbal, physical, sexual). It is possible, however, that being a victim of one type of behavior in a domain increases or decreases the probability of being a victim of another type of violent act from this domain. The findings in the previous section indicate strongly that victimization types may align along the dimension of severity more than along the content-related categories we usually use (e.g., verbal-emotional, threatening, and physical violence). To examine this issue further, we ask, How do different forms of victimization associate with one another, or how they are grouped together in real life?

Further, we ask whether this factor structure is similar across contexts. That is, are victimization behaviors organized similarly for boys and girls, Jews and Arabs, and students in the three school levels (primary, junior high, and high schools)? To illustrate, the various types of victimization among boys may form two groups, mild and serious. For girls, on the other hand, types of victimization may be grouped into verbal and physical. These differences in structure may have significant theoretical and practical implications.

To answer these questions we performed separate factor analyses on students in each of the 18 groups formed by the intersection of gender (male, female), school type (primary, junior high, and high school), and cultural group (Jewish secular, Jewish religious, and Arabs). In Tables 4.4 and 4.5, we present the findings for secondary and primary schools separately because the instruments were not identical in the two settings. The tables show that the various victimization types are associated with two factors;[1] most items are loaded on either Factor I or II, and only a few are loaded on both. The first answer the tables seem to provide is the clear tendency for school victimization to be grouped along the dimension of the frequency of the behavior: Victimization types that are not frequent belong to Factor I, whereas items with higher frequency are associated with Factor II. Given that this dimension of frequency is almost identical to the dimension of severity and potential harm, we can see that being victimized by one type of a moderately violent behavior, such as pushing and shoving, occurs together with being victimized by other types of moderate and less severe violent behaviors, such as being threatened. Being victimized by more severe behaviors, such as being cut with a sharp object, occurs together with being victimized by other behaviors that reflect more severe consequences, such as being injured in a fight and needing medical attention.

Table 4.4. Factor Structure of Victimization Types in Secondary- Schools

	Total Frequency %	Factors									
		Junior High					High School				
		Overall	Male	Female	Jewish	Arab	Overall	Male	Female	Jewish	Arab
A student threatened you with a gun and you saw the gun.	3.5	1	1	1	1	1	1	1	1	1	1
You saw a student in school with a gun.	4.5	1	1	1	1	1	1	1	1	1	1
A student cut you with a knife or a sharp instrument on purpose.	5.7	1	1	1	1	1	1	1	1	1	1
A student threatened you with a knife and you saw the knife.	6.4	1	1	1	1	2	1	1	½	1	2
A student gave you a serious beating.	7.0	1	1	1	1	1	1	1	1	1	1
You were blackmailed under threats by another student (for money, valuables, or food).	7.4	1	1	1	1	1	1	1	1	1	1
Gang members at school threatened, harassed, and pressured you.	8.3	1	1	1	1	1	1	1	1	1	1
You were involved in a fight, were hurt, and required medical attention.	9.7	1	1	1	1	1	1	1	1	1	1
Students threatened you on your way to or from school.	12.0	1	1	1	1	1	1	1	1	1	1
A group of students boycotted you and did not want to play or talk with you.	13.5	1	1	1	1	2	1	1	1	1	½
You were involved in a conflict between veteran Israelis and new immigrants.	14.0	1	1	1	1	1	1	1	½	1	1
A student took your things from you by force.	15.0	½	1	2	½	1	1	1	½	1	1
Students intentionally destroyed or broke your personal belongings.	18.0	½	1	2	2	1	½	1	2	½	1
A student used a rock or another instrument in order to hurt you.	21.6	2	2	2	2	½	2	2	2	2	2
A student tried to intimidate you by the way he or she was looking at you.	21.9	2	½	2	2	2	2	½	2	2	2
You were kicked or punched by a student who wanted to hurt you.	24.8	2	2	2	2	2	2	2	2	2	½

(continued)

Table 4.4. (continued)

	Total Frequency %	Factors									
		Junior High					High School				
		Overall	Male	Female	Jewish	Arab	Overall	Male	Female	Jewish	Arab
You were involved in a fistfight.	25.6	2	2	2	2	2	2	2	1	2	½
A student threatened to harm or hit you.	31.6	2	2	2	2	2	2	2	2	2	2
A student seized and shoved you on purpose.	43.8	2	2	2	2	2	2	2	2	2	2
A student stole your personal belongings or equipment.	45.9	2	2	2	2	2	2	2	2	2	2
You saw a student in school with a knife.	47.1	2	½	2	2	2	2	2	2	2	2
A student mocked, insulted, or humiliated you.	59.1	2	2	2	2	2	2	2	2	2	2
A student cursed you.	73.9	2	2	2	2	2	2	2	2	2	2

Table 4.5. Factor Structure of Victimization Types of Primary Schools

	Total Frequency (%)	Factors				
				Gender		Ethnic Group
		Overall	Male	Female	Jewish	Arab
You saw a student with a gun.	3.7	1	1	1	1	1
A student threatened you with a knife and you saw the knife.	6.8	1	1	1	1	1
You were blackmailed under threats by another student (for money, valuables, or food).	8.9	1	1	1	1	1
You were involved in a fight, were hurt, and required medical attention.	13.8	1	1	1	1	1
A student gave you a serious beating.	15.3	1	1	1	½	1
A student took your things from you by force.	26.9	½	2	2	2	1
Students threatened you on your way to or from school.	28.1	2	2	2	2	½
A student tried to intimidate you by the way he or she was looking at you.	28.4	2	2	2	2	½
You saw a student in school with a knife.	28.8	1	1	1	1	1
A student used a rock or another instrument in order to hurt you.	30.0	2	2	2	2	½
You were kicked or punched by a student who wanted to hurt you.	42.5	2	2	2	2	2
You were involved in a fistfight.	42.6	2	2	2	2	2
A student stole your personal property or equipment.	45.0	2	½	½	2	2
A student threatened to harm or hit you.	48.4	2	2	2	2	2
A student seized and shoved you on purpose.	57.1	2	2	2	2	2
A student mocked, insulted, or humiliated you.	62.2	2	2	2	2	2
A student cursed you.	81.1	2	2	2	2	2

Our second question was whether the structure of interrelationships is universal across different ethnic groups. For instance, if we examine Arab boys, do we get the same pattern of interrelationships as when we look at Jewish boys or at Arab girls? Inspection of the tables strongly suggests that most groups share similar patterns of relationships that we described above.

In a few instances, however, it seemed that for a specific group of students, a certain item was exceptionally loaded on a different factor than in most other groups. When we examined these outstanding cases we concluded that in this group the frequency of that behavior was exceptionally lower or higher than in other groups. See, for instance, being the victim of threats made by another student: In all groups, this is a frequent behavior that is included in Factor II; in the group of high school Arab girls, it is included in Factor I (rare/severe behaviors). Indeed, the relative frequency of "threatening to hurt" in this group (6%) is much lower than in all other groups.

Along with the earlier rankings, these findings suggest that researchers need to look more closely at severity and frequency of behaviors as possible universal dimensions that help explain the phenomenon of victimization across cultures. However, the relative ranking of the behaviors appears to be driven by forces beyond culture, such as severity and pain, creating a relative ordering within each culture that looks very similar, if not the same, even at the item level.

The fact that culture may not have a huge impact on the ordering of victimization levels has great theoretical implications for fields such as anthropology, psychology, social work, education, public health, and medicine. First, it means that the experiences of violence within each culture are probably hierarchically organized in similar ways according to severity (frequency and severity are two sides of the same coin and cannot be separated). Societal norms do not impact the relative hierarchy within or between cultures; order is influenced by the actual frequency rates of each category of behavior and within prescribed boundaries created by the overarching hierarchy in that society.

Against the backdrop of what seem to be universal dimensions of pain/severity, variations and deviations acquire special significance and should lead to further exploration. Thus, if the relative frequency (the rank order) of a certain form of victimization is extremely high or extremely low in a certain group, this suggests that the behavior has special meaning for that group. Consider, for instance, the issue of social exclusion and boycotting, which may rank higher or lower in different cultures. In certain cultures, it may be perceived as similar to other types of social-verbal victimization and its frequency would be as high as other forms of victimization, such as spreading rumors. In other cultures, social exclusion may be used only in extreme cases of hostility, carrying much more meaningful implications and signifying that the victim is being totally cut off from the peer group. Similarly, differences in the relative frequencies of various forms of sexual victimization between genders will help direct attention to the different meanings that these behaviors have for male and female students.

In Tables 4.1–4.5 we rank ordered victimization types by their frequency, overlooking how far apart two types of victimization were in terms of prevalence. Researchers should examine the relative distance between the ranked victimization rates within cultures. For example, it is possible that in different cultures, the distance between rankings 1, 2, and 3 are different than in other countries with the same rankings, even though the same behaviors are ranked high. Thus, whereas in one culture the most frequent victimization type may be reported by 50% of the students and the next most frequent reported by 25% of the students, in another culture the most frequent victimization type may be reported by 40% of the students and the second most frequent by 38%. The study of these issues could provide better understanding of the potential relative role of culture in similarly universally ranked categories. It could also explain why aggression and violence norms and behaviors appear so different in different cultures. Our data suggest that there are differences but also great structural similarities. Both universalities and peculiarities within and between cultures need to be addressed if a viable theory of school violence is to survive and explain victimization in different cultures.

It is not entirely clear why this finding has not been reported in the literature of school or youth violence prior to our study, but we suspect that there are several reasons. First, there is an element of intuitive obviousness in the fact that severity and frequency of behaviors would be driving forces in ranking school violence events. Yet, intervention literatures and theories do not predict such uniformity. In fact, most theories and interventions point to the central role of culture in determining norms of violence and violence levels (see, e.g., de Oliveira, 1998; Feldman, 1998; and reports from a variety of cultures in Watts, 1998). Much of the aggression and violence literature in sociology and psychology assumes that culture is the primary source in establishing aggression levels. If this were true, we would see cultural attitudes creating very different rankings of behaviors that are more "acceptable" in some cultures versus those not "acceptable" in others. Instead, we see that norms appear to impact frequency levels but not relative rankings between violence behaviors.

Another reason this has not been explored has to do with the organization of the violence and victimization literatures. Currently, the violence literature is built on different types of violence behaviors, such as bullying, school fights, sexual harassment, emotional-verbal behaviors, and weapons use. These behaviors are rarely examined together in one study with the same sample. In fact, we cannot find a single study that compares or looks at the relative rankings of more than one kind of violence at the same time. This means that the actual organization (domains) of the violence literature may have served as an obstacle in discovering uniformity in ranked victimization behaviors across and within cultures.

A third reason for the dearth in this kind of research stems from the fact that most inquiries on violence are attempting to describe a category of person, such as a victim or victimizer (rather than a behavior). Therefore, even if researchers include different behaviors, they do not compare these behaviors between different ethnic groups and cultures. A fourth reason is related to the fact that most studies don't have an array of different forms of violence in their questionnaires. Most violence surveys don't have very many questions even within domains of violence. Our study allows such comparisons because we ask over 100 questions altogether (compared with five questions in most other national surveys) and we cover a range of victimization behaviors (about 40 specific questions related to victimization).

Current theories seek either universal or relativistic components of violence rather than attempting to explain what is universal and what might be relativistic. Because culture has become a relativistic concept in the social sciences (in recent years), we think it has been assumed that violence is relative between cultures and there have been few attempts to look at universalities.

We think looking at school violence and other forms of violence as we have could facilitate a greater understanding of the way violence is structured in our society.

KEY FINDINGS AND IMPLICATIONS

A. When all forms of victimization—verbal-social, threats, and physical violence—are rank ordered, overall patterns are extremely similar across gender, ethnicity/culture, school types (primary, junior high, high school), and within and between countries.
   1. We think this commonality in rank ordering of victimization type reflects common global victimization patterns that exist within schools.
   2. Looking at behaviors that deviate from this rank order can be useful to better understand cultural differences.
B. Victimization types fit into two major factor structures: those that are rare and severe, and those that are more common with less severe outcomes.
C. Severity and relative frequency of the types of victimization appear to be a cross-cultural organizing dimension that may keep rankings similar within and across cultures.

NOTE

1. Technically, the initial factor extractions were performed with the principal components method, with subsequent orthogonal Varimax rotation with Keiser normalization. An oblique rotation was also performed for each analysis, but because both rotations yielded very similar results, only the orthogonal solutions are presented. At the first stage, the rotation was performed on components with Eigen values greater than 1. The analyses yielded solutions with three to seven factors, a rather large number that seems to suggest that victimization types are not interrelated much. However, when we explored further, we arrived at a slightly different conclusion. Inspection of Eigen values suggests that in most groups, the first factor explained a large amount of item variance (Eigen values ranging between about

5 and 7), and the second factor explained much less variance (Eigen values in the area of 2). In many groups, these two factors were responsible for the most frequent (appearing in the upper part of the table) and the least frequent (appearing in the lower part of the table) behaviors. All the remaining factors had Eigen values rather close to 1. Using the Catell criterion, we believed we were justified to try a solution with only two factors. Therefore, in the final analyses, the number of factors selected for rotation was forced to be two in all the groups.

Chapter 5

Sexual Harassment

The findings we present in this chapter strongly suggest that victimization by sexual harassment shows different patterns of relationships from other forms of school victimization, which is the major reason we address sexual harassment in a separate chapter. By doing so, we can present some of the distinct features and patterns more comprehensively.

From a theoretical standpoint, sexual harassment is considered a unique form of victimization because, though it shares some commonalties with other forms of school violence, it has characteristics that are quite different (Zeira, Astor, & Benbenishty, 2002). Theoretical discussions and empirical studies on sexual harassment have reflected this complexity. For example, in the school violence literature, sexual harassment is often described as one of many behaviors considered to be part of school violence and student victimization. Yet, surprisingly, other than the data generated from the study in this book, no national study of school violence has explored sexual harassment itself, let alone in conjunction with the many other forms of school violence. Therefore, theorists have very little empirical data concerning within- or cross-cultural prevalence rates of sexual harassment in schools.

Furthermore, the sexual harassment literature demonstrates very little consensus about the theoretical roots of sexual harassment in schools and its connectedness to other forms of sexualized violence (Lee, Croninger, Linn, & Chen, 1996). Some researchers have speculated that sexual harassment is a precursor to dating violence and/or domestic violence later in life (Molidor & Tolman, 1998). Pellegrini (2001) presents a developmental perspective on sexual harassment in schools, suggesting a trend in which, as adolescents move from same-gender groups into cross-gender relationships, they engage in early courtship behaviors that include sexual harassment behaviors.

Others argue that sexual harassment is part of a larger cultural patriarchal pattern and is a reflection of the society's mores and views toward male-female relationships (Fineran & Bennett, 1998; Hand & Sanchez, 2000). The degree of patriarchy in society has been by far the most common theoretical explanation for school-based sexual harassment behaviors. Under this theoretical formulation, sexual harassment victimization is influenced greatly by cultural variables (especially those dealing with social hierarchy and patriarchal issues) as they intersect with gender. Hand and Sanchez exemplify this approach; they write, "In fact, schools serve as hotbeds for cultivating sexual harassment experiences and tactics that children, adolescents, and adults carry into their adult settings. Schools are key settings for the socialization of children into a sexist gender order" (p. 720). This theoretical characterization distinguishes sexual harassment from other forms of victimization, whose patterns appear to be more influenced by gender and age and to a lesser degree by culture (see Table 3.1 for an example of such results for physical victimization).

There is agreement in the sexual harassment literature regarding what kinds of behaviors constitute sexual harassment. These are often described as a diverse set of behaviors that share common goals of humiliating, intimidating, establishing dominance and hierarchy, and victimizing students based on their gender and by psychological and physical sexual means. Sexual harassment behaviors can range in severity from name calling and teasing to sexual assault. There also seems to be agreement that overly persistent and inappropriate attempts by perpetrators to engage in sexual experiences with other students (without the intention of humiliating or shaming the victim) should be labeled sexual harassment. Despite consensus regarding the behaviors undergirding sexual harassment as a concept, there have been few if any empirical explorations into the differences in prevalence of the different types of sexual harassment (e.g., Hand & Sanchez, 2000). Moreover, there have not been any cross-cultural empirical studies of school-based sexual harassment behaviors in cultures that are more patriarchal.

The present study provides a unique opportunity for investigating the cultural context of school sexual harassment. In our sample, the Orthodox Jewish schools and Arab schools have a tendency toward patriarchal values; we would therefore expect to see patterns reflecting patriarchy when compared to Jewish secular schools. The data in the study also allow us to explore different forms of sexual victimization as well as the gender relationships between victim and perpetrator for each type of victimization.

As we did with other types of victimization, in this chapter we first investigate the frequency of specific types of victimization. Careful examination of separate acts of sexual harassment is necessary for a better understanding of the relative contributions of culture, gender, and age. Following our conceptual model, we examine sexual harassment in context and examine the effects of gender, age, and culture. The majority of our analyses center on youth in junior high and high schools. We also present some preliminary data on primary school sexual harassment gathered in our third wave of the national study.

Before we present our data, we should remind the reader that we asked the students to indicate whether they experienced each of the behaviors listed in Table 5.1 *at least once during the prior month.* This is quite different from the question presented to students in the most often cited research on sexual harassment, the national survey of high school students conducted for the American Association of University Women (AAUW, 1993). The AAUW questionnaire asks about "your whole school life." Clearly, one would expect major differences in frequency of reports when a student is asked about experiences occurring over as many as 10 years in school, compared with asking about last month.

We believe that there are also conceptual differences that should not be overlooked when comparisons are made between our study and the AAUW study (1993). We think that recent events are more available to memory. When a student is asked about a period that spans many years we expect that extensive retrieval and information processing is taking place. These processes are more vulnerable to retrospective interpretations and screening. One possible consequence is that older male and female students may look back at similar experiences with a framework influenced by their current age and gender role. Certain experiences may be seen in retrospect by adolescent male students as "horsing around" and not categorized and remembered as relevant to sexual harassment. Adolescent female students, on the other hand, may interpret these behaviors very differently and categorize them as relevant to sexual victimization. Current efforts to address issues of victimization of girls and women in our society and in schools and to sensitize the public to injustice and oppression of girls and women may influence female more than male students to categorize a wider range of behaviors as relevant to sexual victimization.

We return to these issues in our final chapter. In the present context, we caution the reader against direct comparisons between prevalence rates we report here and those cited in other studies.

WHAT TYPES OF SEXUAL HARASSMENT DO ISRAELI CHILDREN EXPERIENCE?

In this section we describe the base rates of different types of sexual harassment in Israeli schools. Table 5.1 shows that the most common sexual harassment behaviors reported by junior high and high school students in Israel are being shown obscene pictures (11.9%), being victimized by a student who touched or tried to touch or pinch in a sexual way without approval (11.5%), and being victimized by a student who tried to "come on" (sexually) and made unwanted sexual comments (10.2%). Slightly less frequent types were being victimized in the bathroom or locker room by a student's peeping (7.1%) and having a student take or try to take one's clothes off (for sexual reasons; 7.9%).

Table 5.1 shows clearly that boys tend to report more sexual harassment than girls. This is most evident in the behaviors of peeping in the bathroom (10% of males reporting vs. 5% of female) and being victimized by another student trying to take one's clothes off (13% vs. 3%). Still, there are behaviors for which the differences in reporting between boys and girls were small.

Table 5.1. Frequency and Rank Order of Sexual Harassment (by gender, grade level, and ethnic group)

	Total		Gender				Ethnic Group				School Level			
			Male		Female		Jewish		Arab		Junior		High	
	%	Rank	%	Rank	%	Rank	%	Rank	%	Rank	%	Rank	%	Rank
A student showed you obscene pictures or sent you obscene letters.	11.9	1	16.0	1	7.9	3	10.6	2	17.1	1	13.7	1	8.7	3
A student touched or tried to touch you or to pinch you in a sexual way without your approval.	11.5	2	12.1	4	10.7	1	11.8	1	10.4	4	12.6	2	9.3	4
A student tried to come on to you (sexually) and made sexual comments that you did not want.	10.2	3	9.4	6	10.9	2	10.3	3	9.8	5	10.1	4	10.3	2
A student tried to kiss you without your consent.	9.9	4	12.5	3	7.2	4	9.1	4	12.8	2	10.1	3	9.5	1
Sexually insulting things about you were written on walls or sexual rumors were spread about you.	8.1	5	9.2	7	6.9	5	7.9	5	8.6	6	9.0	5	6.4	5
A student took or tried to take your clothes off (for sexual reasons).	7.9	6	13.0	2	2.8	7	8.2	6	6.7	7	9.1	6	5.3	7
A student peeped while you were in the bathroom or the locker room.	7.1	7	9.6	5	4.6	6	6.3	7	10.5	3	7.9	7	5.5	6
Any of the above behaviors.	29.1		32.5		25.9		28.9		29.6		32.4		22.9	

In Table 5.1 we can see that high school students tend to report less frequently on several types of sexual victimization compared with junior high students. The most significant differences were much lower reporting in high school of students trying to take off another student's clothes (9% in junior high vs. 5% in high school) and showing obscene pictures (14% vs. 9%).

The comparisons between Jewish and Arab students revealed some large differences. Arab students reported more victimization by another student peeping (11%, vs. 6% among Jewish students) and students showing unwanted obscene pictures (17%, vs. 11% among Jewish students).

The findings we present focus on students in junior high and high school. There are indications from retrospective studies that sexual harassment starts as early as primary school (Bryant, 1993). However, our literature search found only one empirical study that asked primary school students about their experiences of sexual harassment. Murnen and Smolak (2000) presented 11 scenarios of sexual harassment incidents to primary school students and asked them for their interpretations and whether any of the incidents had ever happened to them. The authors report that only about a quarter of the students reported no sexual harassment. The study was based on 73 students from two classes in rural Ohio and cannot be considered representative.

To address this gap in the literature we added four questions regarding sexual harassment to our primary school questionnaire in the 2002 data collection wave.[1] In general, the primary school patterns are very similar to these in secondary schools; thus, the patterns shown in the secondary school data are applicable to primary schools, suggesting that sexual harassment begins very early and so interventions should start before junior high.

PATTERNS OF SEXUAL VICTIMIZATION

We examined several behaviors that are used commonly in research on sexual harassment; they all relate to inappropriate sexual behaviors that cause emotional distress. Some behaviors also vary along the dimension of intent to cause humiliation and harm. The question we raise, however, is whether all these sexual harassment behaviors have similar patterns, or if it is possible, and perhaps important, to make meaningful distinctions among them. Previous chapters showed that other types of victimization were aligned along the severity-frequency dimensions. For other forms of victimization we found that although there were significant differences in frequency of reporting, the patterns were similar for boys and girls, Arabs and Jews, and the various school levels.

Table 5.1 paints a different picture. The examination of the distribution patterns across the various groups reveals many differences. For example, the most frequent reports made by girls were that another student touched or tried to touch them or tried to come on to them. In contrast, among boys, another student showing obscene pictures, trying to take their clothes off, and trying to kiss them were the most frequently reported incidents. Interestingly, in Hand and Sanchez's study (2000), rank orderings among boys and girls were much more similar, except for one major difference: Whereas for girls the most frequently reported victimization was being kissed against their will, for boys being kissed against their will was rank ordered 6th (of 14 behaviors). Being called gay, on the other hand, was the most frequent victimization type for boys and only the 6th for girls.

Among Jewish students, the most frequent reports were that a student touched (or tried to touch) or pinch them in a sexual way without their approval; this behavior was ranked only 4th among Arab students. The rank order of peeping, on the other hand, was much higher among Arabs. These differential patterns suggest the dependence of sexual harassment on mechanisms that are influenced strongly by gender and culture.

In the analyses presented so far there are clear indications that sexual harassment behaviors show different relationship patterns for gender, ethnicity, and school level. Do sexual harassment behaviors belong to different empirical categories? Sexual harassment behaviors may belong to more than one dimension, and perhaps reflect different aspects of the more general phenomenon of sexual harassment. Pellegrini (2001) used a developmental perspective and described behaviors of youngsters in their early attempts at cross-gender relationships. Some of these behaviors are more aggressive in nature (rough play, "pushing and poking" courtship behaviors; Maccoby, 1998) and are a "relatively safe and ambiguous way in which to interact with peers of the opposite sex" (Pellegrini, p. 121).

From our perspective, the most important potential conceptual distinction regarding our list of behaviors is intent of the perpetrator. Some sexual harassment behaviors have the intent of serving the sexual desires of the perpetrator, whereas other behaviors' sole function is to humiliate or shame the victim (some serve both functions). To explore this, we conducted a factor analysis of the scale of sexual harassment, using students as our units of analysis. Table 5.2 contains the results when a two-factor solution was explored.

We can see in Table 5.2 that three of the behaviors seem to relate to one factor: inappropriate and overly aggressive attempts to have sexual interaction, such as making sexual passes or trying to kiss or touch in a sexual manner. With these kinds of behaviors, the goal and intent is most likely to have sexual contact with the victim. The second factor was also of a sexual nature but was more strongly associated with attempts to humiliate and degrade the victim, such as by spreading rumors, peeping/spying, and intentionally showing obscene pictures or sending obscene letters. One behavior loaded on both factors: trying to take off the student's clothes for sexual reasons. This makes sense because taking off someone's clothes could serve the purpose of humiliation in some situations and have sexual connotations in others. For example, when a student walks behind another student and pulls his or her pants down in front of other students, it is clearly a humiliation tactic. This is a common behavior among male students and seems to combine both direct sexual

Table 5.2.   A Factor Analysis of Victimization and Sexual Harassment

	Factors	
	I	*II*
A student tried to come on to you (sexually) and made sexual comments that you did not want.	0.77	
A student touched or tried to touch you or to pinch you in a sexual way without your approval.	0.77	
A student tried to kiss you without your consent.	0.73	
Sexually insulting things about you were written on walls or sexual rumors were spread about you.		0.82
A student peeped while you were in the bathroom or the locker room.		0.60
A students showed you obscene pictures or sent you obscene letters.		0.58
A student took or tried to take your clothes off (for sexual reasons).	0.39	0.56

Note: Variance explained by Factor I was 43.4% and by Factor II was 12.0%.

aggression and an attempt to embarrass boys in front of girls. However, while dating, an overly aggressive sexual advance may stem from an attempt to have sexual contact rather than to cause pain and humiliate the other student.

Further analyses show that boys report more victimization of both types of sexual harassment. The gender gap with regard to "intent to humiliate" types of sexual harassment victimization is much wider; whereas 27% of male students reported being victimized by at least one of these behaviors in the prior month, 15% of female students made such a report. A similar pattern emerges when we compare Arab and Jewish students; Arab students report more of both types of victimization, but the gap between the ethnic groups is larger for intent-to-humiliate types of victimization.

GENDER AND CULTURAL SIMILARITIES AND DIFFERENCES

One of the questions that we asked throughout this study is whether gender differences are similar or dissimilar across contexts. The above findings raise the specific question: Are the gaps between boys and girls in terms of sexual victimization different for Jewish and Arab students? We examined this question separately for the two types of sexual harassment: intent to humiliate and intent to have sexual contact. Would groups in more patriarchal school settings reflect a different pattern with regard to these two kinds of victimization?

Figure 5.1 reveals an interesting picture. Clearly, the gap between the genders in reporting sexual harassment is much wider among Arab students than among Jewish students. Furthermore, the pattern of this gap differs in these two cultures. Among Jewish students, boys and girls report very similar levels of sexual victimization that results from the intent to have sexual contact. The gap between them exists only with regard to behaviors with the intent to humiliate. In contrast, among

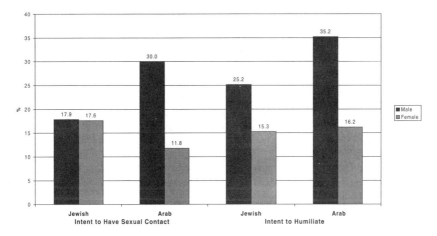

Figure 5.1.   Sexual harassment among Jewish and Arab boys and girls.

Arab students, the differences between the genders are much larger with regard to types of sexual victimization associated with the intent to have sexual contact.

These findings seem to imply that culture is influencing the gender differences in the area of sexual harassment. To test the question of culture and patriarchy further we compared students in Jewish Orthodox schools with students in Jewish secular schools. Figure 5.2 suggests that the gender patterns among students in Orthodox Jewish schools are quite similar to those in the Arab schools. Reports of sexual victimization with the intent to have sexual contact are lower among boys compared to girls in secular Jewish schools; the trend is reversed in Orthodox schools (as is the case

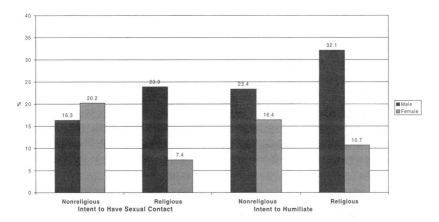

Figure 5.2.   Sexual harassment among male and female Jewish students in religious and nonreligious schools.

in Arab schools), where male students report more sexual harassment with intent to have sexual contact than do female students. These patterns support theories that name patriarchal structures as social contributors to increased victimization.

Taking these findings together, it seems that the sexual victimization of boys is increased in more traditional social contexts. This is expected because both Orthodox Jewish and Arab society place strong restrictions on sexual contact between boys and girls in the junior high and high school years. In fact, all Orthodox Jewish schools and some Arab schools separate boys and girls, making physical contact on school grounds very difficult. The cultural separation and taboos surrounding contact between boys and girls could explain the elevated victimization rates for boys and very low victimization rates for girls in schools that are high on the patriarchal dimension. In this patriarchal social system, boys' desire for sexual contact may be directed at other boys because access to same-sex victims is easier and less detectable to adults.

Sexual harassment as a theoretical concept requires researchers to explore the genders of the victims and perpetrators. One historical problem with the sexual harassment literature is the assumption that only girls are victims of sexual harassment. However, there is very strong international data showing that boys have equal or higher rates of some forms of sexual harassment victimization. There is also an assumption that the perpetrators mainly are male. Knowing the genders of the victims and perpetrators constitutes another important theoretical layer.

VICTIMS AND PERPETRATORS: AN EMPIRICAL EXPLORATION

What sexual harassment behaviors are perpetrated by same-gender students and what victimization types are cross-gender? Table 5.3 distinguishes male and female perpetrators and victims of the behaviors on the sexual harassment scale. The table shows, for instance, that 12.5% of boys were victims of another student trying to kiss them when they did not want to be kissed. Of this group, about 26% reported that the perpetrator was male, 63% that the perpetrator was female, and 11% reported that they were victimized by both. Only 7.2% of girls reported this behavior, and of these about 64% said the perpetrator was male, 31% female, and 6% both.

Table 5.3 presents a rather complex picture revealing some interesting dynamics of sexual harassment in schools. An overall view of the table indicates that, for the sexual harassment behaviors we studied, boys tend to be victims and perpetrators more often than girls. This can be seen most clearly with regard to showing obscene pictures: Boys were victimized twice as often as girls, and the perpetrators against male victims were mostly male. Trying to take off someone's clothes for sexually related reasons is perpetrated against boys four times more than it is against girls, although a rather large proportion of male victims say that female students victimized them.

Table 5.3. Victims and Perpetrators of Sexual Harassment

	Male Victim				Female Victim			
			Perpetrator				Perpetrator	
	Total	Male	Female	Both	Total	Male	Female	Both
	(100%)	(%)	(%)	(%)	(100%)	(%)	(%)	(%)
A student tried to kiss you without your consent.	12.5	26	63	11	7.2	64	31	6
A student touched or tried to touch you or to pinch you in a sexual way without your approval.	12.1	42	47	11	10.7	75	18	8
A student tried to come on to you (sexually) and made sexual comments that you did not want.	9.4	30	56	14	10.9	85	10	5
Sexually insulting things about you were written on walls or sexual rumors were spread about you.	9.2	53	23	24	6.9	35	43	22
A student peeped while you were in the bathroom or the locker room.	9.6	53	35	12	4.6	43	47	10
A students showed you obscene pictures or sent you obscene letters.	16.0	53	27	20	7.9	55	32	13
A student took or tried to take your clothes off (for sexual reasons).	13.0	48	39	13	2.8	45	42	12

Several sexually harassing behaviors are characterized by a cross-gender victim-perpetrator relationship. These behaviors are identical to the group of behaviors we called intent to have sexual contact (Factor 1 in Table 5.2). Here, 63% of the male victims reported that a girl tried to kiss them without their consent (compared with 26% of the boys who said the perpetrator was male), and 64% of the female victims said the perpetrator was male (31% of the girls said the perpetrator was a girl). The phenomenon of cross-gender victimization is stronger for girls. That is, the proportion of girls victimized by boys compared with those victimized by girls is much higher than among boys, who are victimized to a significant degree by other boys.

These findings support our position that student victimization is not the result of a homogeneous group of behaviors having the same meaning. Knowing who is the victim and who is the perpetrator is also important. We suspect that these combinations make qualitative differences and may reflect different intentions and, perhaps, consequences. For example, we think further research is needed to explore the intentions of same-sex and cross-sex sexual harassment. It is quite possible that when boys harass each other there are heavy components of social dominance and public humiliation. However, it is not clear to what extent humiliation and dominance are factors when girls harass boys. Likewise, sexually motivated harassment may play a larger role in cross-gender harassment than was believed previously. These kinds of distinctions and explorations are important for a better understanding of sexual harassment behaviors.

RELATIONSHIPS BETWEEN SEXUAL AND OTHER TYPES OF VICTIMIZATION

The findings presented in this chapter show that patterns of sexual victimization are distinct from patterns of other types of victimization, such as social-verbal and physical, and should be treated separately. Given the differences, how does sexual victimization relate to other types of victimization? Are victims of sexual harassment likely to be victims of other types of violent acts? Is sexual harassment associated more with social-verbal types of victimization, or with physical victimization? The only other study that asked this type of question was conducted by Pellegrini (2001), who examined the relationships between sexual harassment and bullying among seventh-graders in Minnesota. Pellegrini reports that bullying at the start of sixth grade was associated with sexual harassment at the end of seventh grade.

To answer questions about sexual harassment and other aspects of school violence, we explored the relationships between the two dimensions of sexual harassment identified in this chapter and other forms of school victimization. Table 5.4 shows that both dimensions of sexual harassment are associated positively with being a victim of other violent acts. Most of the correlations range between r = 0.30 and

Table 5.4.   Correlations between the Dimensions of Sexual Harassment and Other Forms of Victimization

	Intent to Have Sexual Contact	Intent to Humiliate
A student gave you a serious beating.	0.33	0.40
A student cut you with a knife or a sharp instrument on purpose.	0.36	0.39
You were involved in a fight, were hurt, and required medical attention.	0.33	0.39
You were blackmailed under threats by another student (for money, valuables, or food).	0.32	0.38
You were kicked or punched by a student who wanted to hurt you.	0.30	0.38
Students threatened you on your way to or from school.	0.29	0.38
A student used a rock or another instrument in order to hurt you.	0.31	0.37
Gang members at school threatened, harassed, and pressured you.	0.33	0.37
You were involved in a fistfight.	0.29	0.37
You saw a student in school with a gun.	0.33	0.36
Students intentionally destroyed or broke your personal belongings or equipment.	0.31	0.36
A student took your things from you by force.	0.29	0.35
A student threatened to harm or hit you.	0.26	0.35
A student tried to intimidate you by the way he or she was looking at you.	0.30	0.34
A student threatened you with a gun and you saw the gun.	0.29	0.33
A student threatened you with a knife and you saw the knife.	0.29	0.33
A group of students boycotted you and did not want to play or talk with you.	0.27	0.32
A student seized and shoved you on purpose.	0.23	0.31
You saw a student in school with a knife.	0.26	0.29
A student mocked, insulted, or humiliated you.	0.19	0.24
A student cursed you.	0.17	0.21

0.40. Consistently, sexual victimization associated with intent to humiliate is more closely correlated with other forms of victimization than sexual victimization associated with intent to have sexual contact. The more severe physical victimization forms tend to have higher correlations with sexual harassment. Verbal-social victimization in the forms of mocking, humiliation, insults, and curses have much lower correlations with sexual harassment victimization.

These findings suggest that sexual victimization is not associated with the social-verbal realm. Instead, it is associated with being victimized physically. This is especially true for sexual harassment behaviors with intent to humiliate. Notwithstanding these relationships, sexual harassment is only moderately associated with other types of victimization and should therefore be addressed as a separate phenomenon.

KEY FINDINGS AND IMPLICATIONS

A. Children experience a wide array of sexual victimization behaviors.
B. Victimization by sexual harassment presents differently from other forms of school victimization.
  1. Patterns are far more influenced by gender and culture than those of other forms of victimization.
  2. Age does not have a large impact on sexual harassment behaviors.
  3. Boys report more sexual harassment victimization than girls.
  4. Primary students show victimization patterns similar to patterns of secondary school students.
C. Sexual harassment victimization patterns fit into two distinct categories of victimization that vary in
  1. Intent to humiliate.
  2. Intent to have sexual contact.
D. There is an interaction between gender and culture with different types of sexual harassment.
  1. With intent to humiliate:
    a. Boys are victimized far more often than girls.
    b. Orthodox Jewish students and secular Jewish students show patterns similar to those of Arab students.
  2. With intent to have sexual contact:
    a. Arabs' and Orthodox Jews' pattern are similar, with boys being victimized more often than girls.
    b. Secular Jewish students deviate from this pattern, as girls report slightly more victimization than boys.
E. Sexual harassment victim-perpetrator distinctions fall along expected patterns related to the two types of sexual harassment.
F. Intent-to-humiliate forms of sexual harassment are more similar to other forms of school victimization, and intent to have sexual contact is less related to other forms of victimization.

NOTE

1. In our third wave of data collection (2002), we added sexual harassment in primary schools (grades 4–6) to our investigation. We examined three sexual harassment behaviors that are identical to these we used in our study of secondary school students.

Table 5.5 suggests that reports of sexual victimization start as early as fourth grade. Furthermore, the patterns found among primary school students in 2002 are very similar to the ones we found among junior high and high school students in 1999. Male students reported sexual harassment more often than female students; this is especially true for the reports of students trying to remove the clothes of other students. Also, Arab students reported more often than Jewish students being victims of another student trying to kiss them and that

Table 5.5.   Sexual Harassment in Primary Schools, 2002 Data

	Overall (%)	Gender		Ethnic Group	
		Male (%)	Female (%)	Jewish (%)	Arab (%)
A student tried to kiss you without your consent.	11.7	12.9	10.2	9.2	17.8
A student peeped while you were in the bathroom or the locker room.	11.1	13.0	8.9	9.8	14.1
A student tried to remove your clothes (for sexual reasons).	6.5	9.5	3.4	6.5	6.6
A student tried to touch or pinch you in a sexual manner in private parts without your consent.	18.2	22.9	13.1	14.8	26.4

another student peeped while they were in the bathroom or locker room. These patterns are similar to the patterns found among the older students.

These findings call attention to the literature's relative lack of interest in sexual harassment behaviors in younger children. Most studies and intervention efforts focus on junior high and high school students. Our findings suggest that these behaviors start earlier and seem to follow the same age-gender-culture patterns as sexual harassment in later ages.

Chapter 6

Weapons in School

In this chapter, we examine the issue of weapons in secondary schools. We think this topic requires separate treatment because of its inherent significance and the unique characteristics surrounding weapon use. The presence of firearms and knives in schools is considered one of the most threatening and dangerous aspects of school violence. The mass shootings in U.S. schools heightened public awareness and worries with regard to the use of lethal weapons in schools across the world. In fact, zero tolerance policies mainly target the possession of any kind of weapon on school grounds and dictate severe and uncompromising sanctions for those who violate them.

We examine weapons on school grounds from several vantage points intended to further theory, methodology, and conceptual development of the subject. We focus on areas and issues that are not addressed fully in the literature, and we report on the various modes of exposure to weapons among secondary school students in Israel, including bringing a weapon to school, seeing a weapon on school grounds, being threatened by a student using a weapon, and being injured by a student using a knife or another object. We distinguish between guns, knives, and other objects (such as clubs) and examine how different forms of weapon victimization are associated with student background factors of gender, age, and ethnic group. We explore further how other types of victimization at school are related to bringing weapons to school. Finally, we examine how fear is connected with bringing weapons to school.

THE MANY FACES OF VICTIMIZATION BY WEAPONS ON SCHOOL GROUNDS

Research on youth possession and use of weapons, especially guns, is quite extensive (see reviews in McKeganey & Norrie, 2000; Mercy & Rosenberg, 1998). We think, however, that a sole focus on the possession and use of guns is not warranted. Students can be victimized by weapons in various ways and all of these should be examined. A student may see a weapon on school grounds (and may therefore feel unsafe), may encounter a student who uses a weapon as a threat, or may be injured by a weapon. It is important to consider all forms of victimization because they may have differential effects on the students involved. For instance, Martin and associates (Martin, Sadowski, Cotten, & McCarraher, 1996) report that, compared to their peers, adolescents who perceived that their schoolmates brought guns to school were almost twice as likely to experience fear while at school, were more than three times more likely to exhibit school avoidance behavior, and were more than twice as likely to bring a weapon to school for self-protection. Although seeing a weapon on school grounds may constitute a serious threat, it differs significantly from being a victim of a direct threat with a weapon, and a weapon-related injury represents a much more significant victimization still.

In addition to addressing different forms of victimization, we think it is important to treat different weapons differently. Currently, most U.S. surveys do not distinguish between handguns, knives, and other weapons. For instance, the Youth Risk Behavior Surveillance Survey (YRBS) includes only one weapon-related item: "During the past 30 days, on how many days did you carry a weapon such as a gun, knife, or club on school property?" (for other examples, see Bailey, Flewelling, & Rosenbaum, 1997; Kodjo et al., 2003). To address the differences between various types of weapons, DuRant and his associates (DuRant, Krowchuk, Kreiter, Sinal, & Woods, 1999) modified the YRBS to include two separate questions, one about bringing guns to school and the other referring to "any other weapons (such as a knife or club)." In the present study, we distinguished further between guns, knives (including pocket knives), and other weapons (such as clubs).

Although various types of weapons share much in common, they differ in many respects. Clearly, the potential lethality of handguns differs from that of knives. Weapons also differ in their symbolic role, and their usage is influenced by cultural context. For instance, Kingery, Coggeshall, and Alford (1999) found ethnic differences in preference for weapon: non-Hispanic Blacks preferred guns and Hispanics and non-Hispanic Whites preferred knives. When students use guns regularly for hunting with their parents (Devine & Lawson, 2003), the meaning of bringing a gun to school is different than when the possession of firearms in the community is rare. McKeganey and Norrie (2000) examined weapon carrying by adolescents in Scotland and note that the west of Scotland has had an association with weapon carrying and gang fights for many years, immortalized in the "no mean city" account of life in Glasgow. These authors conclude that it is far from clear why a substantial proportion of young people in Scotland feel the need to carry a weapon.

Israel presents an interesting arena with regard to weapons. Visitors to Israel are often astonished by the number of guns they see in the streets. There are many (male and female) uniformed soldiers carrying their personal rifles on their way to and from their army base. There are also many young Israeli men in civilian clothes who live in the occupied territories (West Bank and Gaza Strip) who visibly carry a rifle or handgun. All this, in addition to police officers who carry handguns and, quite often in recent years, rifles. School guards are often armed with a handgun, intended to protect from outside danger and never to be used against students. Thus, weapons are quite common in everyday life in Israel, are associated with safety and protection from terrorist attacks, and are not seen as a threat. Nevertheless, one needs a license to carry a handgun, and this license is given only to those who are deemed to live in or travel through dangerous areas. Weapon carrying among youth is totally unacceptable and is associated with criminal activities. Thus, despite the extensive presence of guns in Israel, guns in schools are perceived by all as very rare and extremely dangerous.

WEAPON-RELATED BEHAVIORS AS THEY RELATE TO GENDER, SCHOOL LEVEL, AND ETHNIC GROUP

Table 6.1 shows that Israeli students are exposed to knives much more than to guns. Whereas 2.7% of the students said that they brought a gun to school and 3.5% said that another student threatened them with a gun, 5.7% report bringing a knife to school and 6.3% were threatened with a knife. More than a fifth of the students (21.3%) reported being hurt by a rock, a chair, or another object in school. A much smaller number (5.6%) reported being cut by a knife or another sharp object. This trend is similar to that found in the United States; DuRant and his associates (1999) report that whereas 3% of their sample of adolescents report carrying a gun to school, 14.1% reported carrying a knife.

Almost half of the students in our study saw another student with a knife in school. In the first wave of data collection in our study we found similar findings. We were surprised by these high numbers and were concerned that perhaps we were not clear enough in our questions and so students may have reported seeing other students with Xacto knives used in art classes. So we clarified in the second wave of data collection (reported here) that we are asking about knives that are brought to school not for the purposes of art classes. Still, we found in the second wave that almost half of the students reported seeing students in school with knives; high numbers were also evident in a series of studies we conducted in the city of Herzliya (Benbenishty, 2002).

Table 6.1 shows that boys report three to four times more exposure to weapons than girls. Interestingly, not only do fewer girls bring weapons to school and fewer are threatened with a weapon, but fewer girls report seeing weapons in school. These gender effects were found in many other studies on weapons in school. It seems that these weapons are being shown and known mainly to boys involved in violence. For instance, in DuRant et al.'s (1999) study, a higher percentage of adolescent boys (20.2%) reported having carried a knife or club to school than adolescent girls (7.7%).

In previous chapters we saw that students in junior high report more victimization than students in high school. These differences are much smaller with regard

Table 6.1. Weapon-related Behaviors (by gender, grade level, and ethnic group)

			Gender		Ethnic Group		School Level	
		Total	Male	Female	Jewish	Arab	Junior	High
Brought	A gun	2.7	4.1	1.3	2.2	4.5	2.7	2.6
	A knife	5.7	9.1	2.3	4.8	9.2	5.5	5.9
Threatened by	A gun	3.5	5.6	1.3	3.0	5.4	3.2	3.8
	A knife	6.3	10.3	2.5	4.2	14.5	7.2	4.9
Hurt by	A knife or sharp object	5.6	9.4	1.9	5.2	7.4	6.0	4.9
	A rock, chair, other object	21.3	30.3	12.6	21.8	19.6	24.1	16.3
Saw on school	A student with a handgun	4.4	7.6	1.2	4.0	6.1	4.0	4.8
grounds	A student with a knife	46.4	59.2	34.2	47.4	42.7	46.2	46.8

to weapon-related behaviors. The only behavior reported much more by junior high students is being hurt by an object (not necessarily a weapon): 24.1% compared with 16.3% among high school students. In the United States, DuRant et al. (1999) reported no significant relationship between school grade and carrying a gun to school. Still, eighth-grade students were more likely to carry a knife or club to school than sixth- and seventh-grade students.

Arab students report more than Jewish students that they were involved with guns and even more with knives. Whereas 4.8% of the Jewish students said they brought a knife to school, 9.2% of the Arab students make such a report. Similarly, 2.2% of the Jewish students report that they brought a gun to school compared with 4.5% of the Arab students. Interestingly, the percentages of Jewish and Arab students reporting seeing another student in school carrying a knife were almost identical.

The finding that Arab students have more access to guns was very surprising to us, considering the political climate in Israel. Gun control is very strictly regulated among the Jewish population. Because of concerns surrounding terrorism, we assumed that access to guns would be even more difficult for the Arab students. However, there is an illegal underground that makes access to guns easier than we thought originally. Much of the gun use in Arab schools is related to family clan issues, especially in the Bedouin and Druze populations (who serve in the military and have access to guns), but also among other Arab groups.

VICTIMIZATION AND BRINGING A WEAPON TO SCHOOL

After the U.S. and international school shootings, the media made many links between chronic victimization and bringing a weapon to school (and using it). The U.S. Secret Service Report mentioned the relationship between being bullied and bringing a weapon to school and using it (Vosskuil, Reddy, Fein, Borum, & Modselski, 2002). Students who are being victimized in school may be more likely to bring a weapon to school, either for self-defense or for revenge (American

Psychological Association Commission on Violence and Youth, 1993; DuRant et al., 1999; DuRant, Getts, Cadenhead, & Woods, 1995). Furlong, Bates, and Smith (2001) examined the correlation between an item asking how many times the student brought a weapon to school and the School Risk Index. This index tallies the number of risk factors present for the student, such as missing school due to fear of violence, being threatened and injured with a weapon in school, and the use of cigarettes and drugs on school property. The authors combined three data waves that administered the YRBSS in the United States and examined the prevalence of weapon possession and its relation to grade level, ethnicity/race, and gender. The correlations between weapon possession and the various items included in the index were quite low (range 0.13–0.26), but the correlation with the combined School Risk Index was higher (r = 0.36), providing support for the hypothesis that bringing weapons to school is associated with being victimized in school.

Similarly, Paetsch and Bertrand (1999) write that in their sample of youth in Calgary, Canada, students who self-reported weapon possession were more likely to report higher levels of victimization, both at school and while not at school. For instance, of the students who reported having a weapon at school, 49.0% reported a moderate or high level of victimization at school, 22.1% reported a low level, and only 15.7% reported no victimization. The levels of victimization among the students who did not report involvement with weapons were much lower.

The Probability of Bringing a Gun or Knife to School: Comparing Victims and Nonvictims

Following these findings in the literature that indicate a possible connection between victimization and weapons in school, we asked whether Israeli students who are victimized more are more prone to bringing weapons to school. Table 6.2 presents the probability that a student victimized by a specific form of violent act will bring a weapon to school, compared with the probability that a student who was not victimized will bring a weapon. The table shows that students who bring weapons to school tend to be those who are victimized much more than others. For instance, among students who were threatened with a gun, 30.1% brought a gun to school, compared with only 1.7% among the students who were not threatened. Similarly, among students who saw another student with a gun in school, 28.5% brought a gun, whereas among those who did not see another student with a gun in school, the rate was only 1.5%.

The patterns with regard to bringing a knife to school are very similar. For instance, among students who reported receiving a serious beating, 23.7% brought a knife to school; the rate was 4.3% for those who were not victimized in such a way. Among students who saw another student in school with a knife, 10.1% reported bringing a knife to school, but among those who did not see another student with a knife, only 1.7% reported bringing a knife to school.

In Chapter 3, we saw that verbal-social victimization does not follow the same patterns as physical and threat-related victimization. In this chapter again, whereas

Table 6.2. Probability of Bringing Knives and Guns to School among Students Victimized and Not Victimized by Violent Acts

	Probability of Bringing a Gun to School		Probability of Bringing a Knife to School	
	Not Victimized (%)	Victimized (%)	Not Victimized (%)	Victimized (%)
A student threatened you with a gun and you saw the gun.	1.7	30.1	4.8	30.6
You saw a student in school with a gun.	1.5	28.5	4.4	34.2
A student seized and shoved you on purpose.	1.6	20.8	4.3	29.3
A student cut you with a knife or a sharp instrument on purpose.	1.6	20.8	4.3	29.3
A student gave you a serious beating.	1.7	16.0	4.3	23.7
A student threatened you with a knife and you saw the knife.	1.8	15.5	4.5	23.2
You were blackmailed under threats by another student (for money, valuables, or food).	1.7	15.4	4.4	21.6
Gang members at school threatened, harassed, and pressured you.	1.6	14.6	4.3	21.1
You were involved in a fight, were hurt, and required medical attention.	1.7	12.3	3.7	23.8
Students threatened you on your way to or from school.	1.6	10.6	4.1	17.6
A student took your things from you by force.	1.7	8.1	4.4	12.7
A group of students boycotted you and did not want to play or talk with you.	1.9	7.8	4.4	13.7
A student used a rock or another instrument in order to hurt you.	1.4	7.3	3.7	12.9
You were involved in a fistfight.	1.5	5.9	2.8	13.9
A student tried to intimidate you by the way he or she was looking at you.	1.8	5.7	3.9	11.8
You were kicked or punched by a student who wanted to hurt you.	1.8	5.4	3.8	11.4
A student threatened to harm or hit you.	2.0	4.2	3.4	10.5
You saw a student in school with a knife.	1.4	4.0	1.7	10.1
A student mocked, insulted, or humiliated you.	2.7	2.7	4.7	6.4
A student cursed you.	3.0	2.6	4.1	6.2

physical and threat victimization are associated with bringing a weapon to school, verbal victimization in the form of curses and humiliation is not related to bringing weapons to school. It is important to note, however, that being socially isolated and excluded in school is associated with bringing a weapon to school. Thus, among students who reported being socially isolated and excluded, 7.8% brought a gun and 13.7% brought a knife. The rates among students who do not report being socially excluded are much lower: 1.9% brought a gun and 4.4% brought a knife. This confirms many of the media reports in the United States and elsewhere that students were bringing weapons both for self-defense and because they were socially excluded or bullied. This appears to be the case in Israel, as well.

Multiple Forms of Victimization and Bringing a Weapon to School

To get an overall picture of the relationships between victimization and weapon-related behaviors in school, we created a Physical Victimization Index tallying the number of different types of physical victimization that the student experienced in the previous month. Figure 6.1 shows that the prevalence of bringing a weapon to school is highly associated with physical victimization. Whereas the prevalence of bringing a gun to school among students who do not report any type of physical victimization is 1.5%, it goes up to 2.7% for students reporting three types of victimization, to 10.3% among students who report five types of victimization, and to 28.4% among students who report being victims of six types of violent events. The patterns of bringing knives to school are very similar.

Figure 6.1 suggests that the relationship between physical victimization and bringing weapons to school is *not linear*. It seems that there is a qualitative difference between students who report up to three out of the six types of victimization we addressed and students who experience almost all of the different victimization types. This finding calls for focusing efforts to prevent weapons in school on the small group of students who are extreme in their victimization levels. Targeting these students may raise issues of labeling and stigmatizing; nevertheless, we think that spreading the efforts thin among the whole student population may not be as effective as identifying the group of students who are most extreme in their victimization levels and addressing their specific needs.

FEAR AND BRINGING A WEAPON TO SCHOOL.   It is possible that students bring weapons to school because they are being victimized and fear for their safety (May, 1999). We examined this connection and found that missing school due to fear of being victimized is highly related to bringing a weapon to school; whereas 4.4% of the students who did not miss school due to fear reported bringing a knife to school, about 20% of the students who missed school once or twice reported that they brought a gun to school. Among the few students who reported missing school due to fear more than twice in the prior month, almost 40% report that they brought a knife to school. A similar pattern is evident with regard to bringing a gun to school:

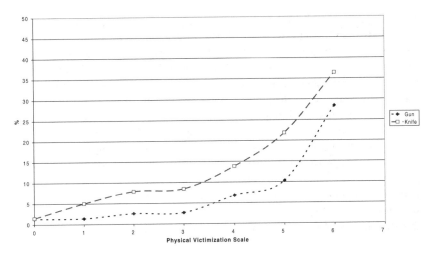

Figure 6.1. The probability of bringing a weapon to school as it relates to physical victimization.

1.7% of those who did not miss school reported that they brought a gun to school, but 34.4% of the students who missed school more than twice reported bringing a gun to school. These findings are similar to these of Simon, Crosby, and Dahlberg (1999), who showed that among students who missed school due to fear, the probability of bringing a weapon to school was six times higher than among those who did not report missing school due to fear. Interestingly, Wilcox and Clayton (2001) report that despite a strong relationship between weapon carrying on school grounds and previous victimization, little evidence was found for the predictive power of school-associated fear.

Clearly, our findings indicate that missing school due to fear is a strong predictor for bringing a weapon to school. Simon and his associates (1999) interpret this finding as a possible indication that this behavior is fulfilling the perceived need for personal safety. They argue, therefore, that if students feel unsafe in school without a weapon, the threat of punishment might be ineffective in deterring weapon carrying in school. The implication is that personal safety should be increased before we can expect students to refrain from bringing weapons to school.

The relationship between being a victim and the act of bringing or using a weapon may not be explained only from an "intent" perspective. For instance, it is not entirely clear if students who bring a weapon are only afraid and a weapon is their means of protection, or if there are also elements of retribution or revenge involved. For example, students who bring weapons because they are excluded socially may be seeking retribution rather than self-defense. A similar point was made by Page and Hammermeister (1997), who indicate that although a common reason youth give for carrying weapons is that they were afraid someone will jump them, there are many indications that weapon carrying is related more to perpetration of criminal activity than to victimization and fear. In a similar vein, Ding, Nelsen, and Lassonde (2002) write that male adolescents who had more experience with guns reported reacting more violently to frustration and also admitted to having participated in greater numbers of violent incidents. These issues need to be explored further to understand better the motivations (fear, revenge, retribution, self-defense, and normative acceptance) that underlie weapons on school grounds.

Clearly, the pool of students who bring weapons to school is much greater than those who actually use those weapons. Nevertheless, understanding the motivations for bringing weapons could further our understanding of lethal violence on school grounds and reduce the overall risk of being injured by a weapon. Our data suggest that being victimized is clearly related to bringing a weapon to school. Therefore, we suggest that strategies to reduce weapons on school grounds should incorporate students' experiences of victimization and social exclusion.

KEY FINDINGS AND IMPLICATIONS

A. There are many ways weapons on school grounds can victimize students. Each can produce different outcomes.
   1. Seeing a weapon.
   2. Being injured by a weapon.
   3. Being threatened by a weapon.
B. There are many types of weapons on school grounds. Each may be used and interpreted differently by various school groups.
   1. Israeli students are exposed more to knives than to guns.
   2. About a fifth of students claimed to have been injured by an object at school.
   3. Compared to girls, boys report three to four times more weapon-related behavior.
   4. Gender patterns in Israel are similar to those in the United States.
   5. Arab students are more likely than Jewish students to report being involved with either guns or knives.
C. There are associations between being victimized at school and bringing weapons to school.
   1. Students who are chronically victimized are more likely to bring guns or knives.
   2. Physical and threat victimization are related to bringing a weapon to school, whereas verbal-social victimization is not.
D. Fear of victimization is a major predictor of which students will bring weapons to school.
E. A sizable proportion of students who do not attend school more than twice a month due to fear are likely to bring either a knife or a gun.

Chapter 7

Student Victimization by Staff

In this book we include victimization by staff as an important aspect of school violence. Very few studies of school violence have included any questions related to students' victimization by staff members. We believe that staff violence should be included in all conceptual and empirical investigations of school violence. However, staff victimization should be treated separately from peer victimization because it may emanate from different social mechanisms, may be associated with different risk factors, and may be amenable to different interventions. In previous chapters we focused on peer victimization. We now examine the many faces of staff victimization and its relationship with various aspects of our model, such as gender, school level, family poverty, and culture.

Our goals in this chapter are multiple: First, we want to raise researchers' awareness of the importance of including victimization by staff members as part of the conceptualization of school violence theory. This can only happen if studies include victimization by staff in their research. Second, we aim to explore the different kinds of staff victimization that may occur in schools. It is possible that different variables impact the various types of victimization. Third, we explore the relationships between age, gender, and culture on student victimization by staff. The child abuse literature in settings outside school suggest that these are essential and important components to consider. Finally, we explore the joint contributions of socioeconomic influences and cultural issues on staff violence. This kind of discussion is very important because ethnicity, culture, and economic issues are often confounded.

BACKGROUND ON STUDENT VICTIMIZATION BY STAFF

To date, the school violence and bullying literature has paid little attention to victimization of students by school staff. It was only in 1999 that Olweus, a pioneer in the study of peer bullying, reported on data he collected on teachers bullying students in Norway in 1985. He wrote: "So far as is known, it is the first scientific investigation of this sensitive topic" (p. 42). Since then there have been further studies, but most of these have used smaller and nonrepresentative samples (e.g., Kim, Kim, Park, Zhang, Lu, & Li, 2000).

Educators and other school staff are important figures in children's lives. They provide children with knowledge and skills that are vital for their psychological and social development. They also serve as role models for normative behavior and social skills. Through interaction with the adults in school, children learn important life lessons in empathy, respect for others, and peaceful conflict resolution. Educational and other school staff are also valuable sources of emotional support for students. Educators thus play a vital role in providing a safe haven and protecting children from harm inflicted in their home and community as well as from victimization in school by their peers. In some cases, however, educators become the source of emotional, physical, and sexual maltreatment. They may insult and humiliate students, assault them, and behave in an inappropriate sexual manner.

Historically, staff victimization of students has been associated with corporal punishment. *Corporal punishment* refers to intentional application of physical pain as a method of changing behavior. In a position statement of the Society for Adolescent Medicine, Greydanus and his colleagues (Greydanus, Pratt, Spates, Blake-Dreher, Greydanus-Gearhart, & Patel, 2003) review the history of the debate on corporal punishment and comment that for many years there was a strong belief that corporal punishment at home and in school has positive effects. Only recently have there been gradual changes in this area; now, some social groups and experts believe that corporal punishment is ineffective and has deleterious effects. Still, 22 U.S. states authorize corporal punishment in schools today (Hyman, Stefkovich, & Taich, 2002; see also the work of Grossman, Rauh, & Rivera, 1995, on the prevalence of corporal punishment among students in Washington State). In Israel, corporal punishment in schools is prohibited. Interestingly, as Sabba (2003) notes, it has been prohibited since the early 1950s, but only recently has there been a renewed effort to address explicitly the issue of staff maltreatment of students.

Based on evidence on the meaning and effects of corporal punishment at home and in school, the position of the Society for Adolescent Medicine is clear: "Corporal punishment in schools is an ineffective, dangerous, and unacceptable method of discipline" (Greydanus et al., 2003, p. 391). Indeed, studies in this area show that staff maltreatment may have significant deleterious consequences for students. Irwin Hyman has been a leader for many years in the efforts to eliminate corporal punishment in U.S. schools. He and his associates (e.g., Hyman, 1990; Hyman & Snook, 1999, 2000; Hyman & Wise, 1979; Hyman, Zelikoff, & Clarke, 1988) investigated a range of educators' victimizing behaviors toward their students, such as ridicule, physical assault, isolation, verbal discrimination, and sexual harassment. Their findings suggest that children who are exposed to these behaviors have a higher likelihood of developing a series of symptoms, such as problems in school, aggressive behavior, fearful reactions, somatic complaints, dependency and regression, and reexperiencing the trauma inflicted by the educator (Educator Induced Posttraumatic Stress Disorder; Hyman, 1990). Some of these negative effects are immediate and short term, whereas others are long-lasting.

In addition to these negative effects on children's psychological well-being, aggressive and violent behavior by educators and school staff may result in a strong social learning effect (Imbrogno, 2000). Students see these aggressive behaviors as legitimate forms of social influence and conflict resolution. Thus, certain practices by the educational staff that have been designed to curb student violence may in fact *increase* the frequency and severity of violence by these students and their peers (Hyman & Perone, 1998).

Given the importance of educators and schools in children's lives, and the possible negative effects of maltreatment by school staff, it is important to note the paucity of studies that assess the prevalence of the various forms of staff maltreatment. Olweus (1999) reports on a study conducted in 1985 of 2,400 students and their teachers in Belzen, Norway. The focus was on teachers bullying students. He found that about 2% of the students could be identified as being bullied by a teacher during the reference period of five months. Olweus concludes that bullying of students by teachers occurs in Norway at much higher frequency than expected.

THE MANY FACES OF VICTIMIZATION BY STAFF

Parallel to the literature on child abuse and maltreatment, three types of maltreatment by staff have been identified: emotional, physical, and sexual.

Emotional

Emotional maltreatment by educational staff is the most commonly experienced form of staff victimization. These behaviors include humiliation of students in public, name-calling, cursing of students and their families, poking fun at the student's appearance and abilities, and similar degrading behaviors. In some cases, the behavior is occasional and infrequent; in other cases, the behavior becomes a pattern of bullying a particular student who has been singled out by a specific staff member (Hyman, 1990).

Physical

Physical maltreatment has many forms. Hyman (1990) lists a range of weapons that teachers employ, such as paddles, rubber hoses, leather straps and belts, switches, sticks, and rods (see Benthall, 1991, for a similar list of methods for physical punishment in Britain in the 1950s). There are also reports of extreme aggression against children that results in serious injury and, in some cases, death (Chianu, 2000). Most physical maltreatment in schools, however, does not involve these severe types of physical punishment. Rather, it includes behaviors such as pushing, shoving, slapping, pinching, punching, and kicking.

Sexual

Sexual harassment of students by staff takes various forms, such as sexual advances, inappropriate comments, and inappropriate touching. It should be noted that *any* contact of a sexual nature between school staff and students (even if "consensual") is unacceptable and should be considered maltreatment (Shakeshaft & Cohan, 1995). Whereas reports of emotional and physical maltreatment are quite common, sexual maltreatment by educational staff is not reported often. Wishnietsky (1991) says that although most of the reports of sexual harassment in educational settings pertain to college campuses, there is clear evidence in the United States of sexual maltreatment in high schools as well (see also Corbett, Gentry, & Pearson, 1993; Shakeshaft & Cohan, 1995). It should be noted that the little empirical research there is in this area is based on retrospective reports made by college students. We could not locate any study that investigated reports of sexual harassment by staff made by students while they were still in high school. Further, the few empirical studies reported in the literature were all conducted in the United States.

STAFF VICTIMIZATION, AGE, GENDER, AND CULTURE

The literature in this area provides several hints as to which groups are vulnerable to victimization by staff. We focus the following literature review on issues that are most relevant to groups in the Israeli educational system.

Gender and Age

The literature clearly indicates that boys are involved in many more disciplinary confrontations with staff and are punished and disciplined more than girls. For instance, Hyman and McDowell (1979) report large gender differences in the incidents of corporal punishment in Vermont for the 1974–1975 school year. In the first grade, boys were more than 9 times more likely to be punished; in the fifth grade they were 10 times more likely to be punished than girls in their grade level (see also a review on gender differences in corporal punishment in Gregory, 1995). We expected, therefore, that the prevalence of reports of staff maltreatment in our sample would be higher among male students.

With regard to age, there seems to be some conflicting evidence. Hyman and McDowell (1979) show that most physical punishment is perpetrated by male staff against male students. Thus, the frequency of such physical maltreatment should be lower in primary schools, in which most teachers are female. However, Youssef et al. (1998) showed that younger children are subjected to *more* maltreatment. Our informal observations suggest very strongly that in Israel the older students are much more vocal and powerful in protecting themselves against authority than younger students and would therefore be less victimized by educational staff. We expect that primary school students in our study will report the highest levels of victimization by staff.

Cultural and Religious Beliefs and Norms

Hyman (1990) shows that corporal punishment in schools has historical roots and is connected to prevailing myths and beliefs about children, their motives, their rights as human beings, and the effective and acceptable ways to "correct" unwanted behaviors (see also Costin, 1978; Groves, 1997; Imbrogno, 2000; Williams, 1979). Certain religious beliefs were shown to be related to acceptance of corporal punishment in school. Hyman mentions the strong belief by certain Christian groups that the "devil should be beaten out of children." Many religious groups interpret some proverbs in the Old and New Testament as supporting corporal punishment (e.g., Proverbs 13:24: "He that spareth the rod hateth his son, but he that loveth him chasteneth him"). It should be noted that there are alternative interpretations to these same proverbs (see Carey, 1994). The public debate on the legality of corporal punishment in Israel also showed that among parties representing orthodox religious groups, there were more proponents of a law permitting some "nonabusive" forms of parental corporal punishment. Therefore, we predict that children who study in Jewish religious schools in Israel will report more physical maltreatment than students in nonreligious schools.

Cultural norms regarding acceptable child-rearing practices are highly associated with corporal punishment in schools. Cultures that are more accepting of corporal punishment by parents tend to permit more corporal punishment in school, because teachers stand in loco parentis. To illustrate, Ellinger and Beckham (1997) report that South Korean parents will consent to their children being punished physically in school if the teacher thinks it will improve the child's performance. The Korean Protection Agency reported that 97% of the children it surveyed have experienced corporal punishment (see also Doe, 2000). Kim and his associates (2000) compared the rates of teacher violence against children in South Korea and China and reported very large differences: Whereas 4.1% of Chinese children reported that their teachers perpetrated serious violence against them, the rate among South Korean children was 43.8%. The authors attribute these differences to very different cultural stances with regard to the acceptability of corporal punishment in school.

Findings on Arab cultures also suggest that corporal punishment in school may be acceptable. Youssef and his associates (1998) studied the prevalence and determinants of corporal punishment in Alexandria, Egypt. They report a high prevalence of corporal punishment, especially among male and younger students. Corporal punishment by teachers in junior high and high school during a period of one year was reported by 80% of the boys and 62% of the girls in the sample. The authors indicate that this type of behavior is highly acceptable in Egypt.

Based on this literature, we expected to find differences in the prevalence of staff maltreatment between Jewish and Arab schools in Israel. Much of the Arab sector in Israeli society is characterized by traditional patriarchal and authoritarian family values (Haj-Yahia, 1997); the use of physical power to express control is an acceptable norm, especially when coming from men and directed toward children and women. Elbedour, Center, Maruyama, and Assor (1997) studied physical and psychological maltreatment in Arab Bedouin schools in Israel. They describe a cultural climate in which the child is seen as the property of the parents, and physical and psychological punishment by teachers is an accepted cultural norm.

Among the Jewish population in Israel there are certain groups that are more patriarchal and have more traditional family values than others. Still, the general orientation among Jews in Israel is Western and liberal. One expression of this orientation is the clear rules and guidelines of the Ministry of Education that ban corporal punishment specifically and urge educators to respect students' feelings and rights. Our hypothesis, therefore, is that children in Arab schools in Israel will report higher rates of victimization (perpetrated by school staff) than children in Jewish schools.

PREVALENCE RATES OF STUDENT VICTIMIZATION BY STAFF IN ISRAEL

Table 7.1 indicates that 16.5% of the students in our sample reported that they experienced at least one type of physical victimization by a staff member in the prior month, almost 29% experienced emotional victimization, and 4.5% were sexually harassed by a member of the educational staff.

Clearly, emotional victimization occurs very frequently. Most frequent is being mocked, insulted, or humiliated by a staff member. Boys tended to report more on being cursed. Also, although Jewish and Arab students reported similar levels of insults and humiliation by staff, Arab students report much more on curses than Jewish students do.

Physical victimization is less common, but the frequency of reports is not negligible: 10% of students were purposely seized or shoved by staff in the prior month, and 9.5% report that they were pinched or slapped by a staff member. Boys were clearly more often victimized than girls: 24% of boys experienced at least one type of physical victimization in the prior month, compared with 9% of the girls. Physical victimization decreases as the students move from primary school to junior high and high school: 12% of primary school students reported that a staff member pinched or slapped them, and 6% of high school students reported the same behavior. The group that experiences the highest levels of physical victimization is the Arab students: 34% of them experienced at least one type of physical victimization in the prior month, compared with 12% of Jewish students.

Table 7.1. Frequency of Staff-Initiated Victimization (by gender, grade level, and ethnic group)

	Total (%)	Gender		Ethnic Group		School Level		
In the prior month, a staff member:		Male (%)	Female (%)	Jewish (%)	Arab (%)	Primary (%)	Junior High (%)	High (%)
Physical								
Seized and shoved you on purpose.	10.9	16.4	5.6	8.7	18.6	12.6	10.6	7.9
Kicked or punched you.	5.5	8.5	2.8	2.7	15.4	7.1	4.7	4.2
Pinched or slapped you.	9.5	14.0	5.4	5.7	23.0	12.3	8.6	6.4
Any physical maltreatment.	16.5	24.0	9.4	11.5	33.8	20.7	15.1	11.2
Emotional								
Mocked, insulted, or humiliated you.	24.7	26.6	23.1	24.4	25.7	25.1	24.7	24.5
Cursed you.	13.4	17.3	9.8	10.2	24.6	14.7	13.0	12.0
Any emotional maltreatment.	28.7	31.9	25.9	26.7	35.4	30.2	28.6	26.8
Sexual								
Made sexual comments to you.	3.3	4.2	2.4	2.7	5.3	*	5.1	5.5
Tried to come on to you (sexually).	2.4	3.2	1.8	2.3	3.1	*	4.2	3.6
Touched or tried to touch you (in a sexual manner).	2.3	3.3	1.3	2.1	3.1	*	3.9	3.4
Any sexual maltreatment.	4.5	5.7	3.4	3.8	7.2	*	7.5	7.1

*Not asked.

Sexual victimization was reported by fewer students: 3.3% reported receiving sexual comments, 2.4% that staff tried to come on to them, and 2.3% that staff touched or tried to touch them in a sexual manner. There is a tendency for Arab students to report more sexual victimization than Jewish students.

In general, the findings indicate that as children move from primary school to junior high and high school, they report less physical victimization. This trend may reflect the growing physical size of the students, which may deter staff from attacking them physically. It could also reflect changes in student-staff relationships as students move from one school level to another. We wanted to see whether these age-related differences are identical for male and female students in Jewish and Arab schools. Figure 7.1 shows that the reduction in physical victimization of students is evident among male and female Arab students but is less pronounced among Jewish students. Among Jewish boys, the drop in physical victimization from one school level to the next is almost negligible.

Why does physical victimization decrease so steeply in Arab schools as students get older but not in Jewish schools? One possible explanation is that the dropout rate among Arab students is much higher than among Jewish students. Consequently, Arab high schools get a more select group of students. This may change the school climate so that the relationships between staff and students are much better than they are at earlier school levels, resulting in lower levels of victimization. Another possibility is that in the Arab culture, as students grow they are treated with more respect and are victimized less. This is especially true for Arab female students, whose level of physical victimization drops dramatically as they move from primary school to junior high. Perhaps the reason for this drop is the strict traditional and cultural prohibition against touching female students of a certain age.

Socioeconomic and Ethnic/Cultural Status

These findings indicate that Arab students experience more staff victimization, which could reflect the different cultural backgrounds of Jewish and Arab students. There is another interpretation, however. In Israel, the Arab minority has a much lower SES than the Jewish majority; the differences between Jewish and Arab students may reflect socioeconomic, rather than cultural, differences. The U.S. literature indicates strongly that school staff victimize students from minority and poor families more than those from higher socioeconomic backgrounds (Dietz, 2000; Hyman, 1990; Hyman & Wise, 1979; Jackson, 1999). Hyman has shown that regions in the United States with high illiteracy and poverty rates and low per student expenditure on education have the highest rates of corporal punishment. African Americans are particularly overrepresented; they make up more than 74% of students receiving corporal punishment (Meier, Stewart, & England, 1989). Analyzing the database on corporal punishment compiled by the U.S. Office of Civil Rights, Gregory (1995) found that African American students were 3.26 times more likely to receive corporal punishment in school than White students. Gregory speculated that there are

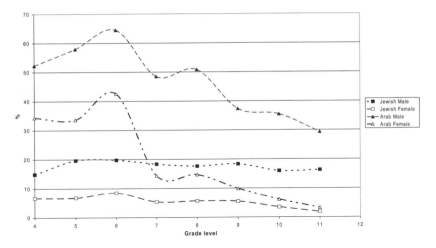

Figure 7.1. Staff-initiated physical victimization (by gender, grade level, and ethnic group).

even stronger biases against African American male students (see also Shaw & Braden, 1990).

Based on the literature, we hypothesize that students in schools characterized by lower SES will report more maltreatment. It should be emphasized that our study examines SES of the student body as a whole. We therefore analyzed the correlations between the socioeconomic characteristics of families in a school and the frequency of maltreatment reported in that school with the school as the unit of analysis. We do not explore whether students in the same school who come from families that are economically disadvantaged are treated differently.

We explored this issue with our data on secondary school students (Benbenishty, Zeira, & Astor, 2002). Because of the major differences between Arab and Jewish rates of maltreatment and because the SES of the Arab and Jewish populations in Israel are very different, we examined the correlations separately for the 108 Jewish schools and for the 41 Arab schools (see Table 7.2).

The overall picture presented in Table 7.2 is complex. It shows that the relations between maltreatment and SES differ among the various forms of maltreatment and between the two ethnic groups. In Arab schools there are very high correlations between family poverty rate and reports of physical and sexual maltreatment. For instance, the correlation of the percentage of families below the poverty line with the percentage of children in the school who reported being kicked or punched by a staff member is r = 0.57 (p < .001), being pinched or slapped is r = 0.53 (p < .01), and for staff members trying to touch in a sexual manner is r = 0.47 (p < .01). The same trend exists, though it is considerably weaker, with regard to the other two socioeconomic indicators (percentage of large families and of families with low education).

Table 7.2.   Correlations between Levels of Student Victimization by Staff in School and SES of the Students' Families

In the prior month, a staff member:	Low Education		Poverty		Large Families	
	Jewish N = 108	Arab N = 41	Jewish N = 108	Arab N = 41	Jewish N = 108	Arab N = 41
Mocked, insulted, or humiliated you.	0.05	0.14	0.06	0.28	0.04	0.16
Cursed you.	0.27**	0.17	0.36***	0.19	0.14	0.06
Grabbed and shoved you.	0.13	0.28	0.23	0.51**	0.16	0.29
Pinched or slapped you.	0.06	0.25	0.18	0.53**	0.18	0.34
Kicked or punched you.	0.23**	0.31	0.31***	0.57***	0.11	0.34
Made sexual comments to you.	0.22*	0.10	0.27***	0.24	0.08	0.18
Tried to touch you in a sexual manner.	0.26***	0.23	0.31***	0.47**	0.19*	0.35
Made sexual advances to you.	0.21*	0.23	0.17	0.45*	0.05	0.39*

*p < .05; **p < .01; ***p < .001

In Jewish schools, the correlations between the socioeconomic characteristics of the families and reports on staff maltreatment are considerably weaker than in Arab schools. The strongest correlations are between the percentage of poor families in the school and children's reports that staff cursed them (r = 0.36, p < .001), kicked or punched them (r = 0.31, p < .001), and tried to touch them in a sexual manner (r = 0.31, p < .001). The percentage of parents with low education had a similar pattern of relationship with staff maltreatment, but the correlations were lower. For instance, the correlation with reports of staff who curse was r = 0.27 (p < .01), with being punched or kicked was r = 0.23 (p < .01), and with a staff member trying to touch in a sexual manner was r = 0.26 (p < .001). In Jewish schools, the rate of large families in the school did not correlate with staff maltreatment.

The strong correlations between socioeconomic characteristics of families and prevalence of maltreatment in school raise the possibility that the differences between Jewish and Arab children that we found (see Table 7.1) reflect the different SES of their families. To examine this possibility, we analyzed the differences between the Jewish and Arab schools after controlling for the variables describing the SES of the students' families. We performed a multivariate analysis of variance with the school as the unit of analysis; the dependent variables were the prevalence of each of the specific behaviors in the school, the independent variable was school ethnicity (Jew or Arab), and the covariant was the percentage of families in the school below the poverty line. The multivariate analysis indicated that overall, the differences between Jewish and Arab schools are significant (although quite small) even after controlling for the SES of the families (F(8,137) = 2.77, p < .01).

Table 7.3 presents the means and standard deviations of the prevalence rates of each of the maltreatment behaviors in school, separately for Jewish and Arab schools.

Table 7.3.   Means and Standard Deviations of Staff Maltreatment Reports Made
by Jewish and Arab Children and Main Effects for Ethnic Group Before and
After Controlling for Socioeconomic Status of Children's Families

In the prior month, a staff member:	Mean % (SD)		Main Effect for Jewish vs. Arab F(1,148)	Main Effect after Controlling for Socioeconomic Variables F(1,148)
	Jewish	Arab		
Mocked, insulted, or humiliated you.	20.73 (8.36)	21.53 (9.14)	0.26	0.65
Cursed you.	10.94 (7.95)	23.68 (11.89)	57.03***	4.82*
Grabbed and shoved you.	7.24 (7.38)	16.83 (10.19)	40.27***	1.19
Pinched or slapped you.	5.94 (7.31)	17.42 (11.70)	51.39***	4.60*
Kicked or punched you.	3.04 (3.75)	11.42 (8.93)	65.54***	0.40
Made sexual comments to you.	4.37 (3.81)	10.72 (7.31)	47.74***	3.07
Tried to touch you in a sexual manner.	3.85 (3.72)	7.64 (6.35)	20.20***	0.08
Made sexual advances toward you.	3.30 (3.10)	6.40 (5.95)	17.08***	0.00

*p < .05, **p < 01, ***p < .001

Means and standard deviations and main effects for ethnic group were correlated before and after controlling for SES of children's families.

It also presents the significance tests for these differences, before and after controlling for the poverty rates among the families in each school. The table shows that
many of the differences in rates of maltreatment between Jewish and Arab schools
disappear after controlling for poverty. For instance, the mean prevalence rate of
reports on being kicked or punched by a staff member is 11.4% in Arab schools and
3.0% in Jewish schools, a strong and highly significant difference (F(1,148) = 65.54,
p < .001). When we controlled for the number of poor families in the school, however, the significant effect of ethnicity on being kicked or punched by staff disap-
peared (F(1,148) = 0.40, n.s.). The only two specific behaviors that showed small
but significant differences between ethnic groups were the rates of victimization by
cursing or pinching. As with the prior analyses, Arab students were more likely to
be victimized than Jewish students, even after controlling for poverty.

These findings raise several important questions. Why would Arab teachers be
more likely to hit Arab students? Why would teachers be more likely to hit students
who have lower SES? What possible theories or hypotheses could be explored to
clarify these questions? Again, SES and ethnic background are confounded variables
in this study, so the reader should be cautious when interpreting them.

First, it is important to start with the assertion that, given the educational training system in Israel, it is impossible that teachers do not know that physically maltreating students is against the law. Thus, our findings cannot be explained on the basis of selective awareness of the policies against corporal punishment.

It is possible that teachers from the same cultural background as the students share the same values as the students and their families concerning the utility of corporal punishment. If corporal punishment is seen as a valuable or useful educational tool by a given culture, the family, teachers, and community may be at odds with the national policy banning corporal punishment. Teachers who victimize children for these reasons may justify their behavior with the goal of improving the child's educational outcomes. If this is the case, national policy should be directed at sensitizing teachers who share those views to the deleterious effects of corporal punishment.

We found that staff are much more likely to victimize children if they have more students from poorer backgrounds. This could mean that the number and magnitude of social and behavior problems presented by the students overwhelm staff, who in turn become abusive to students out of stress. This kind of victimization would be very different because staff members would be aware that their actions are wrong and not helpful to the student. They might be victimizing children in an effort to control the class or because they are personally overstressed by the magnitude of issues presented in the class. If this were the case, additional resources, support, consultation, and strategies to deal with student problems would be most effective.

Yet a third alternative exists. It could be that teachers are aware that victimizing children is wrong and do not agree with cultural norms of the community, but they victimize the children because they see no social consequences for doing so due to the weakness of the child's family and community. In this situation, the teacher would not behave in the same way when in a community that clearly does not allow corporal punishment of children. This kind of victimization by staff is more opportunistic because it is based on a lack of reaction or response by parents and the community, and would require very different policy and intervention than the other two situations. Efforts to empower families and community and to advocate against maltreatment of children from weaker backgrounds would be most appropriate.

We encourage school violence researchers worldwide to incorporate these issues into their studies and theoretical models.

KEY FINDINGS AND IMPLICATIONS

A. Very few countries or studies collect data on student victimization by school staff.

B. The vast majority of victimization is by teachers.

C. There are three main types of victimization by staff:
   1. Emotional
   2. Physical
   3. Sexual
D. Emotional victimization is the most common and impacts about a third of Israeli students every month. Boys are victimized more often than girls.
E. Physical victimization impacts about 16.5% of Israeli students.
   1. Boys are victimized far more often than girls.
   2. Arab students are victimized far more often by Arab staff than Jewish students by Jewish staff.
F. Sexual victimization is reported by 4–5% of Israeli students.
   1. Boys are victimized more often than girls.
   2. Arab students are victimized more often than Jewish students.
G. As children grow older they are victimized less by staff.
H. Staff are more likely to victimize students if they have more students from low SES in their classes.
I. Many of the cultural effects of staff victimization disappear or are greatly reduced when SES is controlled for. What may have been interpreted in the past as being cultural may be SES effects.

Chapter 8

The Influence of Within-School Context on the Subjective Experience of Victimization: Safety, Violence as a Problem, and School Nonattendence Due to Fear

In the first chapters we looked at various aspects and types of victimization and examined their distribution and structure. However, we did not look at how variables within schools impact different forms of victimization. A viable theory of school victimization needs to explain how specific aspects of the school environment, either working alone or in concert, impact different types of victimization. An empirical understanding of how the school environment and victimization experiences impact students' feelings related to their school's safety is also critical. These issues lead to an entirely different set of questions that go beyond victimization prevalence rates and demographics. By their nature, these kinds of queries involve more sophisticated multivariate analyses that explore the *patterns of relationships between school-based variables.* Variables such as school climate, policy, rules, and staff's responses to violence may contribute to student victimization and subsequent feelings or interpretations that impact the experience of school in profound ways.

Hence, we believe it is important to explore how student-perceived school variables impact different forms of school victimization. How do the school climate, teacher support, school rules and policy, risky peer groups, and other school dynamics impact victimization? How do these context variables, combined with students' experience of personal victimization, impact students' feelings of personal safety, their assessment of the violence problem in their school as a whole, and their nonattendance due to fear? These more subjective variables go beyond victimization because they involve how students interpret experiences of the school environment and personal victimization. Clearly, there are many questions researchers could ask about students' subjective views of their school's safety. For example, in any given month, a sizable proportion of students miss school due to fear; currently, though, we do not know what relationships exist between school climate variables, student victimization, and school nonattendance. Likewise, we do not know which school variables and forms of victimization contribute to students' perception of their school as a violent setting. If students believe that their school has a serious school violence problem, we suspect this has a broad impact on their academics and their school experience as a whole. Finally, it is critical to know which school variables and experiences lead students to feel personally safe at school. At face value, these three types of subjective outcomes may appear similar; however, we suspect that they are influenced in different ways by school variables and personal victimization.

This chapter has two major objectives: first, to describe better the role of school variables in victimization; second, to describe how school variables combined with victimization lead to students' subjective interpretations about their school. We selected three interpretive outcomes to serve as examples of research that deals with *the patterns of relationships between theoretical variables* surrounding school victimization. We believe that it is this kind of empirical work that will help researchers develop and test an empirically based theory of school violence.

SUBJECTIVE OUTCOMES OF SCHOOL VIOLENCE

Figure 8.1 represents our theoretical model discussed in this chapter. At the extreme right are three summative or interpretive judgments about the school. The model is exploratory, but it suggests that the subjective outcomes we are exploring may be influenced directly by either the school context or personal experiences of victimization on school grounds. For some outcomes, personal experiences of victimization mediate the effects of the school context (such as school climate or the observation of risky peer group behaviors on school grounds). The following sections describe our expectations of how the variables will behave in relation to the subjective outcomes.

Assessment of the School's Violence Problem

This assessment (labeled School Violence Problem in the model) pertains to the degree to which the students believe their school has a violence problem. One would suspect that students' assessments of an entire school is influenced by a wide array of school variables in addition to their own personal experiences of victimization. For instance, students who are not involved in violence may still observe violent and risky peer behavior and the ineffective responses of staff and conclude that their school has a severe violence problem. An assessment that their school is a violent setting may result in reluctance to identify with their school. It might also have a strong effect on the students' opinion of the need for intervention and their acceptance (or lack of acceptance) of the school's measures to curb school violence (Dwyer et al., 2000; Dwyer, Osher, & Warger, 1998).

Findings from other studies have provided indirect evidence that when assessing the overall safety of the school, children may be influenced by an array of school-related factors, such as school policies against violence, teacher-student relationships,

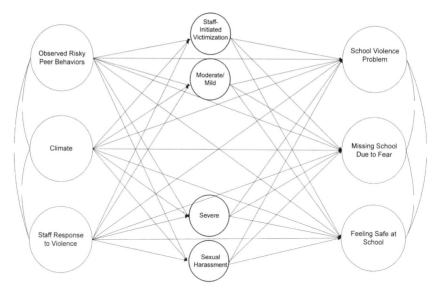

Figure 8.1. Theoretical structural model of direct and mediational effects on students' feeling safe at school, school nonattendance due to fear of violence, and perceived seriousness of the violence problem.

and observed risky peer group behaviors, and may be less influenced by their own experiences. Thus, students who see peers behave in a dangerous manner and staff responding ineffectively may judge that the school has a serious problem, even if they themselves were not victimized. (On the role of risky peer group behavior, see Astor, Benbenishty, Haj-Yahia, et al., 2002; Astor, Benbenishty, Marachi, et al., 2002.) Therefore, we would predict that how students judge the dangerousness of their school is directly related to school climate, teachers support coping, and risky peer behaviors they observe.

Nonattendance Due to Fear of School Violence

The choice to skip school may reflect a strong emotional reaction to violence in school or the feeling that staff are unable to protect them. Fear and school avoidance may directly affect the overall psychological well-being of these children. Further, missing school regularly could negatively impact these children's academic involvement and achievement. In contrast with the way students judge the violence problem in their school, which we believe requires students to look at the whole environment, we predict that student nonattendance due to fear will be mainly influenced by personal experiences of victimization and how the staff react to violence in their schools.

Feeling Safe at School

Feeling safe at school requires more from the school environment than merely being a setting devoid of violent behaviors. A sense of school safety may or may not be directly related to the actual number of violent events on campus. For example, in the United States, many educators have commented to us that in the post-Columbine era, the introduction of metal detectors, security guards, and specialized canine units may have reduced actual violence in their schools but made their schools feel unsafe and "prison-like." (These security measures do not exist in Israeli schools; see the final chapter for an elaboration of this issue.) We believe that the school-based variables contributing to feeling safe at school are different from those contributing to judgments about the school's violence problem, and differ from students' fear of attending school. In contrast with the other two subjective outcomes, we expect a positive and proactive school climate to be the most influential variable in creating feelings of safety.

Prevalence of the Three Outcomes in Israel

With the goal of understanding these subjective outcomes better, we present their prevalence rates by gender, grade level, and ethnic group. Table 8.1 shows that male more than female students tend to miss school due to fear, feel less safe in school, and see the violence problem as more serious. This gender difference is much smaller in primary schools than in secondary schools. Arab students miss school due to fear more than Jewish students. Overall, Arab students also feel less safe and see the problem as more serious than the Jewish students. In junior high, Jewish students report feeling slightly safer than Arab students, but there is a developmental trend for both: Rates among younger students are much higher than among older ones. This age trend is stronger and more pronounced for Arab students. Even so, for each group, three times more students in primary school report missing school due to fear than students in high school. Overall, students in secondary school also assess the violence problem as less serious than do younger students.

These findings lead to the question, What experiences of victimization and what aspects of the school environment influence these outcomes? In the following sections, we explore select variables that have been identified in the school violence literature.

VICTIMIZATION TYPES

In the middle part of our model in Figure 8.1 are victimization behaviors that have both direct and mediating effects on students' feelings of fear and safety and their nonattendance. Based on our analyses in Chapter 4, we have strong evidence that students' experiences of victimization are understood better along the dimension of severity rather than as theoretically or conceptually separate categories. Using the factors presented in Chapter 4, we thus separated victimization by peers at school

Table 8.1. Distribution of Nonattendance Due to Fear (percent), Assessment of the Severity of the Problem (mean, SD), and Feeling Safe in School (mean, SD) by Gender, Grade Level, and Ethnic Group

School Level	Total	Gender		Ethnic Group	
		Male	Female	Jewish	Arab
Primary School					
Nonattendance	15.7	16.2	15.5	14.0	21.1
Severity of the Problem[1]	3.11	3.09	3.13	3.13	3.07
	(1.25)	(2.89)	(1.26)	(1.20)	(1.41)
Feeling Safe in School[2]	2.92	2.89	2.95	2.96	2.80
	(0.94)	(0.97)	(0.92)	(0.88)	(1.10)
Junior High					
Nonattendance	6.5	7.8	5.1	5.7	9.5
Severity of the Problem[1]	2.95	3.11	2.81	2.96	2.93
	(1.32)	(1.30)	(1.33)	(1.27)	(1.48)
Feeling Safe in School[2]	2.81	2.68	2.93	2.79	2.87
	(0.90)	(0.95)	(0.83)	(0.85)	(1.04)
High School					
Nonattendance	4.6	6.0	3.1	4.3	6.2
Severity of the Problem[1]	2.58	2.65	2.51	2.52	2.89
	(1.30)	(1.31)	(1.28)	(1.26)	(1.43)
Feeling Safe in School[2]	2.89	2.83	2.96	2.91	2.81
	(0.88)	(0.94)	(0.80)	(0.86)	(0.96)

[1] On a scale from 1 = no problem or a very small problem to 5 = a very serious problem.
[2] On a scale from 1 = strongly disagree to 4 = strongly agree.

into two main categories of severe and moderate/mild. In Chapter 5 and 7 we saw that sexual harassment and victimization by staff present differently from other forms of victimization at school. Therefore, our model has four types of victimization based on empirical analyses: staff victimization, mild victimization by peers, severe victimization by peers, and sexual harassment by peers (sexual harassment by staff is included in the Staff-Initiated Victimization factor). We believe that each of these forms of victimization is impacted differently by different school variables and in turn influences students' perceptions of their school in different ways.

SCHOOL CONTEXT VARIABLES

We now move to the left side of our model presented in Figure 8.1, which consists of school context factors. The literature in this area identifies many school factors that relate to school victimization and its consequences. Some of these factors create a dangerous and threatening environment; other factors provide a sense of safety and protection, mitigating negative influences. In our model we include variables that belong to both sets of factors.

Observed Risky Peer Behaviors

There are many indications that students are influenced by the behaviors of their peers in school. Exposure to risky and dangerous behaviors on school grounds may contribute to students' fear and their feeling that violence is a problem. For instance, students who see peers bringing guns to school, drinking and using drugs on school grounds, fighting repeatedly, and harassing other students may feel threatened and conclude that the school has a major violence problem. It should be noted that we refer to the observation of behaviors that may not be directed at the reporting student; students may report that they see peers who harass other students but not that they themselves were victimized by these peers. Many studies have corroborated the importance of this set of variables in understanding students' perceptions of school violence (e.g., Astor, 1998; Astor, Benbenishty, Haj-Yahia, et al., 2002; Astor, Benbenishty, Zeira, et al., 2002; Cairns & Cairns, 1991; Griffith, 1995; Guerra & Tolan, 1994; Martin et al., 1996; Olweus, 1993; Slaby, Barham, Eron, & Wilcox, 1994; Wiist, Jackson, & Jackson, 1996).

School Climate

School climate and organization have been shown repeatedly to impact how students behave and feel in school (e.g., Astor, Vargas, et al., 1999; Garrity, Jens, Porter, Sager, & Short-Camilli, 1997; Gladden, 2002; D. Gottfredson, 1990; Hyman & Perone, 1998; Lee & Croninger, 1995; Noguera, 1995; Olweus, 1993; Rigby, 1996; Schreiber-Dill & Haberman, 1995; Stephens, 1994; Wicker, 1968). Schools that are able to create a climate that contains both effective preventive policies and teacher support of students can reduce levels of violence.

Mayer and Leone (1999) argue that "the organization of the school environment plays a critical role as either a facilitator or inhibitor of violence and disruption" (p. 334). They identify two major themes in the literature: discipline and control, and a humanistic approach to students. The literature shows that clear, well-known, and consistently enforced rules regarding discipline and conduct are essential in any schoolwide antiviolence intervention.

Staff response to violent events is another aspect of school climate we address in our model. Students who perceive the school's policies and methods of coping with violence as effective may feel safer in school and sense that their school does not have a violence problem. Students and teachers may have different views on what is a supportive or effective response to violent events. In the educational literature, several authors raised concerns that an adult "top-down" emphasis on rigid discipline and strict rules can have negative ramifications.. Hyman and Snook (1999, 2000) describe the ways an atmosphere of strict discipline and mistrust of students (as demonstrated in searches and other violations of students' rights) can in fact make schools more dangerous. These authors (along with many others) argue that a humanistic and supportive approach can help reduce school violence (see also

Astor, 1998; Astor et al., 2001; Devine, 1996; Lockwood, 1997). This approach may be reflected in students feeling that their teachers are supportive and that students are encouraged to participate in decision making in the school.

We tested our model using a confirmatory latent-variable structural equation modeling (SEM) using the EQS software program (Bentler, 1995), a statistical technique most appropriate for our purposes. In contrast to multiple regression analysis, which examines the relationships between one dependent variable and several independent variables, SEM allows us to examine the complex *pattern of relationships* suggested by our model. Further, this analysis considers the measurement error that is part of data collection instruments. Details of the analysis can become quite technical. For readers who are interested in a higher degree of detail, please refer to Appendix 2 and to a series of papers in which we utilized this technique (Astor, Benbenishty, Zeira, et al., 2002; Benbenishty, Astor, Zeira, et al., 2002).

In the following analyses, we address one overarching question: What are the interrelationships between school context variables of risky peer behavior, school climate and staff's response to violence, and peer and staff victimization on the three types of subjective judgments? Consistent with our book's focus on context, we also explore whether the relationships between the variables in our model are similar for students in primary, junior high, and high schools, for boys and girls, and for Jews and Arabs. These sets of analyses of grade level, gender, and culture are exploratory and meant to contribute to theory development rather than for hypotheses testing. Overall, though, given no extant literature or prior studies to suggest otherwise, we expect the patterns of relationships between school-based variables and each subjective outcome to be similar for each group and context.

FINDINGS

In preliminary analyses we found that the models for junior high and high schools are virtually identical. We therefore combined and analyzed them separately from primary schools, and then compared these two school types.[1]

Secondary Schools

OVERALL MODEL.   Figure 8.2 presents the SEM model pertaining to the combined pool of students in junior high and high schools. The results show high indices of fit.[2] Overall, this means that our general theory of how the school variables are related to victimization and the three subjective interpretations is supported by the data. Furthermore, as we report below, the influence of the variables in the model account for a relatively large amount of the explained variance for these outcomes. This means that, as our model predicted, school variables and personal victimization on school grounds have a relatively large effect on how students feel at and judge

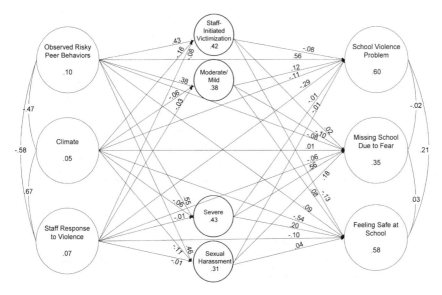

Figure 8.2. SEM of direct and mediational effects on secondary school students' feeling safe at school, nonattendance due to fear of violence, and perceived seriousness of the violence problem.

the school. It also suggests that interventions geared at changing the dynamics in schools (even without family and community interventions) can influence the way students feel about their school.

There are very weak associations between the three subjective outcomes (see Figure 8.2 for details). Our overall results suggest that the three outcome variables are independent entities that are influenced by separate school variables and by very specific forms of victimization.

Assessment of School Violence as a Problem. Overall, the variables in the model predict a lot of variance in this assessment ($R^2 = 0.60$). The model indicates that *students' judgments of the violence problem are mainly associated with perceptions of the risky behaviors of their peers* ($\beta = 0.56$). In addition, judgments of the effectiveness of staff responses to violence contribute to the students' assessment of the problem ($\beta = -0.29$). Personal victimization did not have strong direct or indirect (mediated) effects on students' judgment of their school as a whole; to improve students' judgment of their school, staff would need to show strong effective responses to violence. Most important, the findings show that schools need to focus on a reduction in risky peer behaviors that are witnessed on school grounds.

Missing School Due to Fear. Here, the variables in the model account for about a third of the variance ($R^2 = 0.35$). As expected, school nonattendance is primarily associated with the students' reports of being victims of severe personal victimization

(β = 0.54). It is also associated in a direct but weaker relationship with personal experiences of being sexually harassed by peers (β = 0.18). Risky peer group behaviors on school grounds did not have a direct effect on nonattendance but did have indirect effects that were mainly mediated by severe victimization and sexual harassment. In Chapter 5, our findings showed that sexual harassment victimization was related more to severe victimization, so the connections between sexual harassment, severe victimization, and fear make sense in this model.

Overall, this means that a student's decision not to attend school due to fear of violence is most likely directly related to being a victim at school. These findings suggest that interventions or attempts to increase attendance need to *reduce students' experiences of severe personal victimization at school*. A reduction of risky peer group behaviors on school grounds may indirectly reduce the impact of the effects of severe victimization on fear.

Feeling Safe in School. School variables and personal victimization account for a large amount of the explained variance when examining how safe a student feels in school (R^2 = 0.58). *A positive school climate is the main contributing variable for students feeling safe at school* (β = –0.54). Experiences of severe victimization also contribute to feeling less safe in school (β = 0.20). Risky peer behavior does not have a direct connection to feeling safe in school. However, for feelings of safety, the overall school climate contributes to the largest proportion of the variance.

COMPARISONS BETWEEN ETHNIC GROUPS.   In addition to examining the model for the students in secondary schools as a whole, we asked whether the effects of within-school context would be different for the various subgroups. The analyses comparing all the Arab and Jewish students in secondary schools showed high indices of fit,[3] meaning that our general theory of how the school variables are related to victimization and subjective interpretations is valid for both cultural groups. Although the overall patterns were the same for both groups, there were some important differences in the magnitude of each contributing variable (see Figure 8.3). We describe these differences below.

School Violence Problem. The model explains the variance for judgments about the violence problem much better for Jewish students than for Arab students (R^2 = 0.71 0.35, respectively). For both Jewish and Arab students, the awareness of risky peer behaviors on school grounds is highly related to their assessment that the school has a serious violence problem, but the magnitude of this association is much stronger for Jewish students (β = 0.73 0.43, for Jewish and Arab students, respectively). These differential contributions account for most of the differences between the two groups in amount of explained variance.

Fear. The overall model explains a similar amount of variance for nonattendance due to fear for both Jewish and Arab students (R^2 = 0.35 and 0.28, respectively). The patterns between the two groups mirror our general findings for the combined groups, suggesting that national interventions to reduce fear and increase attendance

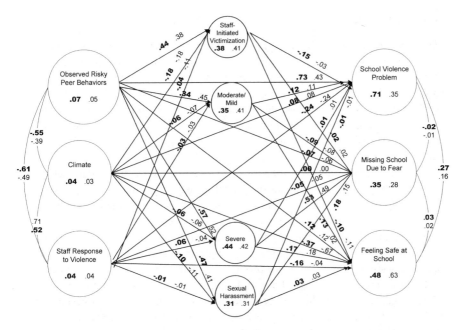

Figure 8.3.   SEM of direct and mediational effects on secondary school students' feeling safe at school, nonattendance due to fear of violence, and perceived seriousness of the violence problem (**Jews**, Arabs).

should focus on the reduction of severe personal victimization for both Jewish and Arab students. Based on our findings, these kinds of interventions are likely to impact both groups' nonattendance due to fear. These findings also imply that fear of attending school is primarily linked to students' direct experiences of severe victimization at school.

Feeling Safe in School. The model explains a large proportion of the variance for both Jewish and Arab students' feelings of safety at schools ($R^2 = 0.48$ and 0.63 for Jewish and Arab students, respectively). The association between positive climate and feeling safe in school was strong for both groups but much stronger for Arab students ($\beta = -0.67$, compared with -0.37 for Jewish students). Both groups were also indirectly influenced by risky peer group behaviors on school grounds (mediated through severe victimization). Nevertheless, whereas Jewish students' feelings of safety were also slightly linked to moderate victimization, Arabs' sense of safety was not associated with moderate victimization ($\beta = -0.13$ and 0.02 for Jewish and Arab students, respectively) and the response of the staff to violence ($\beta = -0.16$ and -0.04, respectively).

There were no real differences between male and female students in secondary schools with the outcomes or the variables in our model.

Primary Schools

The model for primary schools is similar to that of secondary schools but not identical. Because the instrument for primary schools was significantly shorter than that for secondary schools, the model that we tested was not exactly the same. The primary school model did not have the teachers' responsiveness to violent events factor because we did not ask those questions at the primary school level. We also did not ask sexual harassment questions at the primary school level and therefore did not have a sexual harassment factor. Figure 8.4 represents the SEM model for primary schools.

The fit indices of the model for the primary schools show that the model is a good fit.[4] In general, the paths in the model for primary schools show the same patterns as the paths in the model for secondary schools. Safety is mainly influenced by school climate and experiences of severe violence. As with the secondary school findings, nonattendance due to fear is primarily influenced by experiences of severe victimization and indirectly by risky peer group behaviors. Primary school students' assessments of the violence problem in their school had slightly different patterns from the secondary school students'. In secondary schools, the main influence on judgments of the severity of the problem came from the risky peer group behaviors. By contrast, in primary schools, in addition to risky peer group behaviors, the two variables of mild victimization and school climate also had effects on students' judgments of the problem.

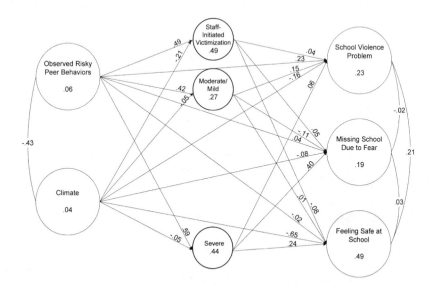

Figure 8.4.   SEM of direct and mediational effects on primary school students' feeling safe at school, nonattendance due to fear of violence, and perceived seriousness of the violence problem.

Compared with secondary schools, the primary school model explains less of the variance on all three dependent variables. Several possible explanations for this should be explored by future studies. Variables that exist within schools play a greater role in secondary than in primary students' assessments. The family, community, and other contexts may be contributing more to younger students' subjective assessments.

This kind of analysis is consistent with theories in developmental psychology. It is possible that students' cognitive and emotional capacity to understand the entirety of school dynamics increases as they grow older. This may be especially true for judging the whole school's problem. It is possible that as children grow older, the crystallization of the victim group becomes more defined and smaller; therefore, for nonattendance due to fear, the predictions become more accurate with secondary school students. As we would expect, primary and secondary school variances for feeling safe are similar.

Overall, the model is a good fit for male and female students (see Figure 8.5).[5] The comparison reveals that there are similar patterns between the variables in the model for the students' assessment of the seriousness of the problem and their views of their own sense of safety. By contrast, for female students, missing school due to fear is more strongly influenced by being victimized in school ($\beta = 0.23$ for male students, 0.50 for female). Additionally, the path from moderate victimization to missing school due to fear is stronger for female students ($\beta = -0.07$ and -0.17 for male and female students, respectively).

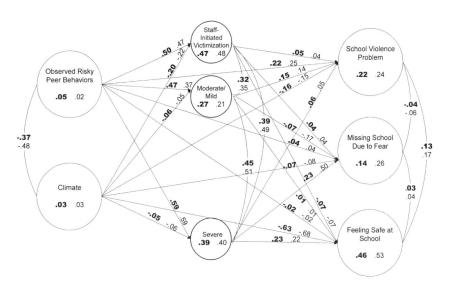

Figure 8.5.   SEM of direct and mediational effects on primary school students' feeling safe at school, nonattendance due to fear of violence, and perceived seriousness of the violence problem (**males**, females).

Overall, the results show that the model is valid for both Arab and Jewish primary school children (see Figure 8.6).[6] However, when we explored specific contributions of school variables, we found some clear differences between the two groups that deserve special attention and call for more in-depth exploration. The differences are small with regard to sense of safety, but much larger with regard to Jews' and Arabs' judgments of the school violence problem and missing school due to fear. This model does not explain as much of the variance for Arab students' views of the violence problem ($R^2 = 0.18$ and 0.34 for Arab and Jewish students, respectively). Furthermore, the paths in the model seem to behave in an unexpected manner for the Arab students: Being victimized by a staff member ($\beta = 0.20$) and severely victimized by a peer ($\beta = -0.13$) are in fact associated with assessing the school as having less of a violence problem. This may reflect a cultural difference that allows for corporal punishment or forms of retribution between peers as a form of social justice. Chapter 7 showed that victimization from staff is more prevalent and accepted in Arab schools, and our qualitative work suggests that corporal punishment is more accepted for educational reasons in Arab schools (even though it's officially banned by Israeli law). For Jewish students, the pattern is in the expected direction ($\beta = -0.22$ and 0.21 for the paths from staff victimization and severe peer victimization, respectively). Additionally, the impact of observed risky peer behaviors on judgments of the school violence problem is much stronger for Jewish students ($\beta = 0.40$, compared with 0.17 among Arab students).

The ability of the model to explain variance in missing school due to fear among Jewish primary school students is very limited ($R^2 = 0.08$, compared with 0.34 for

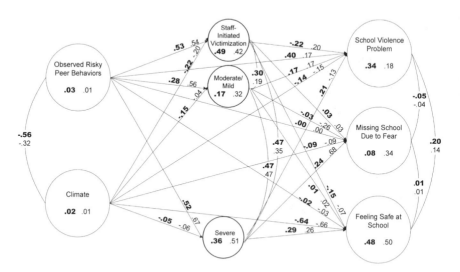

Figure 8.6.   SEM of direct and mediational effects on primary school students' feeling safe at school, nonattendance due to fear of violence, and perceived seriousness of the violence problem (**Jews**, Arabs).

Arab students). For Arab students, as expected, personal severe victimization explains their fear of attending school ($\beta = 0.68$). Interestingly, among Arab students, being the victim of moderate victimization is associated with less fear of attending school ($\beta = -0.26$), despite the fact that being moderately victimized is correlated positively with being severely victimized ($r = 0.47$). This may also reflect cultural differences in the acceptability of certain forms of violence that are seen as horseplay or rough and tumble; victimization from these forms of violence may serve to create greater social group connections in some cultures than in others.

SUMMARY

In this chapter we showed that (1) students' nonattendance due to fear of school violence, (2) students' assessment of school violence as a problem, and (3) students' feelings of personal safety at school are understood better as separate conceptual constructs. These dependent variables are influenced by different social dynamics, organizational factors, and personal victimization occurring within schools. Furthermore, the overall structure of our theoretical model is a good fit for different cultural groups (Arabs and Jews), for both genders, and for primary and secondary schools. Differences between genders and cultural groups emanate mainly from the differential contributions of the independent variables (specific paths) rather than an entirely new theoretical/structural model. These findings are extremely similar to results from our previous analyses conducted on a different data set (Astor, Benbenishty, Zeira, et al., 2002; Benbenishty, Astor, Zeira, et al., 2002) and represent the tenth empirical replication of this model with 10 separate large-scale samples. Therefore, we are confident that the findings reported are reliable and have strong empirical validity.

Overall, the findings reported in this inquiry provide support for the main thesis of this chapter: Social dynamics *within schools*, combined with students' experiences of personal victimization *on school grounds*, have a major impact on children's subjective views of their school context. This study focuses exclusively on the school environment and attempts to explain which school variables contribute to students' views of school violence, nonattendance due to fear of violence, and feeling safe in school. Our model and findings suggest that what students see, hear, know about, and experience on school grounds contributes greatly to their subjective views of the school as a setting.

Implications for Practice

In this study, we found that school climate and observed risk behaviors primarily have an indirect effect on fear that is mediated through the student's own personal victimization. Consequently, interventions that focus exclusively on the school climate may not reduce students' fear of attending school due to violence. To decrease fear effectively, interventions should focus on reducing students' experiences of victimization. Efforts geared toward reducing observed risky behaviors on campus also could indirectly impact nonattendance due to fear.. Nevertheless, intervention strategies for reducing fear should have strong student and teacher components targeting students' personal experiences of severe physical victimization. Interventions geared toward increasing feelings of safety need to focus both on improving school climate and on reducing students' experiences of severe victimization.

Our findings suggest that Israel can increase student school attendance by adopting rather strong cross-cultural and omnibus interventions to reduce severe personal victimization on campus and observed risk behaviors in all schools. These kinds of interventions would impact student fear and assessment of the problem for both Jewish and Arab students. The overall pattern of relationships between the variables for Jews and Arabs and boys and girls was so similar that such national policy and interventions could be effective across all school systems.

This study provides empirical evidence to support the notion that the school environment itself contributes substantially to students' perceptions of a problem, their feelings of personal safety, and their own personal fear. We feel this implication is especially important because school-related variables are under the schools' control. Also, by focusing more precisely on schools as a unique setting, policymakers could gain a better understanding of the unique contributions of the school environment as a normative developmental setting compared with other environments, such as the neighborhood and home.

Implications for Future Research

Our findings were similarly strong for both male and female students. However, our model explained more of the variance for Jewish students' assessments and much less for Arab students'. Future studies should explore possible additional variables in Arab schools that are unique to Arab culture and could contribute more to assessment of a violence problem. Future studies should also explore whether family and community variables impact Arab students' school assessments more than Jewish students'. Clearly, though, for Jewish students' assessments of their schools, the within-school predictors in our model explained over half of the variance for secondary schools and about a quarter for primary schools.

There is ample research suggesting that factors external to the school environment may also affect children's perceptions related to school violence and victimization (e.g., Bowen, Bowen, Richman, & Woolley, 2002; Laub & Lauritsen, 1998). In all likelihood, external factors contribute strongly to children's school-based judgments. In Chapter 10, using hierarchical linear modeling methods, we add contextual variables such as the community, family, and neighborhood to our conceptual model.

KEY FINDINGS AND IMPLICATIONS

A. There is great need for research on subjective interpretations of victimization events and variables within schools.

B. Different subjective interpretive outcomes are influenced by different types of victimization and school variables. In fact, there are only weak associations between these seemingly similar subjective variables.

 1. Students' views of their school violence problem are influenced mainly by the risky peer behaviors they observe on school grounds, as well as by the response of the school staff to violent events.

 2. Students' nonattendance of school due to fear of violence is influenced mainly by their personal experiences of severe peer violence on school grounds.

 3. Schools can reduce victimization that leads to fear by targeting risky peer group behaviors on school grounds.

 4. A student's sense of safety on school grounds is influenced mainly by a positive school climate. These patterns are true for all school levels studied and across ethnicity and gender.

C. This means the overall pattern of relationships between the variables is similar. The amount of influence of each school variable on the three outcomes varies slightly by culture and gender.

D. For these outcomes, the amount of variance explained by within-school variables alone is quite high and impressive.

NOTES

1. Because the instruments used for primary and secondary schools were not identical, we conducted separate structural equation modeling analyses for primary and for secondary schools. We compared the models of junior high versus high school students, boys versus girls, and Jews versus Arabs (all models are available upon request from the authors). The models for junior high and high school were remarkably similar—almost identical. Logically, it made sense to look at secondary schools together as there were no substantive differences between high schools and junior high schools on the overall model. The differences in the paths leading to three variables we examined were also very similar across male and female students. Significantly more differences were found when we compared Jewish and Arab students. Therefore, for the sake of brevity and clarity, we present the secondary students' sample as a whole and focus primarily on the differences between Arabs and Jews, as this represented the greatest number of differences.

2. χ^2 (221, $N = 10,000$) = 2719.93, $p < .001$, NNFI = .995; CFI = .969; SRMR = .024; RMSEA =.034.

3. χ^2(449, $N = 10,000$) = 3020.78, $p < .001$, NNFI = .958, CFI = .966, SRMR = .037, RMSEA = .024.

4. χ^2(142, $N = 5,600$) = 1557.08, $p < .0001$, NNFI = .935, CFI = .956, SRMR = .031, RMSEA = .042.

5. χ^2(309, $N = 5,600$) = 1788.69, $p < .0001$, NNFI = .940, CFI = .951, SRMR = .039, RMSEA = .030.

6. χ^2(278, $N = 5,600$) = 1339.28, $p < .0001$, NNFI = .955, CFI = .963, SRMR = .039, RMSEA = .026.

Chapter 9

Differences in Victimization between Schools

In the previous chapter, we explored the relationships between student-perceived school variables and victimization types. We looked at these within-school dynamics across all schools in Israel, and our findings generalized to the entire student population in Israel. The sets of analyses presented in Chapter 8 are important because they highlight the theoretical patterns between school dynamics and how they contribute to different victimization types. However, schools across an entire country are likely to vary in levels of victimization, which leads us to shift our attention to a different set of questions. Are there schools that have higher rates of victimization than other schools? Do schools differ on some types of victimization and not others? If so, to what degree?

Questions focusing on differences between schools are important for policy and theory questions. If there are only a few schools that have very severe forms of victimization (such as gun use), it would make sense to focus intervention efforts on those schools. Also, perhaps schools with different forms of victimization require a different set of conceptual intervention strategies. In this chapter we ask questions about the *school as a unit*. Most of the literature in this area has neglected this perspective and focused only on student-level views of school victimization, which is surprising because most of the school intervention literature focuses on school-level programs. To understand the dynamics of school victimization, assess the need for schoolwide interventions, and examine the outcomes of such programs, it is essential to explore victimization from a school unit perspective. These kinds of questions explore the variation between schools on specific forms of victimization.

Looking at school victimization by schools as a unit will provide another contextual layer of detailed explication to our dependent variable, victimization. Knowing which kinds of victimization are common across all schools and which are concentrated in a small number of schools is an essential step before exploring the role of contexts. If we find that schools vary widely on different types of victimization, it will then be important to explore the external variables as well as the variables within schools that could help explain why some schools have concentrated or elevated victimization rates.

Here, we combine and aggregate all students' experiences to create a view of the school as a whole. This will help us distinguish between schools that may have only a few students who were victimized, and other schools in which most of the students have been victimized. A whole-school view can also help us identify schools in which students feel safe and perceive their teachers as supportive, and other schools in which there is a consensus among the students that they are unsafe and not supported. In this chapter we explore how schools vary in their levels of student victimization; in the following chapter we will use our theoretical model to guide us in asking what school- and student-level factors explain these variations.

HOW ISRAELI SCHOOLS VARY IN VICTIMIZATION LEVELS

From our daily experiences with schools we know that they vary in their level of violence; some are more violent than others. An intriguing question is whether the rate of violence in schools follows a normal distribution, in which a few schools have high levels of violence and a few have low levels of violence and the rest are somewhere in the midrange. Or perhaps the distribution is skewed and there are a small number of schools that have very high or very low levels of violence that make them stand out as extremes. The answer has implications for policy and practice. For instance, let us assume that that 10% of the students report that they bring knives to school. From a policy perspective, there is a major difference between whether most schools have about 10% of the students bringing knives, a very small minority of schools where many students bring knives, or other schools in which none of the students brings knives. We therefore examine the school-level distribution of the various victimization types reported by the students in each school.

As mentioned, the unit of analysis in this chapter is the whole school. The sample size is 215: 75 primary schools, 62 junior high schools, and 78 high schools. In addition to the means, we examined two parameters of the distribution: (1) a dispersion index that indicates how heterogeneous schools are in terms of their level of violence, and (2) skewness of the distribution, which tells us whether the distribution is normal or skewed in one direction. A high and positive sign of the skewness index means that there are few schools in which the level of violence is exceptionally high, and a negative sign indicates that a few schools have very low rates of violence.

Table 9.1 presents the school-level distribution of the various victimization types. When we examine the dispersion index we see that victimization types that were reported more frequently by the students have a lower dispersion index than victimization types that are less frequent and more severe. The behaviors that have the lowest dispersion index are "A student cursed you" and "A student mocked, insulted,

Table 9.1. School-level Distribution of Victimization

	Mean	Minimum	Maximum	Standard Deviation	Dispersion Index	Skewness
A student cursed you.	75.8	11.7	100.0	18.30	0.24	-1.11
A student mocked, insulted, or humiliated you.	59.7	4.8	91.9	16.12	0.27	-0.70
A student seized and shoved you on purpose.	49.8	1.8	89.3	16.63	0.33	-0.59
A student threatened to harm or hit you.	39.4	0.0	71.4	15.86	0.40	-0.34
A student stole personal belongings or equipment from you.	42.8	1.2	81.5	15.83	0.37	-0.14
You were involved in a fistfight.	33.8	0.0	75.0	14.93	0.44	-0.13
You were kicked or punched by a student who wanted to hurt you.	33.8	0.0	82.1	16.19	0.48	0.00
A student took your things from you by force.	20.1	0.0	50.0	10.82	0.54	0.27
A group of students boycotted you and did not want to play or talk with you.	24.8	0.0	65.1	16.36	0.66	0.29
Students threatened you on your way to or from school.	20.1	0.0	53.8	12.69	0.63	0.41
You saw a student in school with a knife.	35.3	0.0	89.3	18.82	0.53	0.43
A student intentionally destroyed or broke your personal belongings.	16.3	0.0	47.2	9.97	0.61	0.45
A student tried to intimidate you by the way he or she was looking at you.	24.4	0.0	60.2	10.37	0.42	0.50
A student used a rock or other instrument in order to hurt you.	25.8	0.0	71.4	13.55	0.52	0.51
A student gave you a serious beating.	10.9	0.0	39.3	7.99	0.73	0.65
You were involved in a fight, were hurt, and required medical attention.	11.1	0.0	41.4	7.60	0.69	0.89
Gang members at school threatened, harassed, and pressured you.	7.4	0.0	27.8	5.97	0.80	0.91
You were blackmailed under threats by another student (for money, valuables, or food).	7.7	0.0	37.7	6.25	0.81	1.40
A student cut you with a knife or a sharp instrument on purpose.	5.2	0.0	26.8	5.52	1.05	1.41
A student threatened you with a gun and you saw the gun.	3.2	0.0	23.5	3.53	1.11	1.70
A student threatened you with a knife and you saw the knife.	6.7	0.0	42.2	6.87	1.03	1.84
You saw a student in school with a gun.	3.8	0.0	29.4	4.52	1.20	2.25

or humiliated you." The behaviors that showed more variation (the highest dispersion index) are also the rarest: "A student cut you with a knife or a sharp instrument on purpose," "A student threatened you with a gun and you saw the gun," and "You saw a student in school with a gun." In other words, schools tend to be more similar to each other with regard to the less severe victimization types but differ much more from each other when it comes to the more severe behaviors.

When we examine how skewed the distribution is, we find that the more severe types of violence are positively skewed: There are few schools with very high levels of severe violence. Let us illustrate this point with more detailed information about severe violent events in schools. In about a quarter of the schools we examined there were no reports of a student cutting another student with a knife or a sharp object, half of the schools had fewer than 5% of the students making this report, and in more than 80% of the schools the prevalence of this behavior was lower than 10%. However, in 5% of the schools, 20% or more of the students reported being cut with a knife or a sharp object, and in 1% of the schools *more than 25%* of the students reported being cut by a knife or a sharp object.

A similar pattern emerged when we examined reports about being threatened by a knife. In 70% of the schools, fewer than 10% of the students reported such victimization. But in 10% of the schools at least 20% of the students made such a report, and in 1% of the schools *more than 40%* of the students said that someone threatened them with a knife in the prior month.

In our research, we encountered a school that in many ways epitomized the schools at the top of the list of violent schools. We visited the school two years after the quantitative study was conducted and immediately after a new principal was installed (among other reasons, the school hired a new principal because the levels of violence and disarray in the school could not be tolerated by the parents). We heard horrifying stories about the levels of violence evident in the school. The new principal opened a drawer in his desk and revealed a number of weapons confiscated from students, including knives, a loaded gun magazine, and a flammable substance. Although the new principal named the fight against violence as the most important priority of this school, we saw and heard many incidents of violence, including students bringing knives to school to threaten others, students bringing relatives to help them "settle accounts" with other students, and a wide range of vandalism acts. In the year prior to our visit the municipality installed 300 new fluorescent lights; they were all smashed within minutes; in addition, students set fires in various areas of the school, and pulled out many of the electrical fixtures. There were consistent rumors of sexual attacks perpetrated against female students, and many indications that drugs were being distributed on school grounds.

The new principal was trying to change the situation and in the first few months focused on discipline and prevention of violence. Nevertheless, our debriefing of the observers and the visits of the investigators to the site left us with a clear sense of danger and of a disaster waiting to happen.

Implications

The above analyses provide important insights into to how schools differ in terms of their levels of violence and the implications for policy. It seems that schools tend to be quite similar in terms of the less severe and more common forms of victimization, especially social-verbal and moderate physical. Thus, a nationwide campaign targeting these behaviors will be relevant to most Israeli schools. We expect other countries to have this type of skewed distribution.

We strongly suggest that policy and interventions that target *severe* victimization in schools should be much more focused and limited in scope; nationwide campaigns are not relevant to most schools. Clearly, there are a few schools that have extreme levels of severe violence. There is a need to identify these schools and design interventions to address their forms of victimization specifically.

From an empirical and theoretical perspective, it is important to examine community and family variables that may help explain some of the variation in the forms of victimization. In the next chapter, we explore the relative contributions of variables within schools as well as contexts outside the school to understanding violence experienced by students in school.

KEY FINDINGS AND IMPLICATIONS

A. Exploring the variation in victimization rates between schools is an important strategy of analysis.
B. Very few schools have high levels of severe violence.
C. The more severe the violence, the more skewed the distribution of violence in schools.
   1. In about 25% of the schools, there were no reports of students cutting with a knife.
   2. In about 50% of schools, fewer than 5% of students reported being cut with a knife.
   3. In more than 80% of the schools, fewer than 10% of students reported being cut with a knife.
   4. In 5% of schools, 20% or more of the students reported being cut with a knife.
   5. In 1% of schools, over 25% of students reported being cut with a knife.
   6. The same patterns exist with other forms of severe violence.
D. These patterns suggest that policy and resources should be focused on the most problematic schools.

Chapter 10

Schools Embedded in Larger Contexts:
The Matryoshka Doll Theory
of School Violence

Now we come full circle. In Chapter 1 we presented our heuristic model of school violence that served as the road map for this book. Then we explored types of victimization, their patterns, and how within-school variables relate to specific types of victimization. We presented findings showing that students and schools have wide variations in levels of violence. However, within-school variables do not explain all of the variation in school victimization. As depicted in our heuristic model, school settings are embedded in much larger, nested contexts that may impact the kinds of victimization present on school grounds.

According to our theoretical model, victimization in school is the product of many factors that are associated with multiple levels organized hierarchically (nested like a matryoshka doll): individual students within classes, classes within schools, schools within neighborhoods, and neighborhoods within societies and cultures. We therefore propose to view victimization in school as influenced by several nested contexts simultaneously. A similar view was expressed by Welsh, Greene, and Jenkins (1999), who argue that research and intervention efforts have too often been piecemeal, examining specific variables and levels of analysis in isolation from one another. Furthermore, they argue, these past studies have focused on one level of analysis: either determining who are the more violent students or which are the more violent schools.

An effective way of responding to this justified concern is provided by Duncan and Raudenbush (1999). They suggest using multilevel approaches to examine the differential effects of student, school, and neighborhood characteristics. Lee (2000) presents examples of how a multilevel approach can identify school context effects (e.g., school size) on learning. This type of analysis can detect not only the effects of school context variables but also how context interacts with student-level variables. For instance, school size may have different effects on male and on female students.

In this chapter, we use such a multilevel approach to test empirically aspects of our model of victimization in school. Only a handful of studies used a multilevel approach in the study of school violence, including Welsh and his colleagues' (1999) study of school misconduct. These authors examined simultaneously the relative influences of the individual, institutional, and community factors on misconduct with a sample of 7,583 students from 11 junior high schools in Philadelphia, Pennsylvania. Community was conceptualized in two ways: local (the census tract around the school) and imported (aggregated measures from the census tract where the students live). They studied the following predictors of school misconduct: community poverty and residential stability, community crime, school size, students' perceptions of school climate, and individual student characteristics.

The results of Welsh and associates' (1999) research showed that most of the explained variance in student misconduct (94%) was attributable to within-school (individual) factors; school and community-level factors (both local and imported) added only small increments to explained variance (an additional 4.1–4.5%). These findings contradict many other theories, which emphasize the central role of the community in explaining school misconduct. However, the methodological limitations of this important study should not be overlooked. For example, the nonrepresentative sample on the school level included *only 11 schools* from the Philadelphia School District, with a relatively low student response rate (65%). Another limitation is that the dependent variable "school disorder" was measured in a narrow way (four questions), restricting the ability to distinguish among various aspects and manifestations of school violence (for a discussion on this study's limitations, see Hoffman & Johnson, 2000). Nevertheless, the study's findings highlight the importance of examining further the relative role of community and the school on school victimization.

AN EMPIRICAL INVESTIGATION OF SCHOOL VIOLENCE IN A LARGER CONTEXT

We expand Welsh and associates' (1999) research by using a nationally representative sample of students and by exploring the relationships between several types of school victimization and a number of dimensions of the school's ecology. We explore three separate empirically derived categories (presented in Chapter 4) of school violence: mild/moderate victimization (such as being pushed and shoved, or threatened by another student), severe victimization (such as being cut with a knife, or being blackmailed), and verbal victimization (being cursed or humiliated). We ask to what extent these categories are explained by within- and between-school context variables. This analysis involves a focus on school variables that includes the larger societal contexts in which schools are embedded (i.e., family, neighborhood, culture).

We examine several factors that serve as the independent variables in our model. We chose these variables on the basis of extensive review of the literature, some of it presented in this book and some of it in various chapters and papers (e.g., Khoury-Kassabri, 2002). We therefore list these variables here only briefly:

A. Individual factors
   1. Gender
   2. Grade level
B. School context factors
   1. School type (primary, junior, high)
   2. School size
   3. Class size
   4. School climate
      a. School policy against violence
      b. Teacher support of students
      c. Student participation
C. Family context (proportion of families in the schools)
   1. Below poverty line
   2. Low education
   3. Large families
   4. Overall index of social deprivation (a composite index of 1–3)
D. Neighborhood context (percentage of neighborhood members)[1]
   1. Demographic characteristics of school's community
      a. Ethnic origin (e.g., percentage of European descent)
      b. Proportion of population below age 18
   2. SES of school's community
      a. Unemployment
      b. Academic, professional
      c. Working-class families
      d. Low income
      e. Low education
      f. Overcrowded households
E. Cultural context: Jewish and Arab students and schools[2]

DATA ANALYSIS

Our main analytical tool in this chapter is hierarchical linear modeling (HLM), which provides a technique to analyze the effect of individual- and group-level data in nested designs (Bryk & Raudenbush, 1992). In this study, students are nested within schools: The level-1 model represents the relationships between the student-level variables and the dependent variables, and the level-2 model captures the influence of school-level variables.

In this model, school climate operates on two related but separate levels. The ways the individual students perceive and experience their school climate can be related to their unique personal involvement with school violence. For example, students who perceive their teachers as supportive may feel less victimized than students who do not feel supported by staff. This may also work in the other direction, so that students who are involved in violence may be the target of negative sanctions by their teachers, and therefore may feel less supported and perhaps feel that the school's policies against violence are unfair.

In addition to the impact of school climate on the individual level, climate can also influence the aggregated level of the school climate as a whole. The fact that the school has many students who feel that their teachers protect and support them and that the school's policies are effective can have consequences beyond the individual student. For instance, schools with such positive climates may also have more effective staff and organizational structure and stronger community support. These aspects of school functioning may have their own impact, independent of the effects that students' individual perceptions have on violence and victimization.

We explore school climate both on the individual and school levels. This approach allows us to ask whether the effects of school violence can be explained by the ways individual students perceive their school, or by the possibility that the aggregated perceptions of many students create (or reflect) a school atmosphere that influences school victimization (i.e., the whole is more than its parts).

We examined the models for primary and secondary schools separately because we used different questionnaires for each.

Examining Within-School Student-Level Factors

To assess the importance of student-level factors in understanding to what extent students were victimized, we estimated the relationships between gender, age, and climate and victimization. Table 10.1 presents the association coefficients (betas), and Table 10.2 presents the contribution of each factor to the explained variance. Overall, the student-level variables that we employed to predict school victimization do not explain large amounts of variance (between 4.9% and 18.3%). Similar to our find-

Table 10.1. Association Coefficients (Betas) of Student-level Variables

| | Victimization Types | | | | | |
| | Moderate | | Verbal | | Severe | |
	Primary	Secondary	Primary	Secondary	Primary	Secondary
Gender	−0.922***	−1.234***	−0.061*	−0.229***	−0.573***	−0.761***
Age	−0.088	−0.181***	0.036*	−0.060**	0.026	−0.025
Policy	−0.759***	−0.853***	−0.123***	−0.197***	−0.461***	−0.638***
Support	−0.705***	−0.761***	−0.121***	−0.178***	−0.455***	−0.559***
Participation	NA	−0.464***	NA	−0.156***	NA	−0.312***

NA, Not asked. *p < .05; **p < .01; ***p < .001.

Table 10.2.   Within-School Variance Explained by Student-level Variables

	Moderate		Verbal		Severe	
	Primary (%)	Secondary (%)	Primary (%)	Secondary (%)	Primary (%)	Secondary (%)
Gender	4.33	8.91	0.85	2.88	4.29	6.75
Age	0	2.00	1.37	1.85	0	0
Climate	6.71	7.37	2.71	3.47	7.77	11.16
Overall	11.04	18.28	4.93	8.20	12.06	17.91

ings presented in earlier chapters, the tables indicate that male students report more victimization than female students. The largest gender contrasts are with regard to moderate school violence, especially in secondary schools, and the smallest concern verbal victimization. Student's age does not contribute much to explaining variance among students in their levels of victimization; this was especially true with regard to severe victimization. In contrast, school climate, as perceived by the individual student, was a good predictor of the student's victimization level. The school policies and teachers' support of students had stronger predictive power than the student's participation in school decision making.

Examining Variations in Victimization between Schools

In previous chapters we presented data that suggested that schools vary in their victimization levels for specific acts of victimization. To examine this issue in more depth, we now ask similar questions that focus on indices of victimization types rather than individual behaviors (e.g., we examine mild/moderate, severe, and verbal victimization presented in Chapter 4). We used a fully unconditional two-level HLM that provides useful preliminary information on how much variance in student victimization lies within and between schools. (This analysis is equivalent to a one-way ANOVA with schools as random effects.)

Table 10.3 indicates that a considerable proportion of the variance in student victimization is accounted for by variance *between* schools. Variance between schools was almost 19% of the total variance in reports of verbal-social victimization in primary schools; it was about 10% with regard to severe physical victimization and 14% with regard to moderate victimization among secondary schools. The lowest level of between-schools variance was 9%, which was among primary schools with regard to their reports on moderate victimization. It seems that high levels of moderate victimization are quite common in primary schools and these rates do not vary much among schools.

These figures are appreciably higher than the ones reported by Welsh and associates (1999; around 4%), which may be explained by the fact that we used a representative sample that reflects the heterogeneity of the Israeli education system, whereas

Table 10.3.   Proportion of Variance between Primary and
Secondary Schools by Victimization Type (ICC)

Moderate		Verbal-Social		Severe	
Primary (%)	Secondary (%)	Primary (%)	Secondary (%)	Primary (%)	Secondary (%)
8.86	14.12	18.63	14.89	10.19	10.59

Note: The intraclass correlation (ICC) is calculated using the formula: variance between schools / (variance between + variance within).

Welsh et al. studied only 11 schools in one area. These levels of between-school variance strongly support our emphasis on examining the school as an entity embedded in contexts that contribute to variance among schools. Given this between-school variance, what school context factors can best account for this variance?

Table 10.4 presents the association coefficients (betas) of each of the school-level predictors, and Table 10.5 presents the amount of variance explained by predictors in each context. Overall, school-level characteristics were quite effective in predicting school violence. Table 10.5 shows that school-level variables explained best the variance in verbal-social victimization (about 73% in secondary schools and 79% in primary schools). The predictor variables also explained large amounts of variance in severe victimization, about 66% of the variance in secondary schools and 46% in primary schools. The lowest levels of explained variance appeared in the mild/moderate and more frequent type of victimization, especially in primary schools (about 50% and 18% of the variance in secondary and primary schools, respectively).

This set of findings indicates that schools vary in their levels of victimization, and contexts suggested by our model explain a remarkable proportion of these differences. This means that community and family effects do spill over and impact school victimization. However, the overall school climate and organizational variables also make a sizable impact on victimization types. Nevertheless, they do not impact all forms of victimization equally.

Differential Impact of School Variables on Different Forms of Victimization

Taken together, Tables 10.4 and 10.5 show another important pattern: The three types of victimization have very different relationships with school-level variables. In other words, each type of victimization is predicted by different school context characteristics. Furthermore, there are extensive differences between primary and secondary schools. This set of findings suggests that we cannot make sweeping generalizations of how context affects school victimization. More refined models are needed that connect specific types of school victimization with specific context variables. Furthermore, it is possible that certain context variables

Table 10.4. Association Coefficients of School-level Variables

| | Victimization Type | | | | | |
| | Moderate | | Verbal | | Severe | |
	Primary	Secondary	Primary	Secondary	Primary	Secondary
Demographics of school's community						
Percentage of European Jews	-0.132	0.009	0.035	0.147***	-0.139*	-0.103***
Young population	-0.089	0.044	-0.183***	-0.102**	0.150**	0.147***
SES of school's community						
Unemployment	0.159	0.141*	0.030	-0.038	0.114	0.115**
Academic, professional	0.033	-0.065	0.094*	0.105***	-0.138*	-0.123***
Manufacturing workers	0.031	-0.067	-0.153***	-0.167***	0.188**	0.098**
Low income	-0.026	-0.009	-0.189***	-0.158***	0.224***	0.139***
Low education	-0.064	0.020	-0.190***	-0.188***	0.207***	0.188***
House overcrowding	-0.252	0.040	-0.210***	-0.086**	0.127*	0.106**
Ethnic/religious affiliation						
Arab vs. Jewish	-0.362	-0.214	-0.627***	-0.535***	0.428***	0.343***
Family characteristics						
Poverty	-0.061	0.093	-0.246***	-0.201***	0.248***	0.243***
Low education	0.019	-0.035	-0.243***	-0.219***	0.265***	0.178***
Large families	-0.105	0.007	-0.150***	-0.152***	0.090	0.179***
Social Deprivation Index	0.088	0.138*	-0.022	-0.053	0.096	0.130***
School level						
Junior vs. high school	N/A	-0.647***	N/A	-0.280***	N/A	-0.147*
School Characteristics						
Class size	-0.036	0.178**	-0.088*	0.066*	0.072	0.095**
School size	-0.040	0.007	-0.110**	-0.013	0.124*	0.036
Climate						
Policy	-0.401***	-0.404***	-0.006	-0.131***	-0.301***	-0.153***
Teachers' support	-0.481***	-0.355***	0.062	-0.173***	-0.351***	-0.110***
Student participation	N/A	-0.274***	N/A	-0.135***	N/A	-0.052

*p < .05; **p < .01; ***p < .001.

Table 10.5. Between-School Variance Explained by School-level Variables

	Moderate		Verbal		Severe	
	Primary (%)	Secondary (%)	Primary (%)	Secondary (%)	Primary (%)	Secondary (%)
Demographic characteristics of school's community	0	0	33.63	0	6.27	10.95
SES of school's community	0	0.05	15.74	29.07	12.00	9.30
Ethnic affiliation	0	0	29.41	10.38	−0.65	1.71
Family characteristics	0	−0.18	-0.22	2.25	6.40	10.83
School level	N/A	17.57	N/A	15.18	N/A	3.23
School organizational factors	0	0.81	0.60	1.78	−1.16	8.69
School climate	17.57	32.00	0	13.99	23.35	21.46
Overall explained variance	17.57%	50.38%	79.16%	72.66%	46.21%	66.17%

may have different impact in primary schools compared with their impact in secondary schools.[3]

The Unique Contribution of Each Context to Explaining Variance in Victimization

We continue with Tables 10.4 and 10.5 and ask, How does each context contribute uniquely to our understanding of levels of school violence? To answer this question, we added predictors (related to the various contexts that we examined) to the equation sequentially. We entered these predictors in a sequence that follows a hierarchy from the most general context in which schools are embedded to the context within the school, on which schools may have the most direct control (school climate). Because we know that ethnic affiliation and socioeconomic characteristics are strongly associated, we decided to enter first the socioeconomic variables and only in a later stage the ethnic affiliation. This allows us to ask whether the cultural context has an effect that goes above and beyond the effects of socioeconomic characteristics. Because of the differences between the three types of victimization, we review them separately.

VERBAL VICTIMIZATION.   Clearly, greater verbal victimization in school is strongly associated with the school's being embedded in a Jewish, more affluent, and older neighborhood, especially in primary schools. School climate is not related to social-verbal victimization in primary schools but does contribute somewhat to predicting levels of verbal victimization in secondary schools.

This set of findings can be interpreted in several ways. One is to attribute higher levels of verbal victimization among students in Jewish schools in more affluent neighborhoods to the differential expectations of students from different social strata. Perhaps students who come from homes and communities that are characterized by higher education, more prestigious professions, and higher income expect more civil behavior and experience as insult, humiliation, and bad language behaviors that in other environments may go unnoticed. Alternatively, it is possible that because of the students' privilege and hierarchy they feel entitled to use verbal insults.

It is also possible that these findings reflect less verbal victimization in Arab and poor neighborhoods because students from these contexts may be more careful in using these behaviors. In certain cultures and social settings, the power of words is considered stronger than in other settings. For instance, using foul language to characterize one's mother can be taken lightly in one context and be perceived as a major offense in another. This interpretation should be examined further in ethnographic studies that can examine the cultural ramifications and meaning of various types of verbal and social victimization.

Verbal victimization is not associated much with school climate. Efforts to address this issue should be specific to this form of victimization and cannot depend on more generalized tactics to reduce school violence. Social and verbal victimization may need remedies that specifically target interpersonal relationships. These may involve the development and implementation of policy designed to protect students from verbal harm and enhance verbal interpersonal skills, verbal empathy, and verbal assertiveness. Currently, most policies and skill training do not address verbal-social harm as a separate form of violence. As our data have shown, the dynamics for this kind of violence are influenced by different variables from those of other forms of victimization and most likely require a different set of strategies.

MILD/MODERATE VICTIMIZATION.   School climate is the only factor that is associated with moderate school violence. The contexts outside of the school are not related to this type of violence. The implication is that schools have the ability to influence their inner climate irrespective of their surroundings and can reduce the frequency of victimization types that are common in schools. In some ways, we think this is one of the most important types of victimization schools should address. Many of the behaviors listed in the bully/victim literature fall into this category. Some schools may want to target this specific form of violence as a way of maximizing their impact on the largest category of victimization under the school's direct control.

SEVERE VICTIMIZATION.   Severe types of victimization in school are strongly associated with two sets of variables: the socioeconomic characteristics of the school's community (both neighborhood and families) and the school's climate. Schools that are embedded in poor communities and where students' families have low SES have higher levels of severe victimization. This pattern is very similar to what is predicted by previous research and theory about the interplay between the school and its surrounding community (Attar et al., 1994; Brownfield, 1987; Comer, 1980; Dwyer et al., 2000; Earls, 1991; Farrington, 1989; Guerra et al., 1995; Haapasalo & Tremblay, 1994; Hamburg, 1998; Kupersmidt et al., 1995).

Despite this strong impact of the outside context, the within-school context or school climate has its own independent and strong association with severe violence. This impact of school climate on severe violence is on both the individual and the aggregated levels, indicating that the school may have effective means of addressing not only moderate types of school violence but also behaviors that are usually seen as criminal and are perpetrated by individual students who may need to be treated individually.

We now turn to highlight main findings regarding the context variables we examined in this chapter.

SCHOOL CLIMATE.   Earlier, we saw that school climate as perceived by the individual student was associated with the student's level of victimization. Table 10.5 shows that school climate aggregated on the school level was also associated with school violence, above and beyond the effects of the student-level perception. The strongest associations are between aspects of school climate and mild/moderate victimization. Severe victimization is associated with school climate mostly in primary schools; in secondary schools climate is not associated much with severe victimization. This is in contrast to the student-level perception of school climate that is strongly associated with severe victimization in secondary schools.

Positive student-teacher relationships and student participation in decision making are associated with less violence. This involvement in school activities and decision making might enhance students' feelings of belonging to school. Hawkins and colleagues (Hawkins, Catalano, Morrison, O'Donnell, Abbott, & Day, 1992) found that higher levels of bonding to family and school are associated with lower levels of drug and delinquent initiation. According to Smith and Sharp (1994), students should be part of task groups that design and implement interventions to prevent and reduce school violence. By including students, schools provide them with the skills to be assertive, to be supportive of each other, to resolve conflicts constructively, and eventually to help themselves.

Our findings strongly support claims made by many researchers and educators emphasizing the importance of developing a positive school climate to reduce school violence (Colvin et al., 1998; Dwyer et al., 2000; Fraser, 1996; Reinke & Herman, 2002; Stephens, 1994; Welsh, 2000).

SCHOOL LEVEL.   School level (junior high vs. high school) as a school context variable makes a unique contribution to explaining variance between secondary schools in moderate victimization, even after controlling for the effects of students' age. Furlong and colleagues (Furlong, Casas, Corral, Chung, & Bates, 1997) suggest that perhaps the differences in levels of violence between junior high and high schools reflect the stress associated with the transition to secondary school and the comparatively lower social status of younger students. Primary, junior high, and high schools are social contexts that have unique characteristics and differential influences on students. Thus, it is important to try to separate effects of chronological age and the move from one context to another.

In a study conducted by Astor et al. (2001), sixth-graders in middle schools were compared with sixth-graders in elementary K–6 schools. In that study, the elementary school sixth-graders described the school safety in ways similar to other elementary school students, and the sixth-graders in middle school were more similar to other middle school children. Students were very aware of the differential attitude and response of the teachers in the two separate settings. Astor and his associates concluded that the philosophy and size of the school were more influential than age, physical size, and development alone for the sixth-graders in the study. The findings from this study also support the notion that the school contexts of junior high versus high school contribute to victimization above and beyond the effects of age.

SCHOOL AND CLASS SIZE.   The rate of students' reports of moderate victimization in secondary schools was higher in overcrowded classes. According to Walker and Gresham (1997), large classrooms make it difficult for teachers to develop and maintain meaningful relationships with students, especially with students at risk, who need more attention and teacher involvement. Similar points are made by Klonsky (2002), who reviewed the literature in this area. In Israel, one of the main demands expressed by the teachers' union representative on the blue ribbon Vilnai Committee that addressed school violence was to reduce the average number of students in classes. This recommendation and intervention has been made in educational settings in many countries. Our findings provide support for this demand, but it should be noted that the association between class size and school violence is not strong and is limited to mild/moderate victimization in secondary schools.

There were no significant relationships between victimization and school size. These findings are consistent with Welsh et al.'s (1999) and Olweus's (1993) studies but quite different from findings in other studies (G. Gottfredson & Gottfredson, 1985; Lowry et al., 1995; Warner, Weist, & Krulak, 1999). These inconsistencies may reflect the fact that school size alone is not very informative. For instance, some large schools may be divided into several subschools, thus creating protective and intimate environments. The limitations of large schools can be mitigated by low student-teacher ratios (Hellman & Beaton, 1986). Clearly, it is important to examine school size within a wider array of school organization variables that can together explain the effects of school context on violence and victimization.

THE CULTURAL CONTEXT.   Ethnic/cultural differences did not explain variance among schools. We found that the only difference between Arab and Jewish schools was in students' reports of verbal-social victimization. This lack of consistent and significant difference is an unexpected finding, given the many differences between these groups in Israel in their political and socioeconomic status. It is possible that Arab and Jewish schools share similar patterns and the differences we see are mainly socioeconomic rather than cultural.

Another possibility is that the major differences between the two school systems in Israel may have created extremely divergent school ecologies. Perhaps by using the same model to predict victimization in both Arab and Jewish schools we masked the differences between them. If this were true, researchers would need two separate HLM models, one for Jewish and another for Arab schools. Further studies should investigate the possibility that the models predicting school victimization are different across cultural contexts. For instance, it may be that in the Arab culture in Israel the role of the parents in determining violence in the school is more important than in Jewish schools. The area of culture differences is ripe for future research and conceptualization.

CONFOUNDING ETHNICITY AND SES.   Ethnic affiliation had strong predictive power on the severe types of victimization that were more prevalent in Arab schools. However, when we examined the contribution of the ethnic affiliation to severe victimization after controlling for the socioeconomic background of the school's community and students' families, we found that ethnic affiliation explained very little of the variance in levels of victimization in secondary schools and none of the variance in primary schools. This pattern of results is quite similar to our findings (in Chapter 7) on victimization by staff. These findings strongly emphasize the need to disentangle the complex relationships among culture, ethnicity, and socioeconomic factors. Ethnicity may be a more visible characteristic of individual students and of schools, whereas the underlying factors of socioeconomic background may have an important role that is not noticed.

To illustrate, the school with extremely high levels of violence described in the previous chapter is an Arab school located in a mixed-ethnicity (Jews and Arabs) city. The city is a center of crime and drug dealing; substance abusers are being taxied from several neighboring cities to the city's well-known drug-selling spots. Most of the students come from poor, low education, and quite often unemployed families. On their way to school students can see both poor houses and new and expensive cars that belong to drug dealers. As members of an Arab minority in a Jewish state, they often feel prejudice and suspicion, and their prospects for gainful employment and social mobility are quite limited.

Thus, when we examine this school, we find it very difficult to isolate the many ways these students may be disadvantaged. Can we attribute the presence of knives and other types of weapons to cultural norms surrounding weapons? Or should we emphasize the fact that the students come to school from (and return after school to) dangerous neighborhoods in which weapons are quite common? Or perhaps we should examine more closely the school's few resources and low levels of teacher training provided in this municipality. Indeed, natural settings are complex and multidimensional, and we need to take into consideration all these (and many other) ecological factors that operate simultaneously. We believe a more comprehensive and holistic approach is needed to improve the quality of theory.

SUMMARY

The research presented here emphasizes the need for an ecological perspective. It is important to refrain from focusing solely on students at risk. Instead, it is essential to identify the social and school contexts in which school victimization is more prevalent. Our findings indicate that students who are exposed to serious victimization come from families and schools with fewer resources. It is important, therefore, to allocate more resources to these schools.

So far, we have examined our model from the perspective of the student. In the next chapter, we go beyond the students' perspectives to understand our model from multiple perspectives. Clearly, the views of the teachers and principals should impact victimization issues. The challenge of including multiple perspectives should not be underestimated. Currently, there is no theoretical framework for incorporating multiple perspectives in a student-focused theory of school violence. Nevertheless, we provide empirical evidence and practical advantages associated with knowing how multiple perspectives behave with regard to school victimization. The following chapter is the initial empirical attempt to explore the realm of multiple perspectives and school safety.

KEY FINDINGS AND IMPLICATIONS

A. School violence is associated with school, community, and family variables that are organized hierarchically.

B. Student-level variables predict a relatively small amount of the explained variance of victimization (5% to 18%).

C. School-level characteristics explain a very large proportion of the between-school variance for:
   1. Verbal-social victimization (73% and 79% for secondary and primary school, respectively).
   2. Severe victimization (66% and 46% for secondary and primary school, respectively).

D. School level explained a smaller amount of variance for moderate forms of victimization (50% and 18% for secondary and primary school, respectively).

E. Verbal-social, moderate, and severe forms of victimization are influenced differently by different school variables.

F. Verbal victimization in school is associated with the school's being embedded in a Jewish, older population, more affluent context, especially in primary schools.

G. Moderate victimization is associated with school climate. Contexts outside the school are not related to moderate victimization.

H. Severe types of victimization are associated strongly with SES characteristics of the school families and community, combined with the school's climate. Schools that are embedded in low-income communities with high concentrations of students from low-SES families have more severe victimization.

I. School climate is associated with victimization above and beyond student-level perceptions. Its largest impact is on moderate victimization. Climate is associated with severe victimization in primary schools.

J. School level makes a unique contribution to moderate forms of victimization. Junior high schools have more victimization than high schools.

K. School size does not make a difference in victimization; this confirms other studies' findings.

L. Class size does affect moderate forms of school victimization.

NOTES

1. In a previous set of analyses, Khoury-Kassabri (2002) found that in Israel, community crime rates were not associated with any type of school victimization. Therefore, in the present chapter we do not include this aspect of the neighborhood context of the school.

2. We could not examine differences between students in Jewish secular and religious schools because the number of schools in each category was too small for a reasonable statistical power.

3. There is also a possibility that there are other differences between junior high and high schools. We could not test this possibility with our data because we did not observe enough schools.

Chapter 11

One School, Multiple Perspectives on School Safety

In each school, victimization can be perceived from multiple perspectives. Depending on the individual's social role in the school, acts of victimization potentially take on different meanings. Alternatively, it is quite possible that students, teachers, and principals generally see victimization in similar ways. Does divergence or convergence of multiple perspectives in the same school have implications for the safety of the school? To date, there is very little research or conceptual work on multiple perspectives on school violence (see Astor, Meyer, et al., 1999, for one example of a qualitative study exploring multiple perspectives of school violence). We could not find any representative quantitative studies exploring the perspectives of students, teachers, and principals in the same schools.

In previous chapters we focused on the students' reports of their school victimization and their perceptions with regard to school climate and violence. In this chapter we bring in the perspectives of homeroom teachers and principals on these issues and examine the similarity of these three points of view.

These contrasts are important for several reasons. The converging or diverging multiple perspectives of school safety in the same school can help validate (or invalidate) the assessments made by each of the members of a particular school community. Although we expect students, teachers, and principals to have unique vantage points, we also expect similarities between the groups. More important, we believe that research should explore any systematic patterns that exist between students', teachers', and principals' perspectives as they relate to the safety of the school. As far as we know, these kinds of questions have not been addressed in any study.

We have specific hypotheses about the relationships between multiple perspectives and school safety. The degree of similarity between the three perspectives can tell us about how the school is functioning. Large gaps and disagreements between staff and students or between a principal and teachers may indicate that the school does not have a shared mission. This is especially important with regard to how staff respond to school violence. Research from the bullying intervention literature provides some indirect evidence that this might be the case. According to Olweus (1993; see Sullivan, 2000, for a relevant review), one of the most important steps in creating schoolwide safety interventions is reaching a shared schoolwide awareness regarding the seriousness of the problem. Olweus recommends that large gaps in awareness of the problem among school community members should be addressed as part of the design and implementation of these intervention programs.

This does not mean that we expect students, teachers, and principals to have the *same* perspective, even in healthy schools. Clearly, each group is situated in the school's social ecology in different ways. For example, students are likely to see and experience more victimization because more of them are more frequently present in dangerous locations (such as bathrooms, school yards, routes to and from school, and hallways). Conversely, teachers are more likely than principals to see or hear from students about acts of victimization because they have more direct contact with students.

TWO WAYS TO COMPARE MULTIPLE PERSPECTIVES

Multiple perspectives of school constituents can be compared along two different dimensions. Each of these types of comparisons has distinct and independent value in our investigations. The first dimension refers to the question of whether there is a *covariation* among the assessments of the three groups. In other words, do the assessments of students, teachers, and principals go in the same direction when judging the seriousness of their school's problem? This aspect of similarity indicates that the members of the school community share a general sense of whether violence in their school is appreciably higher or lower than in other schools. This may reflect good communication among the various groups in the school and a shared understanding of the situation. In technical terms, we can ask what are the *correlations* between principals, teachers, and students in their assessments. Higher correlations indicate a sense of shared reality that may help achieve agreement on school efforts in this area.

Another dimension of similarity is determined by whether there are *gaps* between the assessments made by the three groups. It is possible that each group has a different assessment of the seriousness of the problem. Teachers and principals may consistently underplay the seriousness of the problem, so that even in schools in which they agree with the students that there is a serious problem (i.e., the correlations between principals and students are high), they may still assess the problem as less serious than their students do. Technically, we focus here on the gaps between the average assessments of the seriousness of the problem made by each of the groups. These gaps in assessments have important policy implications. If principals tend to see their schools as having moderate violence levels, they may not feel the same urgency to act compared with their students, who may feel that levels of violence are much higher. A significant gap between teachers and principals may mean that principals will not authorize the training that their staff feel they need.

In this chapter, we first explore how these groups describe student victimization in school and then turn to their assessments of the seriousness of the problem. We show how strongly the assessments of teachers and principals are associated with important attitudes and behaviors (such as their perceived need for training in this area). We then examine the similarities between the multiple perspectives by (a) presenting the correlations among the three perspectives and (b) analyzing whether there are differences in the average assessments made by each group.

AWARENESS OF VICTIMIZATION ON SCHOOL GROUNDS

How do students' reports of being victimized in school correspond to the staff's and principals' reports of student victimization? School personnel may be unaware of the violent acts that take place in school, and their perceptions may not reflect the reality of what happens to their students. It is possible that certain types of violent acts go entirely unnoticed by personnel. Significant gaps in awareness between students and personnel reduce the chances that all members of the school community reach a common understanding regarding levels of violence in their school.

The design of our study allows us to ask how similar are students, homeroom teachers, and principals in their reports of student victimization in school. Because we can match principals, teachers, and students who are in the same school, we can explore how parallel the reports made by the three groups are. It should be noted that we ask each of the groups a slightly different question. Students were asked to report whether *they* were victimized by certain types of violent acts in the prior month (on a scale of 0 = not at all, 1 = once or twice, 2 = more). Homeroom teachers were asked about the number of times *any of the students* in their homeroom class were involved in a violent act (on a scale of 0 = never, 1 = less than once a week, 2 = once or twice a week, 3 = more than twice a week). Principals were asked how many times *any* student in their school was involved in a violent act in the prior month (on a scale of 0 = never, 1 = once, 2 = twice, 3 = 3–5, 4 = more). The items in each of the questionnaires were similar but not identical because they were created to capture issues surrounding the unique hierarchical role of each group.

To carry out the analyses we used the school-level database, aggregating the reports of all the students in the school, all the reports made by homeroom teachers, and the school principal's report. Table 11.1 presents the correlations between the three groups for each of the items that referred to similar violent acts. The table shows that the correlations between students and teachers are higher than the correlations between students and principals. Most of the correlations between students and teachers were significant and moderate (correlations between r = 0.30 and 0.40). The correlations between students and principals, on the other hand, were quite low. Most of the correlations between teachers and principals were weaker than the

Table 11.1. Correlations between Reports of School Violence by Students, Homeroom Teachers, and Principals

	Teacher-Principal	Student-Principal	Student-Teacher
A student threatened you with a knife and you saw the knife.	0.38	0.18	0.38
A student cut you with a knife or a sharp instrument on purpose.	0.24	0.12	0.30
A student used a rock or another instrument in order to hurt you.	NA	NA	0.41
You were blackmailed under threats by another student (for money, valuables, or food).	0.22	0.14	0.34
A student took your things from you by force.	NA	NA	0.27
A student threatened you with a gun and you saw the gun.	-0.02	0.27	0.16
Gang members at school threatened, harassed, and pressured you.	0.29	0.10	0.35
You were involved in a fight, were hurt, and required medical attention.	NA	0.15	NA
You were kicked or punched by a student who wanted to hurt you.	NA	NA	0.41
A student seized and shoved you on purpose.	NA	NA	0.40
You saw a student in school with a knife.	NA	NA	0.36
A group of students boycotted you and did not want to play or talk with you.	0.14	0.05	0.25
A student intentionally destroyed or broke your personal belongings.	NA	NA	0.49
Students stole personal belongings or equipment from you.	NA	NA	0.27
Students threatened you on your way to or from school.	0.33	0.30	0.44
A group of students jumped on a student and hurt him or her.	0.30	NA	NA
A student tried to kiss you without your consent.	0.09	0.03	0.26
A student touched or tried to touch you or to pinch you in a sexual way without your approval.	0.17	0.06	0.26
A student was sexually assaulted by another student.	0.33	NA	NA
Sexually insulting things about you were written on walls or sexual rumors were spread about you.	0.17	0.21	0.02

correlations between students and teachers, but higher than the correlations between students and principals. This means that, overall, students' perspectives are more similar to teachers' perspectives than to principals' perspectives.

The strongest correlations between students and teachers were with regard to reports about students intentionally destroying and breaking personal belongings (r = 0.49), threats on the way to and from school (r = 0.44), and being hurt by a student using a rock or a stick, and kicked and punched by another student (r = 0.41). The highest correlation between principals' reports of student victimization and students' own reports was with regard to threats made against students on the way to and from school (r = 0.30). The agreement on this issue was also high between principals and teachers (r = 0.38). It seems that threats on the way to school are being reported by the students to the teachers and principals (or are well-known to any member of the school community due to their own personal experiences), and therefore the various groups in school share rather similar views of the magnitude of the problem. It is also possible that students have fewer reservations in reporting victimization that is not taking place in the school itself because they do not risk being labeled a "snitch" by their peers.

The lowest correlation between students' and teachers' reports was with regard to students being victimized by other students spreading sexual rumors or writing sexually insulting things about them on walls (r = 0.02). This may be an indication that teachers and principals are not well aware of this kind of indirect victimization and do not associate graffiti with students feeling victimized. Indeed, not one of the 72 teachers we interviewed in our qualitative study mentioned this form of harassment. This, despite the fact that our observers saw such graffiti on school walls (mainly labeling certain male students as homosexuals).

The Importance of Teachers' and Principals' Assessments of the Violence Problem in Their School

In Chapter 8 we presented a model depicting the interrelationships between aspects of school climate, personal victimization, and students' feelings of safety, fear of attending school, and assessment of how serious the school violence was. We now add the perspectives of homeroom teachers and principals, focusing mainly on how they assess the problem of violence and the risky behaviors of students and staff. Our interest in how teachers and principals view school violence is aroused because we assume that principals and teachers who think the school has no violence problem will not be motivated to get more resources directed to address this problem.

To test this assumption we examined the correlations between these aspects. Table 11.2 indicates that, indeed, the principals' and teachers' assessments of the seriousness of the school violence problem are consistently correlated with their assessments of how well the school is responding to violence. For instance, the correlation of the teachers' assessment of the seriousness of the problem and their assessment of how well the school is responding to violence is r = –0.59, with their

Table 11.2. Correlations of Principals' and Teachers' Assessments of the Seriousness of School Violence and School Policies

	Principals	Teachers
I think that the school copes well with violence.	−0.33	−0.59
Most of the teachers cope well with violence.	−0.36	−0.55
The principal is an educational figure who helps in reducing violence in school.	−0.34	−0.17
The school's management team functions well when dealing with violence.	−0.21	−0.44
Most of the teachers are afraid to break up fights between students.	0.21	0.44
The teachers tend to ignore "low levels" of violence.	0.25	0.41
The teachers who are out in the yard during recess actively prevent and address violence among students.	−0.16	0.02
Most of the teachers choose to ignore violent acts that are not under their immediate responsibility.	0.27	0.51
There is high awareness of the need for violence prevention in school.	0.02	−0.27
Dealing with violence is a major priority for the principal.	0.17	0.10
The principal supports teachers who deal with violence.	0.11	−0.15
We tend to respond only to the more extreme and unusual violent incidents.	0.02	−0.08
I have a feeling that I spend too much of my time dealing with problems of violence.	0.33	0.64
I feel helpless when I am dealing with school violence.	0.33	0.55
I have the right tools for dealing effectively with school violence.	−0.17	−0.51
There is a consistent enforcement of discipline in school.	−0.27	−0.35
There are clear school rules regarding discipline and violence, and these rules are known to teachers and to students.	−0.17	−0.42
The school counselor helps teachers who have difficulty dealing with violence.	−0.11	−0.22
Most of the parents cooperate in efforts to prevent violence.	−0.17	−0.46
The school makes a genuine effort to involve students in the prevention and treatment of violence.	−0.08	−0.20
The school's leadership acts to reveal and to discuss seriously the issue of school violence (doesn't "sweep the problem under the rug").	0.10	0.22
The school involves the police to an adequate degree (not too little and not too late).	0.19	0.27

assessment of how fellow teachers deal with violence is $r = -0.55$, and with how the management team copes with violence is $r = -0.44$. The principals' assessments are in similar directions, but lower than the teachers'. Also, the teachers who think their school has a serious violence problem are to a large extent those who feel that they are helpless ($r = 0.55$) and lack the skills to address the problem ($r = 0.51$).

In addition, there is a clear relationship between how serious personnel view the school problem and the extent to which they are active in prevention and treatment efforts. Principals and teachers were presented a series of possible preventive and treatment measures, such as lecturing on the problem, involving parents, and calling the police. We found that principals' assessment of the seriousness of the problem was associated with how many preventive measures they took (r = 0.47) and also with how many types of intervention they used in the academic year (r = 0.52). Similarly, teachers' reports of prevention and intervention efforts were associated with how severe they thought the school violence was (r = 0.53 with prevention interventions and r = 0.66 with interventions following a violent incidence). Finally, the principals and teachers who thought their school has a serious violence problem were more inclined to say that they needed training in this area (r = 0.38 for principals and 0.68 for teachers).

Comparing Students', Teachers', and Principals' Assessments of the Seriousness of the Problem

How similar are the assessments of students, homeroom teachers, and principals? Table 11.3 presents the mean assessments of students, staff, and principals of the severity of the violence problem in their school and of risky behaviors by student and staff. The table also shows the correlations between these three groups. Clearly, students' assessments differ from teachers' and principals': Students tend to see the problem severity as higher than their teachers and principal do, and they assess all risky peer and staff behaviors as more common than do the other two groups. The means of students' assessments are closer to the means of their teachers' than to their principal's (except for one item: students steal things).

When we interviewed teachers on issues of violence in their school we were able to get a closer look at their assessments. We found that many of them equated school violence with severe and continuous physical aggression. In one high school in Jerusalem a teacher said, "There is no problem of violence, there are incidents." In an Arab village a teacher stated, "There is no problem of violence, sometimes kids hit, there is verbal violence, but there is no problem." A teacher in a Tel Aviv suburb said, "There are fights, it's normal, not irregular, not 'violence.'"

There is a clear trend here: Students and staff differ more on assessments of *staff* risky behaviors and the more severe *student* risky behaviors, especially those that involve weapons and gang activity. None of the principals thought that students brought guns to school; very few of the teachers (mean = 1.01 on a scale of 4) and slightly more students (mean = 1.15) did. Similarly, both teachers and principals assessed that there were very few incidents of staff sexually harassing students (means of 1.01 and 1.02, respectively), but the students had significantly higher assessments (mean = 1.44).

This result is similar to the finding presented earlier, indicating that agreement on other types of sexual harassment is also low. Again, the pattern seems to indicate that certain behaviors, among them sexual harassment, are more secretive in nature and less visible to the staff and principals.

Students, teachers, and principals were closer in their assessment of the extent of student fighting (means of 2.89, 2.65, and 2.60 for students, teachers, and principals,

Table 11.3. Correlations between Assessments by Students, Teachers, and Principals

	Students		Teachers		Principals		Correlations		
	Mean	SD	Mean	SD	Mean	SD	Teacher-Student	Principal-Student	Principal-Teacher
Severity of the Problem	2.72	0.72	2.17	0.77	2.14	0.87	0.56	0.34	0.56
Student risky behaviors:									
Students get into fights.	2.89	0.60	2.65	0.74	2.60	0.82	0.63	0.30	0.52
Students drink alcohol in school.	1.42	0.33	1.11*	0.33	1.05	0.26	0.50	0.39	0.52
Students destroy things (vandalism).	2.80	0.69	2.51*	0.77	2.37	0.91	0.70	0.47	0.43
Students steal things from other students or teachers.	2.37	0.58	2.04	0.61	2.12	0.74	0.61	0.44	0.44
Students use drugs in school.	1.30	0.34	1.12*	0.28	1.06	0.28	0.63	0.40	0.49
Students threaten or bully other students.	2.46	0.66	2.06***	0.69	1.82	0.74	0.64	0.48	0.53
Students bring guns to school.	1.15	0.17	1.01**	0.06	1.00	0.00	0.25	N/A	N/A
Students bring other weapons to school (such as knives, sticks).	1.87	0.53	1.36	0.43	1.30	0.52	0.59	0.42	0.56
There is dangerous gang activity in my school.	1.76	0.49	1.39***	0.49	1.20	0.47	0.49	0.30	0.31
Overall Index of Student Risky Behaviors	1.96	0.38	1.67*	0.37	1.60	0.34	0.70	0.53	0.63
Staff Risky Behaviors:									
Teachers or other staff members come on to, sexually harass, or bother the girls.	1.44	0.33	1.02***	0.07	1.01	0.07	0.23	N/A	0.09
Teachers or other staff members hurt students verbally (insult, humiliate, and curse students).	2.14	0.47	1.51	0.53	1.45	0.61	0.49	0.39	0.36
Teachers or other staff members hurt students physically (slap, pinch, push, etc.).	1.74	0.57	1.29	0.48	1.24	0.52	0.68	0.50	0.57
Overall Index of Staff Risky Behaviors	1.82	0.41	1.27	0.31	1.23	0.33	0.60	0.42	0.50

All significance tests are based on contrast analyses in a repeated measures ANOVA, performed for each set of assessments made by students, homeroom teachers, and principals.

All students' assessments are significantly higher than the assessments made by homeroom teachers and principals ($p < .001$).

* $p < .05$, ** $p < .01$, *** $p < .001$

respectively). Similarly, the gaps between the three groups' assessments of school vandalism were relatively small (means of 2.80, 2.51, and 2.37). Thus, in contrast to secret behaviors such as sexual harassment, fights on school grounds and vandalism are much more public and visible and therefore closer to the awareness of staff and principals.

Examination of the correlations between students' and teachers' assessments reveals strong evidence that these two groups share similar views about their school. Most of the correlations range between r = 0.50 and 0.70 (mean r = 0.55, median = 0.59). The areas in which there seems to be disagreement are students bringing guns (r = 0.25) and staff sexually harassing students (r = 0.23). It should be noted, however, that the correlations with regard to other staff behaviors are quite high. For instance, the correlations among the three groups with regard to staff *physical* victimization of students are high (r = 0.68 between students and teachers, r = 0.50 between students and principals, and r = 0.57 between principals and teachers).

Given the fact that principals did not see students bringing guns to school and saw very little staff sexual harassment, the correlations between students and principals are much lower than between the students and teachers, ranging between r = 0.30 and 0.50 (mean r = 0.36, median r = 0.39). The correlations with regard to staff sexual harassment and students bringing guns are zero. There are also low correlations with regard to gang activity in school (r = 0.30).

Most of the correlations between teachers and principals are quite high, in the range of r = 0.45 to 0.60 (mean r = 0.43, median r = 0.49). The lowest correlations refer to dangerous gang activity (r = 0.31) and staff verbal abuse (r = 0.36).

HOW SIMILARITY IN MULTIPLE PERSPECTIVES RELATES TO SCHOOL VIOLENCE

Now that we have examined the similarities between the multiple perspectives in schools we can turn to our exploratory hypothesis that larger differences between staff and students are characteristic of schools that do not function as effectively and have higher levels of violence. To explore this issue, we divided the schools into four groups on the basis of the students' reports of physical victimization. Table 11.4 presents students', teachers', and principals' assessments of the seriousness of the problem and the correlations between them by levels of school violence.

Our hypothesis was that schools with high levels of victimization will have lower levels of agreement among the three groups. The table indicates that the correlations between teachers and students are indeed lower for schools with high levels of violence. The correlation between teachers' and students' assessments in schools in the lowest quartile of school violence is r = 0.75, in the second quartile is r = 0.52, in the third is r = 0.48, and in schools that are in the upper quartile (in terms of level of physical victimization as reported by students), the correlation between stu-

Table 11.4. Correlations between Students', Teachers', and Principals' Assessments of the Seriousness of the Problem (by levels of school violence)

	Students		Teachers		Principals		Correlations		
	Mean	SD	Mean	SD	Mean	SD	Student-Teacher	Student-Principal	Teacher-Principal
I = Lowest	2.19	(.82)	1.83	(.85)	1.88	(.76)	0.75	0.47	0.61
II	2.66	(.61)	2.19	(.79)	2.34	(.88)	0.52	0.22	0.48
III	3.02	(.45)	2.19	(.81)	2.20	(.55)	0.48	−0.08	0.38
IV = Highest	3.04	(.59)	2.35	(.97)	2.32	(.82)	0.43	0.30	0.59

dents' and teachers' assessments of the severity of the problem is r = 0.43. This trend supports our hypothesis.

With regard to the correlations between the students' and principals' and between the principals' and teachers' assessments, the trend is less consistent. In fact, the correlation between the teachers' and principals' assessments in the first quartile of schools is similar to that between teachers' and principals' assessments in the last quartile (r = 0.61 and 0.59, respectively). Levels of school violence appear to reflect the extent to which students and their homeroom teachers view the violence problem in similar ways. The similarity between assessments by students and principals does not seem to follow a consistent pattern, which may reflect the special nature of relationships between teachers and students in their class.

Overall, the findings suggest that students and teachers are quite close to each other in their assessments, and principals' assessments differ from both. When we examined the principals' assessments there were signs that two separate issues were at play. First, compared to students, principals underestimate the seriousness of the problem; second, principals either do not see the behaviors that students see and experience in school or they interpret them differently, and therefore the correlations between their assessments tend to be quite low.

The fact that principals' perspective is quite different from students' may have negative implications for efforts to reduce school violence. Principals may not know accurately what is happening in their school in terms of violence among students. Coupled with their tendency to underestimate the levels of violence, principals may not act to address issues of school violence. It seems that principals need to become more aware of their students' experiences.

One way to achieve such awareness is through conducting surveys among the students to get their perspectives on the problem and then sharing this information with principals. Our experience has been that, initially, principals tend not to accept findings that indicate high levels of student victimization, especially when violence is perpetrated by staff. However, over time and after repeatedly showing consistent reporting by students, the principals we met were willing to change their views of the situation and showed increased awareness.

THE EXTENT TO WHICH SIMILARITY BETWEEN PERSPECTIVES IS CONTEXT-DEPENDENT

Throughout this book we explore how contexts impact various aspects of school violence. In this section, we ask whether degree of similarity among the various constituents in the school differs across the contexts we studied. It is possible that in certain cultures and school types, the communication among these hierarchically ordered groups is more effective than in others, directly impacting levels of similarity between these three groups. To explore this issue we examined levels of similarity separately for the various groups and contexts we studied.

Comparing Jewish and Arab Schools

Table 11.5 compares levels of agreement in Jewish and Arab schools. The table indicates that although Arab students see the problem as much more serious than Jewish students do (mean = 3.02, compared with 2.60 among Jewish students), the gaps between mean assessments of Jewish and Arab teachers are much smaller (means of 2.28 and 2.13 for Arab and Jewish teachers, respectively). Among principals, the trend reaches an extreme: Whereas Arab students see much more severe violence problems than do Jewish students, Arab principals see the violence problem as less serious in their schools compared to Jewish principals (means = 1.89 and 2.24 for Arab and Jewish principals, respectively).

The correlations between students, teachers, and principals showed no consistent differences in agreement levels between Jewish and Arab schools. It seems, therefore, that the main difference between Jewish and Arab schools is that the Arab principals tend to assess the problem as less severe than one would expect on the basis of the assessments made by the students and teachers. This pattern argues against an interpretation of cultural differences in communication between these two groups. Instead, the findings may indicate that Arab principals are more defensive in their assessment

Table 11.5. Correlations between Students', Teachers', and Principals' Assessments of the Seriousness of the Problem (by ethnic group and school level)

| | Students | | Teachers | | Principals | | Correlations | | |
	Mean	SD	Mean	SD	Mean	SD	Teacher-Student	Principal-Student	Principal-Teacher
Ethnic Group									
Jewish	2.60	(.78)	2.13	(.76)	2.24	(.84)	0.56	0.44	0.57
Arab	3.02	(.52)	2.28	(.70)	1.89	(.95)	0.51	0.31	0.62
School Level									
Primary	2.95	(.58)	2.23	(.73)	2.21	(.94)	0.43	0.18	0.51
Junior High	2.77	(.72)	2.18	(.66)	2.20	(.85)	0.62	0.52	0.55
High	2.45	(.80)	2.11	(.86)	2.00	(.85)	0.61	0.36	0.62

of their school's problem. This pattern may be related to the fact that Arab principals are responsible for schools of a minority group and may be trying to protect their group and tradition by presenting a flawless front to the outside majority group (Abramov, 2003; see Kikkawa, 1987, with regard to Japanese schools).

Comparing Primary, Junior High, and High Schools

In addition to comparing the two ethnic groups in our study, we examined the patterns of similarities between students, teachers, and principals in primary, junior high, and high school. The only major difference between the school levels is a very low correlation between principals and students in primary schools ($r = 0.18$, compared with 0.52 in junior high schools and 0.36 in high schools). This is a surprising finding. We expected principals in primary schools to be closer to their students than principals in the higher school levels, who tend to have more distant relationships with their students. Perhaps principals in primary school base their assessments of the severity of the problem on a different set of cues than do their young students. Perhaps they do not assess correctly how violent behaviors of lower intensity may have a strong impact on the younger students. This may indicate that the more intense interactions and involvement of primary school principals do not necessarily result in their ability to empathize more with these young students and see the world from the students' perspective.

SUMMARY

We have examined the multiple perspectives of students, teachers, and principals and showed that they provide important insights into understanding violence in the context of the school. We showed that the ways teachers and principals perceive the seriousness of the violence problem in their school are strongly associated with their behaviors and attitudes regarding the need for training and interventions. The fact that teachers and principals consistently assess the violence problem as less serious than their students do may result in underestimating the need for interventions to address school violence. Overall, students' perspectives are more similar to teachers' than to principals' perspectives. It seems that student behaviors that are less public are unknown to staff (especially to principals). Finally, we found that school context influences the degree to which multiple perspectives of the various groups in the school's community converge to create schoolwide awareness of school safety.

KEY FINDINGS AND IMPLICATIONS

A. The correlations between students and teachers on reports of violent acts is moderate (0.3 to 0.4).

B. The correlations between students' and principals' assessments were very low.

C. The correlations between teachers' and students' assessments were stronger than those between teachers' and principals'.

D. Principals' and teachers' view of the violence problem in their school is consistently related to how well their school is dealing with violence. Conversely, teachers who think their school has a serious violence problem also feel quite helpless and that they lack skills to address the problem.

E. Students tend to see the violence problem in their school as more severe than teachers and principals do. Nevertheless, teachers' assessments of the violence problem are closer to the students' than the principals', suggesting that students and teachers have more similar views of the school than either group and principals.

F. Similarity of students' and teachers' perspectives on school violence is lower in schools with higher levels of victimization.

G. Similarity between principals' and students' perspectives is lower in Arab schools and in primary schools.

Chapter 12

Revisiting Our Central Thesis: Schools to the Center of the Theoretical Model

The bell rings and within a few seconds an ocean of students spills into the hallway. Students are rushing to their lockers, talking to friends, some meandering aimlessly while others walk with a sense of purpose to their classes. Suddenly, from somewhere in the crowd, a voice yells "FIGHT!" Most students stop what they are doing and energetically attempt to locate the fight. "Where is the fight?" and "Who is fighting?" are their frenzied questions. At the same time, down the hall, a circle of 30 or more adolescents engulfs the two fighting students. Those standing at the back of the circle are stretching their necks to catch a glimpse of the violence—a punch, a kick, or perhaps even a weapon. Some of the students in the circle are watching quietly. Some are cheering the fighters and commenting about the quality of the punches. Finally, after several long minutes, a teacher tunnels through the crowd, screaming, "Break it up! Break it up! O.K., everyone back to class. Break it up. Move aside." Slowly, the crowd begins to dissipate and the fighting students are separated to opposite sides of the hallway. The lone and courageous teacher continues to admonish the few remaining gawkers who continue watching and hoping for another outburst of violence. The disheveled fighters are escorted by the teacher to the vice principal's office. What happens in the office is not entirely known to the students who watched the episode. Likewise, the intervening teacher probably never finds out what happens to the fighting students.

As with our beginning scenario (Chapter 1), the sequence of social dynamics surrounding a relatively common physical assault in a school is probably recognizable to most individuals who attended a secondary school in the United States, Israel, Australia, and many other countries. In fact, it is quite probable that most current students and teachers could recount remarkably similar stories regarding the social dynamics of school fights and other forms of school violence.

We suspect that students', teachers', and principals' descriptions of violent events in their school would most likely contain the following elements: A clustering of many students would surround the fighting individuals and either encourage the fight or merely observe it; very few students or adults would describe a peer cohort response of breaking up or discouraging fights. Students would be quick to point out that the fight and crowd of peers would be more likely (but not always) to dissipate when a teacher or principal appeared. Other than the fighting students, no student in the school would be held directly responsible for the fight. The other teachers would likely view the teacher who intervened as going above and beyond the call of duty; perhaps some would think him or her unwise for attempting to stop a fight with no other teachers for support. Few, if any, students would feel morally responsible for observing the fight and few would expect collective repercussions for the predictable peer group circle around the violence. In most schools, suspension would be the only intervention applied to one or both of the fighting students after an inquiry into who started it. In most cases, suspension would be left to the discretion of the administrator (unless weapons were involved), and consequences would not always be applied consistently in comparable situations. In some cases, the administrators might send the two students back to class after they showed remorse and promised not to fight again.

Because victimization events in schools such as our hypothetical fight seem quite predictable and recognizable, we asked ourselves why these specific dynamics or variables contributing to victimization are not addressed by school violence theory. The same kinds of questions can be asked about other types of victimization covered in this book. We realized that *school* variables in school victimization have been either ignored or are inserted after the fact but not as part of a viable theory of school violence. We are not entirely sure why schools have not been included in the discussion of school victimization.

Although school violence and victimization share much with violence in other contexts, it is difficult to imagine a similar violence dynamic occurring in any other work setting or social institution. In large part, we believe these widely recognizable and possibly cross-cultural patterns stem from the fact that victimization in school settings is more tolerated by society than violence in any other formal social setting. For instance, most work sites would not allow coworkers to fight physically during breaks. Imagine coworkers (such as university professors, doctors, stockbrokers, teachers, salespeople, or politicians) forming circles around their feuding colleagues and encouraging or merely watching them fight. It is unimaginable and borders on the absurd. In fact, if this were allowed to occur in a given work setting, workers would have serious legal recourse against the employer for not stopping the reoccurring violence. Although violence occurs in all settings, when it occurs in most formal institutional settings it is considered an anomaly. Yet, in school settings, many societies appear to have a greater tolerance for (almost daily or weekly) incidents of victimization that are almost unimaginable in other organized institutional social settings. We wonder if this tolerance represents an underlying assumption or belief that the entire victimization/violence process is in large measure part of development, something students grow out of, regardless of the social climate in the school. The previous chapters have presented evidence showing that the school organization, climate, and social dynamics have independent and quite large contributions to victimization in schools. These data challenge an explanation that claims that school violence is exclusively developmental and ignores the contextual influences present in schools.

We had one central thesis in this book: School victimization is a unique, context-bound form of interpersonal violence that should be addressed separately from victimization in other social-developmental contexts. Once we accepted this thesis as the foundation for our work, the school context, with all its physical and social dynamics, became the center of our theoretical model. We believe that the centrality of the school differentiates our work from many others' in the school violence and youth violence literatures. The family, community, culture, and other contexts have spillover influences on events in the school, but in our model, the school-based peer group interactions, teacher-student relationships, school policy, school climate, teachers' response to violent events, and the effects of different forms of school violence (among many other variables) become *primary areas* for investigation. How the school context contributes to or shelters students from different types of victimization is a key question asked in this book. This seemingly slight shift in theoretical focus, putting the school in the center, has profound implications for the kinds of questions asked and the research designs, methods, and analyses needed to answer school violence questions.

For example, with the school at the center of the model, we were obligated to include all forms of victimization that are likely to occur on school grounds. This is a different approach from the current disciplinary focus of studying one type of victimization by conceptual domain (e.g., sexual harassment or bullying). This meant we needed to have an instrument that focused exclusively on victimization on school grounds and represented victimization behaviors that ranged from very mild (and frequent) to extremely severe (and less frequent). Imagining the day, week, or month in the life of a student who is exposed to all or some of these different forms of victimization takes on different meanings and raises further questions that are unanswerable if we select only one type of victimization. Grouping together the range of victimization types, we then needed to ask another series of questions, including:

- Are these forms of victimization really all that different from each other?
- Do victimization types belong together? Do all victimization types follow the same patterns?
- How would those patterns differ by age, gender, and culture?
- Are there some forms of victimization more influenced by culture and others more influenced by age or gender?
- How do school variables influence victimization types?

- How is the influence of those school variables situated with regard to influence from other contexts, such as the community, family, and culture?

Moving the school to the center of the theoretical model also required a nested research design that could complement the school-based instrument and highlight the centrality of the school. Therefore, we constructed a study design that included students within classes, classes within schools, schools within the community, families within communities, and culture surrounding them all. Because the conceptual core was the school, a rather large sample of schools was needed to explore both within- and between-school differences. The shift caused by our central thesis produced a set of findings reported in this book that are, in our opinion, truly unique, and that raise many new questions to be explored by future research.

In this chapter we highlight and elaborate on some of the implications of the major findings we have reported. We do not intend to reiterate all of them, as the last section of each chapter provides such a summation. With this chapter we hope to inspire other researchers and policymakers to engage in further study of school violence using our approach.

Our visual road map in this book was a heuristic model of school violence that puts the school in the center (presented in Chapters 1 and 10). This model assumes that there are multiple faces of school victimization. It also assumes that the school context impacts victimization and mediates the spillover effects of the wider contexts in which the school is embedded. Looking back at our empirical journey, we think that this heuristic representation, along with our findings, helped us gain important insights into school violence. In the following sections, we address some of the school-based variables and the relationships between the school and external variables.

IMPLICATIONS OF THE MULTIPLE FACES OF SCHOOL VICTIMIZATION

Our findings strongly suggest that there are multiple faces of school victimization. Each victimization type has different patterns and is influenced by different variables in separate ways. In our study, we found that there are at least six empirically supported, separate types of school based victimization: verbal-social, mild/moderate, severe, sexual, weapon-related, and staff-initiated. This finding supports our belief that school violence studies should explore a broad spectrum of victimization experiences instead of limiting the exploration to one set of behaviors (such as bullying, crime, sexual harassment, or social victimization). The wide range of behaviors addressed in this study created an opportunity to uncover both what is shared by all these behaviors and what is unique about each of them.

Distinguishing between Verbal-Social, Physical, and Threats

The differences and similarities among the various types of victimization tell important stories that should inform theory, policy, and practice. For example, threats of harm and actual physical victimization share almost identical patterns in terms of their relationships with gender, grade level, and ethnicity. With these kinds of behaviors there is mainly a gender and age effect, and cultural background does not play a major role. By contrast, verbal-social victimization behaves in very different ways from threats and physical victimization. In verbal-social attacks, culture plays a central role. This distinction has important theoretical and practical implications. First, it is commonly stated in the clinical and intervention literatures that verbal victimization serves as a critical precursor to the physical violence escalation process, but the distinct patterns identified here suggest that only threats are candidates for this hypothesis. Other forms of verbal-social victimization, such as cursing and humiliating, appear to occur independently of physical victimization behaviors; if they were connected, we would see similar age and gender patterns that are evident only in threats and physical victimization. The fact that culture is a major contributor to verbal-social patterns is another indicator that they are in fact separate. The vast majority of students in Israel have experienced some form of verbal-social victimization; a much smaller subset also have experienced threats and physical victimization.

Our findings also suggest that gender patterns distinguish verbal-social forms of victimization from physical and threats. The gender gap in both physical and threat types was much larger than in verbal-social. Additionally, the drop in prevalence of victimization as students grow older was not as significant in verbal-social victimization as it was with regard to physical and threat victimization. Clearly, verbal-social victimization is distinct from other types of victimization. We encourage educators to develop policy specifically geared at verbal-social victimization. Researchers should also consider threats as connected with physical violence rather than as another verbal victimization category.

Our findings also suggest that social exclusion does not behave in the same way as verbal victimization. For instance, Jewish more than Arab students report curses and humiliation; the relative prevalence of social exclusion, on the other hand, is higher among Arab students. This pattern suggests the need to expand our investigation of additional forms of relational aggression. As Baldry and Winkel (2003) indicate, "Repeated relational victimization might produce more severe consequences leading even to thoughts about committing suicide" (p. 706).

Severity and Frequency of Physical and Threat Victimization

We were curious as to how physical and threat behaviors would present from a strict empirical perspective rather than from a theoretical stance. When we examined physical victimization and threats, the findings showed that they were grouped into two main clusters: physical and threat victimization types that are more prevalent and mild/moderate in severity and others that have lower frequency but much higher severity in terms of potential damage to the victim. Conceptually, this empirical grouping made sense because in reality, both frequency and severity of victimization are important criteria that students, parents, teachers, and administrators refer to when discussing or evaluating school victimization events. It also made sense theoretically to use frequency and severity as organizing dimensions for different types of victimization.

Many of the insights gained in our research were made possible because we used the empirical categorization of victimization events rather than a preexisting conceptual categorization. Conceptual categories would have masked some of the distinct patterns we report. We encourage other school violence researchers to consider using the empirically derived severity/frequency dimensions as ways to better understand the patterns of victimization on school grounds.

EMPIRICAL REORGANIZATION OF VERBAL-SOCIAL, PHYSICAL, AND THREAT VICTIMIZATION BEHAVIORS.   Based on our empirical analyses, we reorganized three groups of behaviors that were at first conceptually organized as verbal-social, physical threats, and physical victimization into three empirically derived categories: severe, mild/moderate, and verbal forms of victimization. When we conducted factor analyses, we found that verbal-social behaviors were very similar to the mild/moderate category with regard to severity and frequency. However, because verbal-social violence is influenced by culture, and not much by age and gender (whereas mild/moderate victimization is influenced by age and gender and not by culture), we decided to keep verbal-social as a category separate from mild/moderate. Our findings show consistently that treating each of these sets of behaviors separately along the dimensions of severity and frequency is justified. We found that each of these sets is associated differently with student characteristics such as age and gender, and is predicted by a different combination of context variables, both within the school context and in the context of the school's environment. These differences imply that each distinct type of school violence should be addressed in ways that correspond to its unique characteristics.

MILD/MODERATE VICTIMIZATION.   Of all the forms of victimization we explored, school environment had the greatest influence on mild/moderate forms of victimization. There is considerable variation between schools in this category, mainly associated with the schools' climates: how the school responds to violence, to what extent teachers support students, and, to a lesser degree, to what extent students participate in decision making in the school. This finding suggests that schools, even in the violent geopolitical Israeli context, can create safe havens that have lower levels of mild/moderate violence.

The findings show that moderate levels of violence are quite common in most schools. We suggest, therefore, that national policy target the Israeli education system as a whole. This would address much of the pain and suffering by the large majority of Israeli students. Guidelines and training should be developed as preventive measures to address mild/moderate violence in all schools.

We believe that mild/moderate forms of violence should be targeted by most countries, as they appear to constitute the largest category of victimization events that are most susceptible to influence by the school's climate. Nevertheless, the findings indicate that in terms of prevalence, these types of behaviors are appreciably more frequent in Israeli schools than in schools in many other countries. In a series of international studies it was found that Israeli students report higher frequency of this type of violent acts. For instance, Harel and associates (1997; Harel, Ellenbogen-Frankovits, Molcho, Abu-Asbah, & Habib, 2002) compared Israeli students with students in 23 European countries and showed that overall frequency of bullying in Israel is higher than in most of the other countries. Findings in the TIMSS International Test (Akibba, LeTendre, Baker, & Goesling, 2002) also placed Israel as having high levels of this cluster of moderate violent behaviors.

Our findings may provide a ray of hope for many in the Israeli public. Knowing that school climate can impact mild/moderate forms of victimization may help educators, the public, and policymakers focus on what can be done on school grounds. To date, educators and many others in the Israeli public have lamented the loss of authority that starts at home and continues in schools. The frequent and very public complaint is that parents in Israeli society have lost their authority and as a result cannot provide parental support for the schools' disciplinary actions when students misbehave in school. A book that emphasizes the "restoration of parental authority" (Omer, 2000) received wide attention in the Israeli public in general and among educators in particular. The popular press adds to this sentiment with frequent reporting of lack of discipline in schools and stories about creative and destructive pranks pulled by students.

The concern with lack of parental authority may be warranted. However, our findings show that when schools create a positive climate and clear teacher/administrator protocol, mild to moderate forms of violence are vastly reduced. Thus, schools should focus on what can be done within the school, and not give up on their efforts because they feel they do not get the kind of parental support they need.

VERBAL-SOCIAL VICTIMIZATION.   This category of victimization is distinct from others in several important ways. First, it is very prevalent in Israeli schools. Second, it does not show the same gender or age patterns that mild/moderate victimization does. Third, culture appears to be more prominent with this type of victimization. Whereas physical forms of victimization seem to be associated with lower SES, verbal-social is associated with higher SES and with Jewish students more than Arab. Based on our experiences in both Jewish and Arab schools, we believe that these verbal forms of victimization may not be tolerated in Arab schools because they are signs of disrespect. By contrast, Jewish Israeli schools may tolerate verbal victimization because they do not define these behaviors as forms of school violence. We often encounter teacher and principal groups that question whether verbal victimization is indeed a form of school violence. In our participant observations, we noticed that in some schools the teachers appeared to be desensitized to verbal violence, or so used to hearing curses and bad language that they hardly noticed it and did not remark on it in the interviews.

In fact, about a quarter of all Israeli students report that they were victims of verbal insults and humiliation directed at them by their teachers. If staff in Jewish schools do not consider verbal victimization a form of school violence, they may not feel the need to address these kinds of behaviors unless the threshold of physical contact is crossed. In this case, verbal-social victimization is not even on the radar screen of the school, despite its being the most prevalent form of school victimization. Clearly, verbal victimization affects most students; it starts at a young age, is high for both boys and girls, and remains stable throughout development. Awareness of the negative consequences of and cultural norms against verbal-social victimization can impact this form of victimization.

Although social isolation is a form of verbal-social victimization, culture affects it differently than it affects the behaviors of cursing and humiliation. Social isolation is more prevalent among Arab students and appears to have cultural meaning that needs further exploration; in many of our analyses, this variable stood out. We do not have a clear explanation of why it would be more prevalent in Arab schools, but we suspect it is another important distinction between the Arab and Jewish schools.

SEVERE VICTIMIZATION.   In contrast with mild/moderate victimization, severe victimization is influenced more by family and neighborhood socioeconomic conditions; like mild/moderate, it is also influenced by the school climate. In our study, severe victimization was associated strongly with fear of attending school. In other studies, severe victimization led to posttraumatic responses and, in extreme cases, to suicide or shooting fellow students in school.

Severe victimization is relatively rare; this was true in our study and in many studies conducted across the globe. Our findings over the three waves of data collection show that the rates of severe victimization (such as receiving a serious beating, being blackmailed by a gang, or being cut by a knife) have low frequencies (e.g., 5.7% for being cut by a knife). This, of course, does not diminish the seriousness with which we need to approach these behaviors, given their severe outcomes for the victims and their potential for even more severe and even lethal consequences.

The general public and educators are often under the impression that severe victimization is extremely frequent. We believe these are effects generated by the media, which tend to focus on severe forms of violence. This, in turn, creates a strong public sentiment that these extreme cases are actually representative of many more cases. On the one hand, such media attention contributes to negative public sentiment regarding youth and adds to myths regarding their uncontrollability. On the other hand, one could argue that the media's intense focus on extreme events has raised the international community's overall concern about school violence issues in general, which is bound to have positive effects.

In the United States, the concern with extreme and severe violent acts in schools focuses mainly on the use of weapons, especially guns. Much of the intervention effort is invested in profiling potential shooters and in identifying predictors of which *individual students* may engage in these acts. However, one can argue that this effort to find potential shooters diverts attention from creating safe school environments free of the other severe victimization types that students experience. Our findings suggest that from a public policy or district resource perspective, focusing on entire schools in addition to helping individual students will yield results that help a much large segment of the student population.

We suggest an approach that focuses on entire schools rather than individuals. We found that the distribution of schools with severe types of victimization is highly skewed: There are a few schools with an inordinate number of reports on severe victimization, including exposure to weapons, and many more that have few or no incidents. It seems, therefore, that the highest potential for extreme consequences of school violence is with this select group of schools. It is important to target the schools with the more extreme rates of severe violence and address the school as whole. Clearly, individual students with potential for severe violence may exist in all schools. Nevertheless, by focusing on a small group of schools and working with them to reduce the potential for severe violence, we may increase the probability for a significant reduction in risk for extreme victimization.

The analyses indicate that schools embedded in low-income communities with high concentrations of students from low-SES families are subject to more severe forms of victimization. This finding helps direct allocation of resources in a more deliberate manner to schools with the greatest number of potential victims. When targeting schools in these areas, it is essential to focus on the resources they need to create a school environment that can prevent the spillover from the external context, rather than create an atmosphere of blame and prejudice against students in these schools.

WEAPONS AND SEXUAL HARASSMENT.   In addition to examining a range of behaviors that are studied in the school violence and bullying literature, we added two more areas that are usually studied separately: weapon use and sexual harassment. Our findings indicate that these are indeed separate dimensions that do not show the same patterns as other aspects of school violence. At the same time, studying them alongside other types of victimization enriches our understanding of these behaviors when they occur on school grounds.

Weapon Use. The possession and use of weapons on school grounds is very troubling. The well-publicized shootings in U.S. schools reverberate throughout the world and raise concerns among parents and policymakers everywhere. We know from U.S. Department of Education statistics that the zero tolerance gun laws seem to be decreasing the number of students who bring weapons onto school grounds (Kaufman et al., 2001). Israel does not have a zero tolerance weapons law.

The issue of weapons in Israel in general and in schools in particular is quite complex. On the one hand, due to the security situation of the country, the prevalence of guns in public is extremely high. Soldiers who are on their way to their military bases or returning home, police officers, security guards placed in most public places, and citizens who live or travel in places considered dangerous carry shotguns and handguns in the streets. Schools are protected by armed guards; their mission is to protect against outside attacks on the school, not violent crime by students. Thus, from many perspectives, weapons are not as much symbols of violence as they are symbols of protection against violence. On the other hand, in contrast to the United States, there is no ideology regarding freedom to own a gun as a civil right. To own a gun, a person needs to show that he or she is in danger from a terrorist attack. Except for special circumstances, citizens cannot get a gun for self-protection against crime. Students are not allowed to carry guns, even in the most dangerous areas. Consequently, students' involvement with weapons, especially guns, in school is considered by school staff and the public as extremely rare and, when it exists, highly alarming.

Because of its importance, we treated the possession and use of weapons separately from other aspects of school victimization. We propose a view that differentiates among various modes of exposure and different types of weapons. Our findings support the notion that there are more students who see, hear about, and are threatened by weapons than bring a weapon to school or have been injured by weapons. These findings support our call for research and policy not to be limited to students bringing weapons to schools. Students who hear a rumor about a weapon in school or see a student concealing a gun or who are verbally threatened by a weapon should be considered a target population for interventions. Such victimized students may be paying an emotional price, even if no weapon has actually passed the school's gate. There is a need to broaden the scope of interventions related to weapons in school to include this group of victimized students.

Furthermore, we presented data showing that the students who bring weapons to school are often the students who have been victimized on school grounds, which points to the fact that there are dynamics and events *on the school grounds* that contribute to weapon use. Finally, the findings suggest strongly that schools should focus not only on firearms but on the whole range of weapons that can physically (sometimes lethally) harm members of the school community.

Sexual Harassment. In our book we have treated sexual harassment in a dual way: We considered it as an element of school violence and as a separate and unique phenomenon that should get special attention. Our empirical findings indicate strongly that there are two aspects to this issue: one that is quite consistent with other aspects of victimization in school and revolves around the intent to humiliate the victim, and another that presents quite differently and entails intent to have a sexual encounter that the victim does not want.

Current research in this area lumps together different sexual harassment behaviors and does not attend to its different components. We think that further conceptual and empirical work should be directed to describing the various dimensions of sexual harassment in school. This examination is important for reasons of conceptual and theoretical clarity; the identification of the links between cultural beliefs, social structures, and sexual harassment will be enhanced if we are able to distinguish between certain behaviors that are related to more general aggression and those that have a unique sexual intention that may reflect the special role of sexuality with regard, for instance, to different gender-role expectations in a society. Our finding of a strong interaction between gender and culture with regard to sexual harassment with intent to have sexual contact suggests that further research in this area may reveal some interesting mechanisms that connect society's norms, values, and social organization with sexual harassment by adolescents in school.

Along this line of research it is important to study how school context impacts students' sexual behavior. For instance, our findings in this area indicate a strong impact on adolescent girls in religious all-girl schools: This context has clear implications for these girls' sexual victimization. Our qualitative study also suggests that when boys and girls in a traditional patriarchal group (such as the Bedouin) study in the same school (i.e., the same context), there are many informal ways in which their interaction is restricted and supervised.

From a policy and practice point of view, the distinctions among various aspects of sexual harassment have implications for better planning of educational and preventive work in this area. For instance, we showed that different groups are vulnerable to different dimensions of sexual harassment. This should help refocus and sharpen educational messages to address the issues relevant to specific groups. In the context of Israeli schools, for instance, boys more than girls are victimized with the intent to humiliate; however, Arab boys report much more victimization with sexual intent than do Jewish boys, and Jewish female students are victims of sexual harassment much more often than their Arab female peers. These factors should be reflected in the different educational and preventive work in different schools.

STAFF-INITIATED VICTIMIZATION.   Ours is the first nationally representative study that included victimization by staff as part of a study of school violence. Currently, other countries focus only on student-initiated violence; this is theoretically, pragmatically, and empirically problematic because, as we found, staff victimization does exist, does strongly affect students (as Hyman shows), and is not negligible (as we show). From an emotional and psychological perspective, the effect of victimization by staff can be long-lasting and extremely damaging, many times more than peer victimization. The lack of systematic research interest may be the reason why (as far we know) there are no systemwide interventions that focus directly on preventing and dealing with staff violence. We strongly urge researchers, policymakers, and educators to collect data on victimization by staff members.

The lack of attention to staff-initiated victimization is a serious gap in the school violence literature; we think this stems from the fact that corporal punishment is banned in most districts, states, and countries. This is true in Israel as well. However, as our results show, physical and emotional victimization continues to occur despite the sanctions against it. The absence of data or theory on teacher-student victimization may also reflect the tendency to blame the students and not the powerful group in the school.

From our experience, teachers unions and teachers themselves have been especially resistant to the idea of collecting data on victimization by teachers. We encourage teachers to be part of the process of preventing teacher-initiated abuses on school grounds. We think it is important for every profession to be part of the process of monitoring its members' behavior and coming up with guidelines that help reduce victimization by staff. Research in this area may have several complementary goals: determining base rate data on the magnitude of the problem, identifying vulnerable groups, and assessing change over time, similar to what we have done. Researchers should also situate this behavior within larger theoretical frameworks, identifying cultural, social, and psychological mechanisms that bring about such behavior, especially in certain groups. Thus, we need to explore questions such as:

- Is staff-initiated victimization a reflection of power relations in the school context?
- Do these staff behaviors reflect cultural norms regarding child-rearing practices?
- To what extent do these behaviors reflect lack of effective coping mechanisms or resources for alternative behaviors?

Answers to some of these questions would be very helpful in designing national and local policies aimed at eliminating staff-initiated violence toward students.

CROSS-CULTURAL, CROSS-AGE, AND CROSS-GENDER SIMILARITIES AND DIFFERENCES IN THE STRUCTURE OF SCHOOL VICTIMIZATION

We believe that the similarities among diverse cultural, age, and gender groups are some of the most intriguing and important findings reported in this book. We found that the structure of specific victimization types in school follows a very simple and powerful pattern, ordered by the dimensions of frequency and severity and consistent among all the groups we studied in Israel. Furthermore, it was very similar to the structure we found when we examined findings from California.

The similarity between rank order of specific behaviors and factor structures is important because the school violence literature, as well as other violence literatures, has been focused primarily on base rates of specific victimization behaviors for different groups. Given the different base rates for the different groups, theories have often taken a culturally relativistic view of the role of culture on violence. Current violence theories would not expect boys, girls, Jews, Arabs, older, younger, Israeli, and American students to have virtually identical rankings of each type of violent behavior—that floors and ceilings of each type of behavior move up or down with regard to the base rates of each, but their relationship to each other stays the same for all groups. That is, despite different base rates, there are common patterns of relationships and structures within the school and society that keep the relationships among the different types of violence the same. It could be that the dynamics of a school are so similar and familiar (teacher-student relationships, schoolyard behaviors, peer group interactions, etc.) that they would be recognizable to people from very diverse cultures. It is also possible that this kind of ranking exists for other forms of violence, such as family violence.

We examined these issues of school victimization structure and of similarities and dissimilarities among three cultural groups in Israel and compared them with a sample in California. We were able to replicate these structures in our work in Israel, both in the third wave of our national study (Benbenishty, 2003) and in a series of regional studies in Herzliya, Israel. It is important to expand this line of research to other countries; if researchers from many different countries and cultural contexts use a shared list of victimization types, the accumulated database will help identify universal themes, as well as culturally unique characteristics.

The basic similarity in patterns across groups provides an effective backdrop for efforts to identify cultural and group differences. When a certain victimization type is rank ordered differently in two groups, it raises the possibility that there are some meaningful differences that should be explored further. For instance, we found that social exclusion has a different rank order in Jewish than in Arab schools. One would need to investigate the different meaning that such victimization has in these different cultures. We also found that the various types of sexual harassment did not follow this pattern; the rank order of the items we used was quite different across genders and cultural groups. This pattern strongly suggests that for different groups, these victimization behaviors have different meanings.

THE INFLUENCE OF SCHOOL VARIABLES AND OTHER CONTEXTS ON VICTIMIZATION

Our work focuses on victimization within the school context, especially the ways the within-school context impacts the students. The school is embedded in larger contexts that have important influences on levels of school violence. The "school within context" then becomes a central unit of analysis. Most of the research in this area focuses on individual students and their experiences of victimization; only a handful of studies looked at schools and asked why certain schools have higher levels of violence than others. Our study highlights the limitations of this common approach: We show how important it is to view the school as a whole and to understand how the contexts in which schools are embedded influence their levels of victimization. We recommend, therefore, that in future studies considerations of sample and analytical plans include descriptions of victimization experienced by individual students and also focus on school sites as units of analysis. This approach will no doubt stimulate more thinking on how school-level variables influence levels of victimization.

To illustrate, we are conducting a mixed-method study of nine schools that were identified in our quantitative analysis as experiencing either much higher or much lower levels of victimization, considering the characteristics of the students' families and their communities. When we tried to understand differences between schools, rather than between students, we searched for school-level characteristics that distinguish them. One area we identified was the principals, their educational and social philosophy, and their relationships with their staff and with the students' parents. Based on our observations so far, we believe that these school-level issues are central to understanding why individual students in these schools are being victimized and to designing efforts to reduce and prevent school violence.

As we discussed in our preface, we do not think that the context in which the school is embedded always has direct and immediate impact on the students and on levels of victimization in the school. It really depends on the kind of victimization. For example, in our study, verbal-social behaviors filtered in from the home and community, in part, because these behaviors were not considered school victimization by the teachers. However, mild/moderate victimization was influenced by what was happening in the school. With severe victimization, it was a combination of both within-school context and the family and community context. We envision the school environment as encircled by a semipermeable membrane that mediates and sometimes blocks outside influences. Schools also generate their own dynamics separate from and often unrelated to external influences.

The findings presented in this book show quite a complex and nontrivial picture of how within-school and external contexts are associated with victimization. We found that to understand better the victimization that an individual student experiences, it is important to understand the school context, such as whether the school implements a policy against violence, how supportive the staff is, how peers behave in school, and whether it is a primary or secondary school. Furthermore, knowing that the student is in a school that serves a specific cultural group, that the families of the students in this school are well educated, and that the school neighborhood is mostly blue-collar workers all help predict how likely students are to experience victimization.

These influences of the multiple contexts in which the school is embedded are not uniform across the various victimization types. The question of how context impacts victimization in school should be rephrased to: What contexts influence which victimization types? For instance, our findings suggest strongly that poverty among students' families and in the school neighborhood is associated with levels of severe victimization in school but not with moderate victimization. Also, poverty has an inverse relationship with verbal victimization, as opposed to the relationship it has with severe victimization.

Israel provides a good example of the complexity of the interaction between context and school violence. During the years in which we conducted our studies,

Israeli society experienced extreme acceleration in political violence, and suicide bombings became almost daily events. These major changes in context did not simply translate into an immediate increase in school violence. Context is mediated by many mechanisms that work sometimes to offset, sometimes to enhance the influence of the context. Thus, we think that there are strong indications that when terrorist attacks were more frequent and deadly, school staff responded by getting closer to and supporting and protecting their students in ways they did not do in the past. These behaviors may, in fact, have reduced levels of violence within the school when the outside became so much more dangerous.

One theory that may be relevant to understanding the effects of violence in the larger context on school violence is the work by Landau and Beit-Hallachmi (1983; Landau, 1988). According to their theory, when the individual and the public are under stress, they react aggressively. The cause is not the stress itself, but the negative feelings it brings about in the individual. Landau showed that social stress factors, such as difficult economic situations (including high unemployment levels) and military emergencies, influenced the level of crime. In Israel, social statistics show that national levels of interpersonal (murder and armed burglary) and intrapersonal (suicide) aggression were positively correlated with measures of social stress. According to this theory, the mechanism that mediates between stress coming from the social context and individual aggressive behavior is perceived social support (Landau, 1998). That is, when an individual feels support and social solidarity, outside stress is not translated into aggressive behavior; it is only when solidarity breaks down that stress (due to social circumstances) leads to aggressive behavior.

We think that school climate, especially teacher support, may be playing a similar mediating role with regard to school violence: When the outside context (e.g., exposure to community violence) creates stress, school climate may prevent the negative consequences of this stress. This, of course, is an example of one possible mechanism that can explain how school climate mediates the effects of the outside context. Other theories (such as theories of social capital and collective efficacy) may also prove useful in explaining the interaction between school context and student social and antisocial behaviors (see, e.g., Cartland, Ruch-Ross, & Henry, 2003).

The Special Role of Culture

Israeli society creates an interesting setting for the study of how culture influences school victimization. The Israeli educational system is structured so that Arabs, secular Jews, and Orthodox Jews attend different schools. This allows us to compare students who are in independent cultural settings, although all of them are, of course, part of the Israeli education system. Our findings show that the effects of culture are quite complex and are not uniform across the many faces of victimization that we explored here.

In certain areas, the similarity across cultural groups is astonishing. For instance, when we examined physical victimization among Jewish and Arab boys and girls across grade levels, we saw that, whereas boys were victimized more often than girls and students in lower grades were victimized more often than others, the Jewish and Arab students experienced very similar levels of victimization across genders and grade levels. In other areas, cultural groups were remarkably different in their overall victimization rates. For instance, levels of weapon possession and victimization by knives were highest for Arab students.

Furthermore, in some areas, the findings showed strong effects of interactions between gender and culture. A major example of such cultural influence was found with regard to gender differences in sexual harassment. The gaps between boys and girls in their reports on sexual harassment with the "intent to have [unwanted] sexual relations" were different across the cultural groups we studied. In Jewish religious and Arab groups, boys reported much more often than girls that they had been victimized, whereas among secular Jewish students, the trend was different. This pattern of findings indicates that cultural contexts not only influence base rates of behaviors but may also impact gender and developmental trends of victimization. Clearly, our previous question—How does culture influence school violence?—should be replaced by a series of much more refined questions. We should be asking about the different effects of culture on specific aspects of school violence and the interaction between culture and individual factors such as gender and age.

Frequently, culture is confounded and associated strongly with other contextual factors. Thus, when we examined differences in victimization by gender, we found that levels of victimization among female students in the Orthodox school system dropped sharply when they entered junior high; the reason is probably the fact that in this cultural group, boys and girls study in separate schools. This situation implies that when we examine cultural influences, we should be aware of the fact that different cultures may create different contexts for the individuals, and these contexts may be mediating the effects of culture in addition to impacting individual students directly.

The difficulty in separating culture from other contexts becomes even clearer when school violence is studied in different countries. In a recent book on school violence (Smith, 2003), scholars from 17 European countries presented their findings. In the introduction to each of the chapters, a rudimentary description of the educational system of each country was presented. These presentations revealed similarities and many substantial differences among these countries, some of which relate to the ideology regarding the function of the school in society and the relative roles, the professional authority, and the power positions of parents, students, teachers, and principals vis-à-vis each other (see, e.g., the chapter by Debarbieux, Blaya, & Vidal, 2003). To take but one other dimension, there are significant variations with regard to the age composition in schools in various countries. For instance, in Italy primary schools are for children ages 6 to 11, in Ireland children enter primary schools at the age of 4, and in Finland at the age of 7. Such age differences may have substantial implications for school violence. For instance, having children who range widely in age within the same school building may expose younger students to much more violence from older students than those in schools in which younger students are separated physically. It would be quite difficult to attribute differences in rates of bullying in these educational settings to different cultures before we acknowledge and identify how these age- (and development-) related issues influence levels of school violence.

We think that researchers sometimes take for granted the culture and context with which they are familiar and attribute their findings solely to gender and age effects or universal human developmental trends. They may not give enough attention to the possibility that what they find is a result of the interaction between the characteristics of the context and these individual factors. For instance, in an impressive multimethod longitudinal study, Pellegrini and his associates (Pellegrini, 2001; Pellegrini & Bartini, 2000; Pellegrini & Long, 2002) examined heterosexual relationships, aggression, and sexual harassment during the transition from primary to middle school. To examine and explain patterns of violence-related behaviors and their changes over time, the authors used developmental and dominance theories. For our purposes, it is instructive to observe that in their discussion of the findings the authors do not refer to the sociocultural and organizational contexts of the schools they studied. For instance, one might ask whether the gender and developmental effects would have been similar if the students were predominantly lower-class Hispanics rather than middle-class European Americans. Would the findings have been different had the transition to middle school occurred in seventh grade (as is the case, for instance, in Israel) rather than sixth grade? We think that school violence research would benefit from increased attention to the ways more universal developmental trends interact with context to impact school violence.

It should be noted that we examined differences between three cultural groups that have separate educational systems. One would expect that when students who belong to different cultural groups meet in the same school, culture may influence victimization in additional ways. For instance, the relative power of the various cultural groups that make up the school population, the intergroup relationships, and the proportion of students from each group may have a strong influence on the type and magnitude of school violence. Recent European reviews (Smith, 2003) suggest strongly that the presence of minority groups in schools (such as Gypsies and migrant workers), their proportion in school, and their interaction with the majority group strongly influence issues of school violence. Future research should include these school-level cultural variables in attempts to understand how culture and cultural differences impact school violence.

In many places around the world, cultural differences are associated with other sociopolitical characteristics. Issues of power, poverty, deprivation, and political oppression are often interwoven when we explore cultural differences, especially within the same society. In Israel, for instance, any comparison between Jews and Arabs has to take into account not only different cultural values, heritage, and belief systems but also major political conflicts, power imbalance, and significant gaps in socioeconomic and political status. It is important, therefore, to try to disentangle, as much as possible and when possible, issues of culture, relative power, access to resources, discrimination, and so on.

One such area of interest is victimization by staff. Violence by adults against children is strongly associated with the norms of society and of cultural groups (Hyman, & Wise, 1979). For instance, Ellinger and Beckham (1997) report that in South Korea, parents encourage teachers to use corporal punishment, whereas in China, the norms are quite different (Kim et al., 2000). In Israel, we found that Arab students report much higher incidents of physical victimization by staff than do Jewish students. Explanations based on cultural norms seem appropriate in explaining this strong and consistent finding. Still, when we examined the relationship between staff physical victimization of students and the SES of the students' families, we found an association, even after controlling for culture. This raises the possibility that the underlying mechanisms may relate not only to cultural beliefs but also to other sociopolitical variables, such as lack of resources. Hyman's (1990) analysis of available data seems to indicate that educators may use corporal punishment selectively and target the weaker and poorer students in their classes. Consequently, future research should try to parcel out and distinguish between direct impact of cultural aspects and the impact of other context variables that are either influenced by these cultural aspects (such as separation between genders) or are correlated with them in certain societies (such as the correlation between ethnicity and poverty).

THE MULTIPLE OUTCOMES OF SCHOOL VICTIMIZATION

The literature provides examples of outcomes of victimization in school that relate mainly to long-term consequences of being severely bullied over time. In this book, we addressed several outcomes that were rarely studied before, namely, the overall assessment of the severity of the school violence problem, how safe the student feels in school, and whether students miss school due to fear. Chapter 8 provides strong support for this emphasis on proximal and immediate responses of students to the school context.

We found that each of the outcomes we studied is associated with a different set of within-school context variables and types of victimization. For instance, we found that students' nonattendance of school due to fear of violence is influenced mainly by their personal experiences with severe peer violence on school grounds, whereas their assessment of the severity of violence is associated with risky peer group behavior, and their sense of safety correlated mainly with school climate. The clear implication of these findings is that in order to address the array of outcomes associated with school violence, it is important to deal with many aspects of the school's context.

One of the findings that has a special significance for interventions focusing on school violence is the fact that risky peer group behaviors had a stronger impact than personal victimization on assessments of the seriousness of the problem. Most interventions try to reduce incidents of personal victimization so that students do not suffer the negative outcomes of violence. Our findings emphasize the effects of school violence on students who are not the direct targets of violence but are only bystanders or spectators exposed to others' violent behavior. For instance, a small group of students engaging in violent behavior may be victimizing another small group of students but creating a schoolwide atmosphere of violence. Future interventions should not neglect these indirect effects of violence and should target risky peer group behaviors that create a violent atmosphere in school.

We studied only a subset of the many behaviors, feelings, and cognitions that are the outcomes of school violence. Among the additional outcomes that should be studied, we would emphasize performance. The literature has presented clear associations between violence, both on school grounds and in the community, and poor academic performance (see a critical review of the literature in McEvoy & Welker, 2000). Surprisingly, however, despite many informal and anecdotal observations tying victimization (especially severe victimization) to academic difficulties, systematic research in this area is lacking. We think that more research attention should be paid to the relationship between violence in school and academic achievement. This research should explore questions on two levels: whether victimized students are more likely to do less well academically, and whether students in schools characterized by high levels of school violence are more likely to have lower academic performance.

MULTIPLE PERSPECTIVES AND AWARENESS

Throughout most of this book, we have focused on the students' perspectives. However, our model with the school in the center strongly suggests that the other members of the school community make important contributions to school violence and that their perceptions, attitudes, and behaviors influence how the school contexts interact to influence school violence.

Our findings suggest strongly that educational staff and principals may not be aware of victimization experienced by students. Their awareness is influenced by the extent to which they are exposed to various violent events occurring among students; some of these events are more covert than others, and the importance staff attach to certain events impacts whether administrators know about them. We also showed that awareness may have important consequences: Personnel's assessments of the severity of the violence problem are associated with the degree to which they are involved in prevention and treatment efforts.

One method to increase the awareness of staff and principals that we suggested in Chapter 11 is to conduct student surveys and inform personnel about students' experiences and perceptions. We have evidence that suggests that this strategy is effective. Following our national study reported here, we engaged in a series of dissemination and public education efforts intended to increase awareness of adults (e.g., policymakers, parents, and educational staff) regarding victimization experienced by children in schools. School violence, indeed, became a "hot issue," albeit for a short period. In the third wave of our national study, conducted three years after the work reported here, awareness of school violence among educators was much higher. Principals and homeroom teachers reported many more prevention and intervention activities. The assessments of the severity of the problem were also significantly higher than previously. In fact, although staff and principals assessed the problem as more severe than in our earlier surveys, students felt that the problem was less severe; consequently, their perspectives were much closer to each other than before. We think that this situation is helpful to efforts to address school violence, and it was brought about to a large extent by exposing staff and principals to information gathered from students in national and regional surveys.

MONITORING AND RESEARCH

We conducted three consecutive representative national studies of school violence that examined students and schools in a range of grades and cultural groups. We think that the ongoing impact of our national studies on perceptions and behaviors in this area is another example of the power of monitoring. The term *monitoring* is used to describe a process of tracking issues of concern systematically and over time. Examples of extensive monitoring efforts in this area come mainly from the United States, where the CDC is monitoring many indicators of crime and victimization. The U.S. National Center for Educational Statistics and the Bureau of Justice Statistics have been publishing an annual report, *Indicators of School Crime and Safety* (see, e.g., DeVoe et al., 2002; Kaufman et al., 2001). The foreword to one report states the rationale: "Accurate information about the nature, extent, and scope of the problem being addressed is essential in developing effective programs and policies" (DeVoe et al., 2002, p. 5). This report compiles statistics from several resources that provide an annual snapshot of various aspects of school violence and allow for comparisons over time. The most recent report demonstrates that sizable improvements have occurred in children's safety in schools over the past 10 years.

Frequently, the power of monitoring is overlooked. When we started our work in this area we encountered many policymakers, teachers, and even colleagues who felt that monitoring would not be useful. Their sentiment was captured in the statement "I know there is violence in our schools, I do not need research for it. I need research that will tell me what should be done about it." We believe that there is strong evidence to suggest that monitoring is, indeed, quite useful.

The fact that we systematically collected similar data using similar methods and instruments several times over the years provided information with far-reaching implications. Presented to the public and policymakers, our findings showed the magnitude of the problem, its characteristics, multiple perspectives and perceptions, current practices, and more. It helped identify what the more pressing issues are and who the more vulnerable groups are. Our studies helped to base public and professional discourse on agreed-upon figures. The question at issue shifted from What is the situation? to Given what we now know about the situation, how do we change it? Over time, this national monitoring also showed areas of change (both progress and regression), which groups became more or less vulnerable, and so on. Such findings led to many significant developments, among them structural changes (such as adding counselors to primary schools and creating regional teams to address school violence), new policy guidelines (such as new policies regarding staff-initiated violence), the development and dissemination of interventions, and an overall bumping up of this issue in the priority list of the Israeli Ministry of Education.

Monitoring should not be limited to the national level. Following our national studies, we developed a methodology to link monitoring on the national, regional, and school levels (Benbenishty, Astor, & Zeira, 2003). In this approach, each school in a district conducts a survey of school violence and climate. All schools in the district use the same instruments and methods so that all of the information is aggregated on the district level. This process is repeated annually. The information is analyzed and feedback is provided to all participants. Each school gets a thorough assessment of violence in that school. This information empowers the school leadership to plan interventions on the basis of a valid and reliable assessment of the site. On the district level, a comprehensive and detailed picture of the region emerges, which describes both the district as a whole and the relative situation of each school within the district. Furthermore, because instruments and methodology are similar to those used on the national level, comparisons between district and national statistics are possible. Thus, the district leadership is empowered to make policy decisions and choices regarding which programs to adopt for the district as a whole and for particular schools on the basis of comprehensive and comparable data.

Clearly, the data provided by monitoring efforts are important. We believe, however, that the monitoring process itself has many important implications. For instance, the impact on policymakers and practitioners of monitoring findings is much stronger than is the case with one-shot research projects because everyone involved knows that within a specified period of time, the same issues will be reexamined. Therefore, the efforts to address and change issues identified in the surveys are much more focused on producing noticeable changes in future surveys.

Another important consequence of monitoring processes is their empowering effects on students. Surveys among students become a way of bringing their voices to the attention of all other members of the community. Students may find these surveys to be their opportunity to express what they think about their school and their community. In our monitoring of a district in Israel, students had the opportunity to describe not only their experiences of victimization by peers and staff, but also to express their feelings and provide details regarding how safe they felt in their neighborhood and why. The voices of almost all students in the district could not be ignored by public officials and school professionals.

WHERE DO WE GO FROM HERE?

We have presented a theoretical framework and empirical data that we gathered to examine school violence in context. We showed how our studies were instrumental in enriching our understanding of the interrelationships between various contexts and aspects of school violence. Clearly, despite the many insights gained by our work so far, there are many limitations and gaps in knowledge that should be addressed in future studies. We noted some of these gaps and directions for future research in the relevant chapters. In the following sections, we want to highlight briefly what we think are important elements of the future research agenda.

Multiple Research Methods

The complexity of the theoretical framework we presented requires that the range of research methodologies be expanded greatly in future studies. Our studies are limited by a focus on students' self-reports. It is important to complement this method with a range of data collection techniques, such as observations, personal diaries, and in-depth interviews. These techniques will provide validity checks on students' self-reports and, more important, will add data not available through self-reports.

Further, we believe that mixed-method studies, combining both quantitative and qualitative designs and techniques, are essential in this area. Mixed-method studies, in addition to their well-known strengths (Greene & Caracelli, 1997), may have a special role in this area due to the multilevel nature of school violence. We think that quantitative studies based on large-scale representative national samples are an effective way of detecting trends, associations, and structures of a range of victimization types. These studies can also use quantitative data on neighborhoods and schools to identify the role of these contexts in school violence. However, to understand better the role of neighborhoods, schools, and contexts within schools, qualitative case studies may prove very useful (see, e.g., Behre, Astor, & Meyer, 2001; Devine, 1996). These studies can help identify and describe factors that are not readily captured in available statistics. For instance, such studies can help introduce a historical perspective and present current situations in light of changes over time. A case study of a school may help to reveal how changes in the ideology of the new principal affect a growing emphasis on religious values as a buffer against peer violence, or how gradual changes in the demographic makeup of the students' families shift the balance of power between school management and the PTA in ways that influence how staff support students.

Longitudinal Designs

In this book we used cross-sectional data to describe age-related trends. Clearly, longitudinal designs add more significant information on developmental trajectories.

Research on aggression and delinquency has used longitudinal designs quite effectively over the years. Traditionally, the focus has been on individual developmental trajectories; given our theoretical framework, we think that these longitudinal designs should also incorporate information on context to understand better the interaction between individuals and contexts. This type of design may prove especially useful when individuals are followed as they move from one context to another, either as part of natural development (such as moving from primary to middle school; see Pellegrini, 2001; Pellegrini & Bartini, 2000), or due to life events (such as a change in school due to a family move).

Longitudinal studies of individuals are quite common; we could not identify, however, longitudinal studies of *schools*. Our conceptual framework and experiences with many schools direct us to ask how schools change over time, how these changes are associated with the context outside of the school, how they relate to changes in personnel, what are the changes in school climate, and whether these changes are associated with changes in levels of school violence. Studies that use a nested design and conduct longitudinal studies of students in schools over time will allow us, perhaps for the first time, to examine simultaneously (and assess the relative contribution of) several effects: the contributions of the individual student, class, and school; the effects of the interactions between student, class, and school characteristics; the effects of student age and cohort; and the effects of changes in the school over time.

We think that such studies are feasible, especially within the framework of monitoring presented earlier. Consider a district or region that monitors regularly the achievements of students and schools. This monitoring system could be enhanced by adding references to school climate and school violence. Over time, the accumulated database could provide a wealth of systematic information that could answer many of the questions we raise. It should be noted that identifying schools and classes as units of analysis requires data gathering not only on students but on teachers and on the school as a whole. For instance, the level of training of each teacher in areas related to school violence is an important piece of information in attempts to understand why students in certain classes are involved more in school violence, and in suggesting possible venues of interventions aimed at reducing school violence.

Adding More Perspectives

Chapter 11 showed how valuable are multiple perspectives on school violence. We think that this line of research should be continued and expanded to include more members of the school community. For instance, noneducational staff (e.g., secretaries, maintenance, and guards) can provide important input. Also, the perspectives and roles of supervisors and other district-level officials may be helpful in portraying a richer picture of the school, its internal and external contexts, and the interaction between these contexts and school violence.

One of the most important perspectives that should be added to studies of school violence is that of the students' parents. Studies in the United States have shown that parents of students in public schools are very concerned about school violence (Rose & Gallup, 2000). Parents' awareness of school violence and their reactions to it may be major contextual influences on schools; their levels and types of involvement may affect school violence directly. In our national studies we found that many principals were frustrated because they were not able to engage parents in efforts to address school violence. Principals, teachers, and students also reported that in several schools parents entered school grounds and verbally and physically attacked students and staff whom they believed to be responsible for hurting their children. In our monitoring project we found that concerns about parents' reactions to school violence were quite important for school personnel and district officials in planning and decision-making processes regarding school violence. We believe, therefore, that this neglected area of research can help us understand better how parents, a critical element of the school context, interact with the school on issues of violence.

Cross-national Studies

Israel provides an interesting setting for cross-cultural study in school violence, having separate (but similar in many structural respects) educational systems for its main cultural groups. To continue to explore the interplay between culture, religion, and school violence, cross-cultural studies should cover many more countries and cultural settings. We envision an international network of school violence researchers who are systematically exploring the similarities and differences in how school violence plays out in different cultures. Such a network can help build a shared instrument sensitive to the wide range of contexts present in such an international study and designed to include specific and concrete types of school violence to allow direct comparisons between countries. Such a study can compare base rates of specific behaviors across countries so that each country can put its school violence levels in perspective.

The focus of such a cross-national study, however, should not be on comparing base rates, but on identifying differences and similarities in structures and in the interplay between context and school violence. Thus, one would compare the relative frequency of each of the specific behaviors in the different countries to identify behaviors that have similar ranking and others that show marked differences between cultures. Such differences may be the impetus for qualitative studies that explore how specific behaviors gain special meanings in certain cultures.

Furthermore, a series of such studies can identify similar and different patterns of relationships between context and violence. For instance, in certain cultures exposure to community violence is highly associated with victimization in school; other cultures are shielding schools better and are more successful in making schools safe havens for children. Such findings may provide helpful insights not only about the mechanisms that underlie school violence but also about effective ways to address this problem and reduce victimization in school.

Finally, an international study on school violence will affirm a global commitment to protect children from harm. International cooperation that harnesses both science and deep concern for the welfare of children may be an appropriate response to today's global assault on the well-being and sometimes the mere survival of children around the world.

Appendix 1

Research Instruments

STUDENTS' QUESTIONNAIRE

Victimization

We would like to ask you about the behaviors of other students toward you.[1] We are asking you about what really happened to you, and not what you have heard about others.

For each of the following behaviors, please tell us whether it happened to you at school during the prior month. Use the following scale:

1–Not at all   2–Once or twice   3–Three times or more

A student seized and shoved you on purpose.

You were involved in a fistfight.

You were kicked or punched by a student who wanted to hurt you.

A student used a rock or another instrument in order to hurt you.

A student took your things from you by force.

You were involved in a fight, were hurt, and required medical attention.

A student gave you a serious beating.

A student cut you with a knife or a sharp instrument on purpose.

A student threatened to harm or hit you.

A student tried to intimidate you by the way he or she was looking at you.

Students threatened you on your way to or from school.

Gang members at school threatened, harassed, and pressured you.

You were blackmailed under threats by another student (for money, valuables, or food).

A student cursed you.

A student mocked, insulted, or humiliated you.

A group of students boycotted you and did not want to play or talk with you.

You saw a student in school with a gun.

You saw a student in school with a knife.

A student stole your personal belongings or equipment.

A student intentionally destroyed or broke your personal belongings.

A student threatened you with a gun and you saw the gun.

A student threatened you with a knife and you saw the knife.

Sexual Harassment*

In this part, we are asking you about the behaviors of other students toward you related to sexual harassment. We are interested in what really happened to you, and not about things that you heard about others.

For each of the following please indicate:

Did it happen to you in the prior month in school?

If it did happen, who did this to you (1–a boy; 2–a girl; 3–a boy and a girl)?

A student peeped while you were in the bathroom or in the locker room.

A student took or tried to take your clothes off (for sexual reasons).

A student tried to "come on to you" (sexually) and made sexual comments that you did not want.

Sexually insulting things about you were written on walls or sexual rumors were spread about you.

A student tried to kiss you without your consent.

A student touched or tried to touch you or to pinch you in a sexual way without your approval.

A student showed you obscene pictures or sent you obscene letters.

Observed Risk Behaviors in School

Please indicate to what extent each of following regularly occurs in your school. In each of your responses use the following scale:

1–Not at all   2–A little   3–Some   4–Quite a bit   5–Very much

Students get into fights.

Students drink alcohol (wine, beer) in school.

Students destroy things in school, draw graffiti on walls, damage furniture.

Students steal things from other students or teachers.

Students use drugs on school grounds.

Students threaten or bully other students.

Students bring guns to school.

Students bring other weapons to school (such as knives, clubs).

*The boys sexually harass the girls (make obscene suggestions, touch, peep).

Outsiders (adults) enter the campus during the school day and threaten, harass, or get into fights with students or teachers.

*There is dangerous gang activity in my school.

*Teachers or other staff members come on to, sexually harass, or bother the girls.

Teachers or other staff members hurt students (slap, pinch, push).

Teachers or other staff members curse, insult, or verbally humiliate students.

School Climate

Please indicate how you usually feel in your school. Select one of the following options:
1–Strongly disagree   2–Disagree   3–Agree   4–Strongly agree

I feel very safe and protected at this school

**My school is a safe and protected place.

**In my school there are gangs (groups of violent students who harass and bully other students).

I can trust most adults in this school.

I have close and good relationships with my teachers.

When students have an emergency (or a serious problem), an adult is always there to help.

My teachers are fair.

I am comfortable talking to teachers when I have a problem.

**Teachers in my school are nice to students.

*My teachers respect me.

When students break the rules, they are treated firmly but fairly.

It pays to obey the rules at my school.

The rules at my school are fair.

Teachers do a good job of protecting students from troublemakers.

In my school there are clear and known rules against violence.

*When I complain about somebody hurting me, the teachers help me.

*In my school there are clear and known rules against sexual harassment.

*When boys sexually harass the girls, the teachers interfere in order to stop it.

*In my school the teachers are afraid of the violent children.

*In my school staff disregard the student representatives.

*In my school students play a significant role in taking care of violence problems.

*Staff in my school make efforts to involve students in important decisions.

In my school students participate in making important decisions and in making the rules.

Victimization by Staff

In this section, we ask you about behaviors of school staff (teachers, principal, secretaries, janitors, etc.). We are asking you about what really happened to you, and not what you have heard about others.

For each of the following behaviors, please tell us:

Did it happen to you in the prior month in school?

If it did happen, who did this to you (1–a teacher/principal; 2–other staff)? You may mark both.

A staff member:

Seized and shoved you on purpose.

Kicked or punched you.

Pinched or slapped you.

Mocked, insulted, or humiliated you.

Cursed you.

*Made sexual comments to you.

*Touched or tried to touch you (in a sexual manner).

*Tried to come on to you (sexually).

Severity of the School Violence Problem

What is the magnitude of the school violence problem in your school?

A very small problem or not a problem at all.

A small problem.

A medium-level problem.

A large problem.

A very large problem.

Missing School Due to Fear

How many times did you skip school because you were afraid that someone would hurt you on the way to or from school or at school?

0–Never.

1–Once.

2–Twice.

3–More than twice.

Bringing Weapons to School*

Did you bring a weapon to school?

1–No.

2–Yes. Which? (mark all that apply)

Firearms (like a gun).

Switchblade knife, knife, razor blade.

Brass knuckles, bat, club.

Stick, board, rock.

PRINCIPALS' QUESTIONNAIRE

School Policies and Climate Relevant to School Violence

Please indicate, for each of the following claims, how well it describes your school. Use the following scale:

1–Strongly disagree   2–Disagree   3–Agree   4–Strongly agree

Most of my teachers cope well with violence.

There is a high awareness of the need for violence prevention in school.

Treating violence is an important part of the school's mission.

The teachers tend to ignore "low levels" of violence (e.g., shoves, threats, and verbal abuse).

Dealing with violence is a major priority for me.

I support teachers who deal with violence.

We tend to respond only to the more extreme and unusual violent incidents.

The school counselor helps teachers who have difficulty dealing with violence.

Most of the parents cooperate in the efforts to prevent violence.

I have all the right tools for dealing effectively with school violence.

I believe that as the school's principal I am playing an important role in reducing levels of violence in school.

The school makes a genuine effort to involve students in the prevention of violence.

I have a feeling that I spend too much of my time as a principal dealing with problems of violence.

The teachers who are out in the yard during recess actively prevent and address violence among students.

There is consistent enforcement of discipline in school.

The school's leadership functions well when dealing with violence.

Most of the teachers are afraid to break up fights between students.

A major part of school violence is due to high academic demands and pressure.

I think that the school copes well with violence.

The limitations that the Ministry of Education puts on punishments and sanctions that I can use reduces the effectiveness of our coping with violence.

The school's leadership acts to reveal and to discuss seriously the issue of school violence (doesn't "sweep the problem under the rug").

The school involves the police to an adequate degree (not too little and not too late).

There are clear school rules regarding discipline and violence, and these rules are known to teachers and to students.

I feel helpless when I am dealing with school violence.

A major part of school violence starts with "joking around."

The Ministry of Education's regulations make it hard for me to deal with school violence.

Most of the teachers choose to ignore violent acts that are not within their immediate responsibility.

Observed Risk Behaviors in School

In each of your responses, use the following scale:
1–Not at all   2–A little   3–Some   4–Quite a bit   5–Very much

To what extent do the following behaviors happen at your school?

Students get into fights.

Students drink alcohol in school.

Students destroy things (vandalism).

Students steal things from other students or teachers.

Students use drugs in school.

Students threaten or bully other students.

Student bring guns to school.

Students bring other weapons to school (such as knives, sticks).

Overall, there is a violent atmosphere in school.

Outsiders (adults) enter the campus during the school day and threaten, harass, or fight with students and staff.

There is dangerous gang activity in my school.

Teachers or other staff members come on to, sexually harass, or bother the girls.

Teachers or other staff members hurt students verbally (insult, humiliate, and curse).

Teachers or other staff members hurt students physically (slap, pinch, push).

Severity of the School Violence Problem

What is the magnitude of the school violence problem in your school?

A very small problem or not a problem at all.

A small problem.

A medium-level problem.

A large problem.

A very large problem.

Violent Behaviors in School

We wish to know about violent behavior in your school during the prior month. Please consider events that happened in school, on the way to school, during recess, or during classes. For each of the following, please estimate the number of times it happened during the prior month. Please use the following scale:

$$0 \quad 1 \quad 2 \quad 3–5 \quad 6+$$

Youth who don't belong to school entered the school and threatened or hit someone.

A student punched, kicked, or bit a teacher.

A student cut or wounded a teacher.

A student threatened another student or teacher with a knife.

A student threatened another student or teacher with a gun.

A student threatened a teacher with a chair, rock, or other object.

A student intentionally cut another student with a knife or a sharp instrument.

A student came to school with a gun.

A student blackmailed another student.

A student insulted or humiliated another student (verbally).

Gang members threatened and pressured a student.

A teacher slapped, pinched, or shoved a student.

A teacher insulted, cursed, or humiliated a student (verbally).

A student got hurt during a fight and needed medical attention.

Students threatened other students on the way to or from school.

There was a conflict between students from different ethnic groups.

Insulting sexual rumors about a student were spread in school.

The police got involved due to thefts or acts of vandalism.

A group of students jumped on a student and hurt him or her.

A student tried to kiss another student against his or her will.

A student was suspended for more than a day due to violent behavior.

A student was sexually assaulted by another student.

A group of students ostracized (socially isolated) a student.

The police got involved because a student was hurt.

A parent attacked a student in school.

A parent attacked a staff member in school.

A parent threatened a staff member in school.

There was a conflict between immigrant students and Israeli-born students or between religious and nonreligious students.

A student touched (or tried to touch) another student in a sexual manner.

Training, Programs, and Educational Projects Relevant to School Violence

A. Did you ever attend a training that addresses the prevention and treatment of school violence?
   1. No (move on to question H).
   2. Yes.
B. Please name the training: _____
C. When did it take place?
   1. During this school year.
   2. ____ years ago.
D. Total number of academic hours spent on training: __
E. Where was it held?
   1. In school.
   2. Out of school.
F. Who was the target of the training?
   1. The school as a whole.
   2. School principals.
G. Please evaluate the training using the following scale:
   1–Strongly disagree   2–Disagree   3–Agree   4–Strongly agree

   1. The course taught me relevant knowledge.
   2. The course fit my needs.
   3. The course contributed to my ability to deal with violence.

4. I recommend that course to other principals.
Further comments: _____
_____
_____

H. Did you have enough training on school violence during your formal training in college or at the university?
1. Didn't receive any training at all.
2. Got insufficient training.
3. Got sufficient training.
I. Do you think you need to have training in this area?
1. Not at all.
2. Somewhat.
3. Very much.
J. Do you think your teachers need to have training in this area?
1. Not at all.
2. Somewhat.
3. Very much.
K. What, in your opinion, is the most important issue that needs to be addressed in such training?

Interventions

A. Did your school have any educational programs or projects on school violence during the past two years?
1. No (move on to question G).
2. Yes.
B. Please name the program: _____
If more than one program took place, please indicate the most important one. _____
C. When did it take place?
1. This school year.
2. In the previous school year.
3. Two years ago.
D. Who delivered the program in school?
1. Teachers.
2. The school's counselor.
3. Someone else from within the school.
4. A combination of the above.
E. Who participated in the program?
1. The entire school.
2. A single grade.
3. A few classes.

F. Please evaluate the program/project using the following scale:
   1–Strongly disagree   2–Disagree   3–Agree   4–Strongly agree

   1. The program suited the students' needs.
   2. The program emphasized relevant issues and skills.
   3. The program contributed to reduction in violence.
   4. I recommend using the program.
   Further comments: _____
   _____
   _____

Prevention of School Violence

Please circle each of the activities in which you have participated during the past year:

1. You were part of a community group formed to deal with community violence.
2. You organized a staff team to prevent/deal with school violence.
3. You appointed a teacher or a vice principal to enforce discipline.
4. You worked with the students' representatives or with another group of students on promoting nonviolent behavior.
5. You prepared or helped to prepare a schoolwide program to address the issue of school violence.

We wish to learn about your activities designed to prevent or deal with violence in your school. For each of the following actions, please indicate how many times you carried out this activity in your school during this school year. Please use the following scale:
   1–Not at all   2–Once or twice   3–Three times or more

Prevention:

You brought up the subject of violence in front of the parents.

You consulted the school psychologist or counselor on how to prevent violence.

You held an educational program in school that dealt directly with the subject of violent behavior in school.

You asked for additional resources to deal with school violence.

You spoke to the PTA on how to handle school violence.

You spoke in front of a group of students on the subject of school violence.

You took training that dealt directly with violence prevention.

You consulted the school's supervisor on how to prevent violence.

You consulted the teachers on how to prevent violence.

Responses to a violent incident:

You organized or helped organize educational activities or discussions due to a violent event in school.

You spoke in front of a group of students on the subject of school violence.

You spoke to a student about his or her violent behavior.

You made sure the police got involved due to a student's violent behavior.

You suspended a violent student.

You directed, guided, and consulted with a teacher on how to deal with violence in his or her class.

You invited parents for a discussion of their child's involvement in school violence.

You called the police due to a parent's violent behavior.

You punished a student for his or her violent behavior.

You made students fix or buy equipment and furniture that they vandalized.

You wrote to a student's parents or talked to them on the phone due to their child's violent behavior.

You made sure that a member of your school staff who harmed students would be removed from your school.

You punished a whole class due to a violent event.

You worked with the students' representatives or with another group of students to respond effectively to the violent event.

You made sure that a violent student would be transferred from your school.

Were there other preventive actions or coping strategies that you used? _____
_____
_____

Relationships with Others

In this part, we ask you to evaluate you relationship with others who might be relevant to dealing with school violence. Please use the following scale:

1–Not at all   2–A little   3–Some   4–Quite a bit   5–Very much

PTA (or other group of parents):

1. Are involved in dealing with violence in my school.
2. Show willingness and effort to help me cope.
3. Put additional unnecessary pressure on me.
4. Make a significant contribution to effective coping with violence.

Support staff (counselors and psychologists):

1. Have adequate knowledge and skills to help.
2. Invest the time necessary to address the issue.
3. Cooperate with me on this issue.
4. Initiate educational activities and programs in this area.
5. Make a significant contribution to effective coping with violence.

Local district supervisor(s):

1. Show willingness and effort to help me cope.
2. Provide the necessary resources.
3. Understand the educational needs of the school.
4. Make a significant contribution to effective coping with violence.

Supervisors from the Ministry of Education:

1. Provide the necessary resources.
2. Provide knowledge and skills that I use to deal with violence.
3. Recognize the importance of the issue.
4. Back me up adequately.
5. Understand the educational needs of the school.
6. Put additional unnecessary pressure on me.
7. Damage my educational authority as a principal.
8. Make a significant contribution to effective coping with violence.

Police:

1. Put additional unnecessary pressure on me.
2. Respond effectively to my requests.
3. Understand the educational needs of the school.
4. Damage my educational authority as a principal.
5. Make a significant contribution to effective coping with violence.

Needs

One of the important goals of this study is to identify the needs of principals in dealing with school violence. Please specify your needs regarding prevention of school violence in the following areas.

Staff/personnel:

Training, guidance, information, knowledge, programs:

Other resources:

Authority and autonomy:

Cooperation with support staff (counselors, psychologists):

Cooperation with district supervisors:

Cooperation with supervisors from the Ministry of Education:

Cooperation with the community, including police and local municipality:

Other needs:

Demographics

For the purpose of this study, we need a few details about you and your school. We remind you again that all our analyses are aggregated so that your responses are kept confidential. Please do not write your name on this form.

Gender:
  1. Female
  2. Male
Did you/do you work in special education?
  1. Yes
  2. No
Number of years as a teacher:
  1. Up to a year
  2. 2–3
  3. 4–5
  4. 6–10
  5. 11–20
  6. More than 20
Number of years as a principal:
  1. Up to a year
  2. 2–3
  3. 4–5

4. 6–10
5. 11–20
6. More than 20

Number of years as a principal in this school:
1. Up to a year
2. 2–3
3. 4–5
4. 6–10
5. 11–20
6. More than 20

Degree:
1. College/teaching seminar
2. B.Ed.
3. B.A.
4. M.A.
5. Religious education
6. Other

Dear teacher,

Dealing with the problem of violence is one of the important missions of the education system. We wish to hear about your experiences, thoughts, and ideas in this matter and especially about your suggestions regarding ways that you think we could and should prevent violence in school and treat it when it exists.

We are very interested in what you think!

Characteristics of the School

Number of classes in school: _____

Number of students who study in school this year: _____

Number of teachers who work part time or more:_____

Number of teachers with a bachelor's degree _____ a master's degree_____ a Ph.D._____

What is the yearly turnover rate (percentage of teachers who leave each year)?

What is the percentage of students whose parents immigrated to Israel from the former Soviet Union in the past 10 years?

What is the percentage of students whose parents immigrated to Israel from Ethiopia in the past 10 years?

In your estimate, what is the percentage of students in your school whose family income is below the poverty line?

School Structure

Elementary (first through sixth grade).

Elementary (first through eighth grade).

Junior high.

Junior and senior high.

Senior high school.

Gender composition of school

Boys and girls study together in mixed classes.

Boys and girls study in separate classes.

Boys only.

Girls only.

Please add any additional details about the school that you think are relevant.

HOMEROOM TEACHERS' QUESTIONNAIRE

Observed Risk Behaviors in School

In each of your responses, use the following scale:
1–Not at all   2–A little   3–Some   4–Quite a bit   5–Very much

To what extent do the following behaviors happen at your school?

Students get into fights.

Students drink alcohol in school.

Students destroy things (vandalism).

Students steal things from other students or teachers.

Students use drugs in school.

Students threaten or bully other students.

Students bring guns to school.

Students bring other weapons to school (such as knives, sticks).

Overall, there is a violent atmosphere in school.

Outsiders (adults) enter the campus during the school day and threaten, harass, or fight with students and staff.

There is dangerous gang activity in my school.

Teachers or other staff members come on to, sexually harass, or bother the girls.

Teachers or other staff members hurt students verbally (insult, humiliate, and curse).

Teachers or other staff members hurt students physically (slap, pinch, push).

Severity of the School Violence Problem

What is the magnitude of the school violence problem in your school?

A very small problem or not a problem at all,

A small problem.

A medium-level problem.

A large problem.

A very large problem.

Violent Behaviors in School

We want to know about violent behaviors among students in your class in the prior month. Please consider events that happened in school, on the way to school, during recess, or during classes. For each of the following, please estimate the number of times one of your students was involved in such an event during the past month. Use the following scale:

0   1   2   3–5   6+

Students jumped on a student and hurt him or her.

Students ostracized (socially isolated) a student.

A student was sexually harassed by another student.

A student was sexually assaulted by another student.

A student blackmailed another student.

A student came to school with a gun.

A student forcefully took things from another student.

A student got hurt during a fight and needed medical attention.

A student intentionally cut another student with a knife or a sharp instrument.

A student kicked or punched another student in order to hurt him or her.

A student mocked, insulted, or humiliated another student (verbally).

A student punched, kicked, or bit a teacher.

A student stole personal belongings or equipment from another student.

A student threatened another student with a gun.

A student threatened another student with a knife.

A student threatened to hurt or hit another student.

A student touched (or tried to touch) another student in a sexual manner.

A student tried to kiss another student against his or her will.

A student used a rock or another object in order to hurt another student.

Gang members threatened and pressured a student.

Insulting sexual rumors about a student were spread in school.

Students threatened other students on the way to or from school.

There was a conflict between immigrant students and Israeli-born students.

There was a conflict between students from different ethnic groups.

Please estimate how many of the violent acts done by your students are known to you.

I think I know about all or almost all of the violent acts.

I think I know about the majority of them.

I think I know about a small number of them.

I think I don't know about the violent acts in which the students in my class are involved.

Violence against Teachers

This section investigates violent acts by students against teachers in the prior month. For each of the following please indicate:

Did it happen to you?

Did it happen to other teachers in school?

Please use the following scale:
1–Not at all   2–Once or twice   3–Three times or more

A student cursed a teacher.

A student intentionally shoved a teacher.

A student threatened to hurt a teacher.

A student punched, hit, kicked, or bit a teacher.

A student cut a teacher with a sharp object.

A student threatened a teacher with a knife.

A student threatened a teacher with a gun.

A student hurt a teacher with a chair, rock, or other object.

A student made sexual comments to a teacher or came on to him or her sexually.

A student stole things from a teacher.

A student destroyed personal belongings of a teacher.

If you were physically attacked or verbally threatened, who was the perpetrator?

Don't know who it is.

A student.

A student's parent or other family member.

A stranger who doesn't belong in school.

A member of a youth gang.

A teacher from the school.

Another staff member.

Someone else (who?).

How worried are you about your personal safety in school?

1. Not at all.
2. A little.
3. Very much.

Did you ever think of quitting your profession due to the problem of school violence?

I've never thought about quitting my profession.

Rarely, once a year, or less often than that.

The thought of quitting my profession crosses my mind often.

I intend to leave this school due to the problem of violence.

During this academic year, have you taken any of the following measures to protect yourself against violence in school? (circle all the apply)

You stayed with a group of teachers in order to increase your personal safety.

You left money and valuables at home so they wouldn't be stolen.

You avoided coming to school events after school hours or avoided staying alone in school after hours.

You stayed at home.

You stayed in the teachers' lounge until certain students left the building.

You avoided interfering in a fight between students so that you would not get hurt.

You turned to the police.

You brought a whistle, a horn, or pepper spray to school.

You brought other items that could be used for self-defense (what?).

Other (specify).

What do you think are the three major factors that have the largest impact on the reduction and prevention of school violence, and the three factors that contribute most to increase in school violence?

Additional comments: _____
_____
_____

Training, Programs, and Educational Projects Relevant to School Violence

    A. Did you ever attend a training that addresses the prevention of school violence?
       1. No (move on to question H)
       2. Yes
    B. Please name the training: _____
    C. When did it take place?
       1. During this school year.
       2. __ years ago.
    D. Total number of academic hours: __
    E. Where was it held?
       1. In school.
       2. Out of school.
    F. Who was the target for the training?
       1. The school as a whole.
       2. A substantial number of teachers from my school attended.
       3. Only I, or a small number of teachers from school, attended.

G. If you did take part in such a training course, please evaluate it using the following scale:

1–Strongly disagree   2–Disagree   3–Agree   4–Strongly agree

1. The course taught me relevant knowledge.
2. The course fit my needs.
3. The course contributed to my ability to deal with violence.
4. I recommend that course to other teachers.

Further comments: _____

_____

_____

H. Did your class participate in any educational program/project on the subject of school violence?
1. No (move on to the next section)
2. Yes
I. Please name the program/project:
J. When was it held?
1. During this school year.
2. Last year.
3. Earlier.
K. Who conducted the program in school?
1. Teachers.
2. The school's counselor.
3. Someone else from within the school.
4. A combination of the above.
L. Please evaluate the program/project using the following scale:

1–Strongly disagree   2–Disagree   3–Agree   4–Strongly agree

1. The program suited the students' needs.
2. The program emphasized relevant issues and skills.
3. The program contributed to a reduction in class violence.
4. I recommend using the program.

Further comments: _____

_____

_____

Prevention of School Violence

We wish to learn about your activities to prevent or deal with violence in your class. For each of the following actions, please indicate how many times you carried out this activity in your class during this school year. Please use the following scale:

1–Not at all   2–Once or twice   3–Three times or more

Prevention

1. You held an educational program in the classroom that dealt directly with the subject of violent behavior in school.
2. You consulted with the school management on how to prevent violence in the classroom.
3. You consulted with the school psychologist on how to prevent violence in the classroom.
4. You consulted with the school counselor on how to prevent violence in the classroom.
5. You ran educational activities and class discussions on the issue.
6. You worked with students' representatives or a group of students from the class on this subject.
7. You brought up the subject of violence in front of the parents.

Responses to a violent incident:

1. You talked with a student about his or her violent behavior.
2. You punished a student for his or her violent behavior.
3. You punished the whole class due to a violent event.
4. You ran educational activities or discussions in class due to a violent event.
5. You sent a student to the principal.
6. You wrote to a student's parents or talked to them on the phone due to the student's violent behavior.
7. You invited a student's parents to come in for a discussion of their child's violent behavior.
8. You made sure that a student from your class would be suspended from school due to his or her violent behavior.
9. You consulted the counselor.
10. You consulted the principal and the management team.
11. You consulted the psychologist.
12. You made sure the police got involved.

Training and Support

A. Did you have enough training on school violence during your formal training in college or at the university?
  1. Didn't receive any training at all.
  2. Got insufficient training.
  3. Got sufficient training.
B. Do you think you need to have training in this area?
  1. Not at all.

2. Somewhat.

3. Very much.

C. Do you feel you get enough help, support, and guidance when you have difficulties in dealing with school violence?

1. I don't have any difficulties, I don't need help.

2. I don't receive any help.

3. I receive little help.

4. I receive sufficient help.

School Policies and Climate Relevant to School Violence

Please indicate, for each of the following claims, how well it describes your school. Use the following scale:

1–Strongly disagree   2–Disagree   3–Agree   4–Strongly agree

Most of the teachers cope well with violence.

There is a high awareness of the need for violence prevention in school.

Preventing violence is an important part of the school's mission.

The PTA is involved in attempts to prevent violence.

The teachers tend to ignore "low levels" of violence (e.g., shoves, threats, and verbal abuse).

Dealing with violence is a major priority for the principal.

The principal supports teachers who deal with violence.

We tend to respond only to the more extreme and unusual violent incidents.

The school counselor helps teachers who have difficulty dealing with violence.

Most of the parents cooperate in the efforts to prevent violence.

The principal is an educational figure who helps in reducing violence in school.

I have all the right tools for dealing effectively with school violence.

The school makes a genuine effort to involve students in the prevention of violence.

A major part of school violence is due to students' being bored.

Most of the teachers serve as educational figures who help prevent violence in school.

Most of the teachers are afraid to break up fights between students.

I have a feeling that I spend too much of my time as a teacher dealing with problems of violence.

The teachers who are out in the yard during recess actively prevent and address violence among students.

There is a consistent enforcement of discipline in school.

The school's leadership functions well when dealing with violence.

A major part of school violence is due to high academic demands and pressure.

I think that the school copes well with violence.

The school's leadership acts to reveal and to discuss seriously the issue of school violence (doesn't "sweep the problem under the rug").

The school involves the police to an adequate degree (not too little and not too late).

There are clear school rules regarding discipline and violence, and these rules are known to teachers and to students.

The school's leadership invests too much time and too many resources dealing with school violence.

I feel helpless when I am dealing with school violence.

A major part of school violence starts with "joking around."

Most of the teachers choose to ignore violent acts that are not within their immediate responsibility.

Demographics

For the purpose of this study, we need a few details about you and your school. We remind you again that all our analyses are aggregated so that your responses are kept confidential. Please do not write your name on this form.

Gender:
1. Female
2. Male

Did you/do you work in special education?
1. Yes
2. No

Number of years as a teacher:
1. Up to a year
2. 2–3
3. 4–5
4. 6–10

5. 11–20

6. More than 20

Number of years as a teacher in this school:

1. Up to a year

2. 2–3

3. 4–5

4. 6–10

5. 11–20

6. More than 20

Degree:

1. College/teaching seminar

2. B.Ed.

3. B.A.

4. M.A.

5. Religious education

6. Other

Role in the school (mark all relevant):

1. Teacher

2. Homeroom teacher

3. Grade-level coordinator

4. Principal

5. Other

NOTES

1. The original format of the Hebrew version is not maintained in this translation.

*Included in Primary School Version only.

**Included in Secondary School Version only.

Appendix 2

Details of the Structural Equation Analyses

The reported analyses were performed using variance-covariance matrices with pairwise deletion of missing values. Two alternative methods of dealing with missing values were used: listwise deletion and estimation using expectation-maximization method. All three methods yielded very similar results.

In the analyses, three indicators per latent construct were used, unless a construct was indicated by a single item. In the latter cases, the measurement error of a single indicator was provided to the program, assuming reliability of 0.80. In cases of multiple indicators, using the accepted approach of parceling (Bandalos, 2002; Stacy, Bentler, & Flay, 1994), each latent variable was indicated by one third of the items that make up the scale. Item parcels were constructed so that their kurtosis statistic would be minimized. To achieve this, items with largest kurtosis were combined with items with smallest kurtosis, and so on. In spite of these, many of the observed variables were nonnormally distributed due to the nature of the phenomena under investigation (victimization). To overcome this violation of SEM assumptions, we employed a maximum-likelihood estimation method with robust standard errors (Hu & Bentler, 1999) together with the Satorra-Bentler rescaled chi-square statistic (Satorra & Bentler, 1994, 1999). This statistic compensates for multivariate nonnormality of variables. Difference between two *scaled* chi-squares doesn't distribute as chi-square. Therefore, in computing significance of differences between models, we used the Satorra-Bentler scaled difference test (Satorra & Bentler, 1999).

Following recommendations of Hu and Bentler (1999), we report fit indexes of two types: Non-Normed Fit Index (NNFI, also known as TLI) and Comparative Fit Index (CFI), and two indexes of misfit: Root Mean-Square Error of Approximation (RMSEA) and Standardized Root Mean-Square Residual (SRMR). NNFI and CFI close to or above 0.95 combined with RMSEA below 0.07 and SRMSR below 0.09 are considered indicative of acceptable fit.

The model presented in this chapter tested two types of hypotheses: direct effects of independent on dependent variables and mediated effects. Following Kenny, Kashy, and Bolger (1998, p. 10), we considered two pieces of evidence as compatible with a mediation hypothesis: (1) a significant correlation between an independent variable and a mediator, and (2) a significant indirect effect of the independent on the dependent variable.

Following the test of a model for the whole sample, we proceeded to testing differences between subgroups, such as male students versus female. The multigroup analysis is done in several steps. First, all factor loadings, paths, and covariances are constrained to be equal in two groups, and we tested the hypothesis that the same model is valid for both groups. Second, selected constraints on paths are released one at a time to test whether the model fit could be improved by postulating differences in paths between groups. The constraints to release were selected by inspection of paths in a multigroup model where they were unconstrained. Those paths were selected for testing for which standardized coefficients were different by at least 0.10 in two groups. It should be noted that in SEM, difference between paths in two groups is tested using unstandardized coefficients. A difference of 0.10 in standardized values could be insignificant, while a much smaller difference could be significant. We preferred this approach to ensure that only meaningful differences were chosen as candidates for analysis. After each of the differences were tested one by one, we tested a model in which all paths with significant differences between groups were left unconstrained for equality and assessed improvement in fit over the fully constrained model.

JUNIOR HIGH AND HIGH SCHOOLS

Sample

The initial sample consisted of 10,400 respondents (Rs). They came from 162 different schools, 405 classes. Those respondents who had more than five missing values on 26 observed variables used in the analysis (see below) were deleted from the database. The resulting file had 10,150 respondents. All analyses were performed on data with pairwise deletion of missing data.

Measures

BACKGROUND DATA
Four dummy variables were constructed:

1. School type, distinguishing between junior high (marked 1) and high school students.

2. Religious-nonreligious, comparing between religious Jewish (1) and other students.
3. Culture/ethnicity: Arab schools' students received value 1 on this variable.
4. Gender (with value 1 assigned to boys).

RISKY PEER GROUP BEHAVIOR

Using a scale with 14 items measured on a 1–5 scale (5 meaning high level of risk), a factor analysis performed on these items showed that the first factor was responsible for most of the variance (Eigenvalue of 6.10) and the next ones were much weaker (Eigenvalues 1.31, 1.11). In principal components, all items were heavily loaded on the first factor. Consequently, we treated the items as constituting one scale. Preliminary tests of the measurement model showed that the two items with the smallest distribution (3 and 4) reduced the internal consistency of the measurement; they were deleted from the analysis. The alpha of the overall risk scale was 0.89.

RIS1 Students get into fights.

RIS2 Students drink alcoholic drinks (like wine, beer).

RIS5 Students bring other weapons to school (such as knives, clubs).

RIS6 Students destroy things in schools, put graffiti on walls, damage furniture.

RIS7 Students steal things from other students or teachers.

RIS8 Students threaten or bully other students.

RIS9 There is dangerous gang activity in my school.

RIS10 The boys sexually harass the girls (make obscene suggestions, touch, peep).

RIS11 Outsiders (adults) enter the campus during the school day and threaten, harass, or get into fights with students or teachers.

RIS12 Teachers or other staff members curse, insult, or verbally humiliate students.

RIS13 Teachers or other staff members hurt students (slap, pinch, push).

RIS14 Teachers or other staff members "come on to" the girls, sexually harass, or bother them.

CLIMATE

Using a scale with 21 items with 1–4 response scale (4 meaning positive climate), factor analysis showed that all of these items could be best explained by one factor (Eigenvalue 9.20, with the next factors of 1.29 and 1.08 only). Nevertheless, we decided to use our theory-based categorization of the items and constructed three indicators. Three negatively worded items (10, 14 and 15) were unrelated to the others in item analysis and they were deleted. The overall alpha of the remaining 18 items was 0.94. Three indicators were formed in the following way:

I. Policy

CLIM1   When students break the rules, they are treated firmly but fairly.

CLIM2   My teachers are fair.

CLIM3   It pays to obey the rules at my school.

CLIM4   The rules at my school are fair.

CLIM5   Teachers do a good job of protecting students from troublemakers.

CLIM6   When I complain about somebody hurting me the teachers help me.

CLIM7   In my school there are clear and known rules against violence.

CLIM8   In my school there are clear and known rules against sexual harassment.

CLIM9   When boys sexually harass girls, the teachers interfere in order to stop it.

II. Participation

CLIM11   In my school, students participate in making important decisions and in making the rules.

CLIM12   In my school students play a significant role in taking care of violence problems.

CLIM13   Staff in my school make efforts to involve students in important decisions.

III. Teacher support

CLIM16   When students have an emergency (or a serious problem), an adult is always there to help.

CLIM17   My teachers respect me.

CLIM18   I can trust most adults in this school.

CLIM19   I have close and good relationships with my teachers.

CLIM20   Teachers in this school care for the students.

CLIM21   I am comfortable talking to teachers when I have a problem.

STAFF RESPONSE TO VIOLENCE

Staff response was measured with a single item: Overall, in your opinion, how are the principal and teaching staff dealing with violence when it occurs in your school? This item was measured on a 1–4 scale. It was reverse-coded so that 4 meant effective coping.

VICTIMIZATION BY STAFF

This scale consisted of eight yes-no items:

STF1 Seized and shoved you on purpose.

STF2 Kicked or punched you.

STF3 Pinched or slapped you.

STF4 Mocked, insulted, or humiliated you.

STF5 Made sexual comments to you.

STF6 Tried to come on to you (sexually).

STF7 Cursed you.

STF8 Touched or tried to touch you sexually.

The items were recoded as 1 (yes) and 0 (no). In cases where a respondent referred to at least one item in the scale, meaning that he or she read the item and responded, the missing values in the rest of the items were turned to 0 (assuming that a blank means no). The alpha of the entire scale was 0.80.

STUDENT-INITIATED VICTIMIZATION

Mild/Moderate Victimization
This subscale of the victimization scale consisted of all of the nine items that were identified as mild/moderate aggressive behaviors in the exploratory factor analysis:

RAGR2 A student used a rock or another instrument in order to hurt you.

RAGR9 A student threatened to harm or hit you.

RAGR11 You were involved in a fistfight.

RAGR12 You were kicked or punched by a student who wanted to hurt you.

RAGR15 A student seized and shoved you on purpose.

RAGR18 A student tried to intimidate you by the way he or she was looking at you.

RAGR19 A student cursed you.

RAGR20 A student mocked, insulted, or humiliated you.

RAGR23 A student stole your personal belongings or equipment.

These items were recoded as 1 (at least once) and 0 (no). In cases where there were missing values in some, but not other, items in the scale, they were converted to 0. The alpha of the total scale was 0.82.

Severe Victimization
This subscale of the victimization scale consisted of nine items identified as severe behaviors in the exploratory factor analysis:

RAGR1 A student cut you with a knife or a sharp instrument on purpose.

RAGR3 You were blackmailed under threats by another student (for money, valuables, or food).

RAGR7 A student threatened you with a gun and you saw the gun.

RAGR8 A student threatened you with a knife and you saw the knife.

RAGR10 Gang members at school threatened, harassed, and pressured you.

RAGR13 A student gave you a serious beating.

RAGR14 You were involved in a fight, were hurt, and required medical attention.

RAGR17 You saw a student in school with a gun.

RAGR24 Students threatened you on your way to or from school.

These items were recoded as 1 (at least once) and 0 (no). In cases in which there were missing values in some, but not other, items in this scale, they were converted to 0. In a preliminary analysis of the measurement, item 8 was found to reduce the internal consistency and was removed. The alpha of the total scale with the remaining eight items was 0.83.

Sexual Harassment
These behaviors were assessed with seven yes-no items, recoded as 1 (at least once) or 0 (no):

SEX1 A student tried to kiss you without your consent.

SEX2 Sexually insulting things about you were written on walls or sexual rumors were spread about you.

SEX3 A student peeped while you were in the bathroom or the locker room.

SEX4 A student touched or tried to touch you or to pinch you in a sexual way without your approval.

SEX5 A student tried to come on to you (sexually) and made sexual comments that you did not want.

SEX6 A student took or tried to take your clothes off (for sexual reasons).

SEX7 A student showed you obscene pictures or sent you obscene letters.

Missing values were treated as described above. Alpha was 0.80.

SEVERITY OF THE VIOLENCE PROBLEM
Severity of student victimization at school was measured with a single item: What is the magnitude of the school violence problem in your school? The 1–5 response scale was coded so that high values meant high severity.

NONATTENDANCE DUE TO FEAR

This subject was measured with a single item: Have you stayed at home because you were afraid that someone may hurt you? The scale was 0 = no, 1= once, 2 = twice, 3 = more.

FEELING SAFE AT SCHOOL

We measured this subject with a single item: I feel very safe and protected at this school. The 1–4 response scale was reversed-coded, so that high values meant low level of feeling safe.

PRIMARY SCHOOLS

Sample and Measures

The initial sample consisted of 6,013 respondents. They came from 77 different schools, with three grades (4 through 6) sampled in each school.

Those respondents who had more than three missing values on 22 observed variables used in the analysis were deleted from the database. The resulting file had 5,675 respondents. All analyses were performed on data with pairwise deletion of missing data.

The indicators were constructed in ways similar to the ones described for the secondary schools.

References

Abramov, T. (2003). *Multiple perspectives on school violence: Principals, teachers and pupils* (in Hebrew). Unpublished master's thesis, Department of Psychology, Hebrew University of Jerusalem.

Adams, T. A. (2000). The status of school discipline and violence. *Annals of the American Academy of Political and Social Science, 567,* 140–156.

Ahmad, Y., & Smith, P. K. (1994). Bullying in schools and the issue of sex differences. In J. Archer (Ed.), Male violence (pp. 70–83). New York: Routledge.

Akibba, M., Le Tendre, G. K., Baker, D. P., & Goesling, B. (2002). Student victimization: National and school systems effects on school violence in 37 nations. *American Educational Research Journal, 39*(4), 829–853.

Allen-Meares, P. (2004). An ecological perspective of social work services in schools. In P. Allen-Meares (Ed.), *Social work services in schools* (4th ed., pp. 71–94). Boston: Pearson.

Allen-Meares, P., & Fraser, M. W. (2004). Introduction. In P. Allen-Meares & M. W. Fraser (Eds.), *Intervention with children and adolescents: An interdisciplinary perspective* (pp. 1–8). Boston: Pearson.

American Association of University Women (AAUW). (1993). *Hostile hallways: The AAUW survey on sexual harassment in America's schools* (Research Report 923012). Washington, DC: Harris/Scholastic Research.

American Association of University Women (AAUW). (2001). *Hostile hallways: Bullying, teasing, and sexual harassment.* Washington, DC: Author.

American Psychological Association Commission on Violence and Youth. (1993). *Violence and youth: Psychology's response. Summary report of the APA Commission on Violence and Youth.* Washington, DC: Author.

Anderson, M., Kaufman, J., Simon, T. R., Barrios, L., Paulozzi, L., Ryan, et al. (2001). School-associated violent deaths in the United States, 1994–1999. *JAMA: Journal of the American Medical Association, 286* (21), 2695–2702.

Astor, R. A. (1998). Moral reasoning about school violence: Informational assumptions about harm within school subcontexts. *Educational Psychologist, 33,* 207–221.

Astor, R. A., Benbenishty, R., Haj-Yahia, M., Zeira, A., Perkins-Hart, S., Marachi, R., et al. (2002). The awareness of risky peer group behaviors on school grounds as predictors of students' victimization on school grounds: Part II—Junior high schools. *Journal of School Violence, 1* (3), 57–66.

Astor, R. A., Benbenishty, R., Marachi, R., Haj-Yahia, M., Zeira, A., Perkins-Hart, S., et al. (2002). The awareness of risky peer group behaviors on school grounds as predictors of students' victimization on school grounds: Part I—Elementary schools. *Journal of School Violence, 1* (1), 11–33.

Astor, R. A., Benbenishty, R., Pitner, R., & Zeira, A. (2004). Bullying and peer victimization in schools. In P. A. Meares & M. W. Fraser (Eds.), *Intervention with children and adolescents: An interdisciplinary perspective* (pp. 471–448). Boston: Pearson.

Astor, R. A., Benbenishty, R., Zeira, A., & Vinokur, A. (2002). School climate, observed risk behaviors, and victimization as predictors of high school students' fear and judgments of school violence as a problem. *Health Education and Behavior, 29* (6), 716–736.

Astor, R. A., & Meyer, H. A. (1999). Where girls and women won't go: Female students', teachers', and social workers' views of school safety. *Social Work in Education, 21,* 201–219.

Astor, R. A., & Meyer, H. A. (2001). The conceptualization of violence-prone school sub-contexts: Is the sum of the parts greater than the whole? *Urban Education, 36,* 374–399.

Astor, R. A., Meyer, H. A., & Behre, W. J. (1999). Unowned places and times: Maps and interviews about violence in high schools. *American Educational Research Journal, 36,* 3–42.

Astor, R. A., Meyer, H. A., & Pitner, R. O. (2001). Elementary and middle school students' perceptions of safety: An examination of violence-prone school sub-contexts. *The Elementary School Journal, 101,* 511–528.

Astor, R. A., Pitner, R. O., Benbenishty, R. & Meyer, H. A. (2002). Public concern and focus on school violence. In L. A. Rapp-Paglicci, A. R. Roberts, & J. S. Wodarski (Eds.), *Handbook of violence* (pp. 262–302). New York: Wiley.

Astor, R. A., Vargas, L. A., Pitner, R. O, & Meyer, H. A. (1999). School violence: Research, theory, and practice. In J. M. Jenson & M. O. Howard (Eds.), *Youth violence: Current research and recent practice innovations* (pp. 139–172). Washington, DC: NASW Press.

Attar, B. K., Guerra, N. G., & Tolan, P. H. (1994). Neighborhood disadvantage, stressful life events, and adjustment in urban elementary-school children. *Journal of Clinical Child Psychology, 23,* 391–400.

Bailey, S. L., Flewelling, R. L., & Rosenbaum, D. P. (1997). Characteristics of students who bring weapons to school. *Adolescent Health, 20* (4), 261–270.

Baldry, A. C., & Winkel, F. W. (2003). Direct and vicarious victimization at school and at home as risk factors for suicidal cognition among Italian adolescents. *Journal of Adolescence, 26,* 703–716.

Bandalos, D. L. (2002). Structural equation modeling: Foundations and extensions by Kaplan D. *Journal of Educational Measurement, 39* (2), 183–186.

Batsche, G. M., & Knoff, H. M. (1994). Bullies and their victims: Understanding a pervasive problem in the schools. *School Psychology Review, 23* (2), 165–174.

Behre, W. J., Astor, R. A., & Meyer, H. A. (2001). Elementary and middle school teachers' reasoning about intervening in school violence: An examination of violence-prone school sub-contexts. *Journal of Moral Education, 30,* 131–153.

Benbenishty, R. (2002). *Monitoring school violence in the city of Herzliya: A research report* (in Hebrew). Jerusalem: Hebrew University Press.

Benbenishty, R. (2003). *A national study of school violence in Israel 2002* (in Hebrew). Jerusalem: Israeli Ministry of Education.

Benbenishty, R., & Astor, R. A. (2003). Violence in schools: The view from Israel. In P. K. Smith, (Ed.), *Violence in schools: The response in Europe* (pp. 317–331). London: Routledge Falmer.

Benbenishty, R., Astor, R. A., & Zeira, A. (2003). Monitoring school violence at the site level: Linking national, district, and school-level data. *Journal of School Violence, 2* (2), 29–50.

Benbenishty, R., Astor, R. A., Zeira, A., & Vinokur, A. (2002). Perceptions of violence and fear of school attendance among junior high school students in Israel. *Social Work Research, 26* (2), 71–87.

Benbenishty, R., Zeira, A., & Astor, R. A. (2000). *A national study of school violence in Israel* (in Hebrew). Jerusalem: Israeli Ministry of Education.

Benbenishty, R., Zeira, A., & Astor, R. A. (2002). Children's reports of emotional, physical and sexual maltreatment by educational staff in Israel. *Child Abuse and Neglect, 26* (8), 763–782.

Benbenishty, R., Zeira, A., Astor, R. A., & Khoury-Kassabri, M. (2002). Maltreatment of primary school students by educational staff in Israel. *Child Abuse and Neglect, 26* (12), 1291–1309.

Benthall, J. (1991). Invisible wounds: Corporal punishment in British schools as a form of ritual. *Child Abuse and Neglect, 15,* 377–388.

Bentler, P. M. (1995). *EQS structural equation manual.* Los Angeles: BMDP Statistical Software.

Berrill, K. (1990). Anti-gay violence and victimization in the U.S.: An overview. Violence against lesbians and gay men: Issues for research, practice, and policy. [Special issue]. *Journal of Interpersonal Violence, 5,* 274–294.

Besag, V. (1989). Bullies and victims in schools: A guide to understanding and management. Philadelphia: Open University Press.

Borg, M. K. (1999). The extent and nature of bullying among primary and secondary school-children. *Educational Research, 41*(2), 137–153.

Bosworth, K., Espelage, D., & Simon, T. (1999). Factors associated with bullying behavior in middle school students. *Journal of Early Adolescence, 19,* 341–362.

Boulton, M. J. (1993). Aggressive fighting in British middle school children. *Educational Studies, 19,* 19–39.

Boulton, M. J., & Underwood, K. (1992). Bully/victim problems among middle school children. *British Journal of Educational Psychology, 18,* 117–127.

Bowen, G. L., Bowen, N. K., & Richman, J. M. (2000). School size and middle school students' perceptions of the school environment. *Social Work in Education, 22,* 69–82.

Bowen, G. L., Bowen, N. K., Richman, J. M., & Woolley, M. E. (2002). Reducing school violence: A social capacity framework. In L. A. Rapp-Paglicci, A. Roberts, & J. Wodarski (Eds.), *Handbook of violence* (pp. 303–325). New York: Wiley.

Bowers, L., Smith, P. K., & Binney, V. (1994). Perceived family relationships of bullies, victims and bully victims in middle childhood. *Journal of Social and Personal Relationships, 11*(2), 215–232.

Bragg, R. (1997, December 3). Forgiveness, after 3 die in Kentucky shooting; M. Carneal opens fire on fellow students at Heath High School in West Paducah. *New York Times,* p. A16.

Bronfenbrenner, U. (1979). Basic concepts. In U. Bronfenbrenner (Ed.), *The ecology of human development* (pp. 3–15). Cambridge, MA: Harvard University Press.

Brownfield, D. (1987). Father-son relationship and violent behavior. *Deviant Behavior, 8,* 65–78.

Bryant, A. L. (1993). Hostile hallways: The AAUW survey on sexual harassment in American schools. *Journal of School Health, 63* (8), 355–357.

Bryk, A. S., & Raudenbush, S. W. (1992). *Hierarchical linear models: Applications and data analysis methods.* Newbury, CA: Sage.

Burcky, W., Reuterman, N., & Kopsky, S. (1988). Dating violence among high school students. *School Counselor, 35,* 353–358.

Cairns, R. B., & Cairns, B. D. (1991). Social cognition and social networks: A developmental perspective. In D. J. Pepler & K. H. Rubin (Eds.), *The development and treatment of childhood aggression* (pp. 249–278). Hillsdale, NJ: Lawrence Erlbaum.

Cano, A., Avery-Leaf, S., Cascardi, M., & O'Leary, K. (1998). Dating violence in two high school samples: Discriminating variables. *Journal of Primary Prevention, 18,* 431–446.

Caplan, M., Weissburg, R. P., Grober, J. S., Sivo, P. J., Grady, K., & Jacoby, C. (1992). Social competence promotion with inner city and suburban young adolescents: Effects on social adjustment and alcohol use. *Journal of Consulting and Clinical Psychology, 60,* 56–63.

Carey, T. A. (1994). Spare the rod and spoil the child: Is this a sensible justification for the use of punishment in child rearing? *Child Abuse and Neglect, 18* (12), 1005–1010.

Carnegie Council on Adolescent Development. (1993). *A matter of time: Risk and opportunity in nonschool hours.* New York: Author.

Cartland, J., Ruch-Ross, H. S., & Henry, D. B. (2003). Feeling at home in one's school: A first look at a new measure. *Adolescence, 38* (150), 305–319.

Catalano, R. F., & Hawkins, J. D. (1996). The social development model: A theory of antisocial behavior. In J. D. Hawkins (Ed.), *Delinquency and crime: Current theories* (pp. 149–197). New York: Cambridge University Press.

Centers for Disease Control and Prevention (CDC). (1996). Youth risk behavior surveillance: United States, 1995. *Morbidity and Mortality Weekly Report* (pp. 32–40). U.S. Department of Health and Human Services. Washington, DC: Author.

Centers for Disease Control and Prevention (CDC). (1998). Youth risk behavior surveillance: United States, 1997. *Morbidity and Mortality Weekly Report, 47. SS-3.* U.S. Department of Health and Human Services: Washington, DC: Author.

Centers for Disease Control and Prevention (CDC). (2000). *Youth risk behavior surveillance: United States, 1999.* Washington, DC: U.S. Department of Health and Human Services.

Chianu, E. (2000). Two deaths, one blind eye, one imprisonment: Child abuse in the guise of corporal punishment in Nigerian schools. *Child Abuse and Neglect, 24* (7), 1005–1009.

Coie, J. F., Lochman, J. E., Terry, R., & Hyman, C. (1992). Predicting early adolescent disorder from childhood aggression and peer rejection. *Journal of Consulting and Clinical Psychology, 60,* 783–792.

Colvin, G., Tobin, T., Beard, K., Hagan, S., & Sprague, J. (1998). The school bully: Assessing the problem, developing interventions and future research directions. *Journal of Behavioral Education, 8* (3), 293–319.

Comer, J. (1980). *School power.* New York: Free Press.

Corbett, K., Gentry, C. S., & Pearson, W. (1993). Sexual harassment in high-school. *Youth & Society, 25* (1), 93–103.

Costin, L. B. (1978). The dark side of child rights: Corporal punishment in the school. *Social Work in Education, 1* (1), 53–63.

Crick, N. R., & Grotpeter, J. K. (1996). Children's treatment by peers: Victims of relational and overt aggression. *Development & Psychopathology, 8* (2), 367–380.

Dawkins, J. L. (1996). Bullying, physical disability and the pediatric patient. *Developmental Medicine and Child Neurology, 38* (7), 603–612.

Debarbieux, E., Blaya, C., & Vidal, D. (2003). Tackling violence in schools: A report from France. In P. K. Smith (Ed.), *Violence in schools: The response in Europe* (pp. 17–32). London: Routledge Falmer.

de Oliveira, W. (1998). Normalcy and deviance: Youth and culture of violence in Brazil. In M. W. Watts (Ed.), *Cross-cultural perspective on youth and violence* (pp. 27–38). London: JAI Press.

Devine, J. (1996) *Maximum security: The culture of violence in inner-city schools.* Chicago: University of Chicago Press.

Devine, J., & Lawson, H. A. (2003). The complexity of school violence: Commentary from the U.S. In P. K. Smith (Ed.), *Violence in schools: The response in Europe* (pp. 332–350). London: Routledge Falmer.

DeVoe, J. F., Peter, K., Kaufman, P., Ruddy, S. A., Miller, A. K., Planty, M., et al. (2002). *Indicators of school crime and safety: 2002.* U.S. Departments of Education and Justice. NCES 2003–009/NCJ 1967653. Washington, DC.

Dietz, T. L. (2000). Disciplining children: Characteristics associated with the use of corporal punishment. *Child Abuse and Neglect, 24* (12), 1529–1542.

Ding, C. S., Nelsen, E. A., & Lassonde, C. T. (2002). Correlates of gun involvement and aggressiveness among adolescents. *Youth & Society, 34* (2), 195–213.

Dodge, K. A., Pettit, G. S., & Bates, J. E. (1994). Socialization mediators of the relation between socioeconomic status and child conduct problems. *Child Development, 65,* 649–665.

Doe, S. S. (2000). Cultural factors in child maltreatment and domestic violence in Korea. *Children and Youth Service Review, 22* (3–4), 231–236.

Duncan, G. J., & Raudenbush, S. W. (1999). Assessing the effects of context in studies of child and youth development. *Educational Psychologist, 34* (1), 29–41.

DuRant, R. H., Getts, A. G., Cadenhead, C., & Woods, E. R. (1995). The association between weapon-carrying and the use of violence among adolescents living in or around public housing. *Journal of Adolescence, 18,* 579–592.

DuRant, R. H., Krowchuk, D. P., Kreiter, S., Sinal, S. H., & Woods, C. R. (1999). Weapon carrying on school property among middle school students. *Archives of Pediatrics & Adolescent Medicine, 153* (1), 21–26.

Dwyer, K. P., Osher, D., & Hoffman, C. C. (2000). Creating responsive schools: Contextualizing early warning, timely response. *Exceptional Children, 66,* 347–365.

Dwyer, K. P., Osher, D., & Warger, C. (1998). *Early warning, timely response: A guide to safe schools.* Washington, DC: U.S. Department of Education.

Earls, F. (1991). Not fear, nor quarantine but science: Preparation for a debate of research to advance knowledge about causes and control of violence in youths. *Journal of Adolescent Health, 12,* 619–629.

Elbedour, S., Center, B. A., Maruyama, G. M., & Assor, A. (1997). Physical and psychological maltreatment in schools: The abusive behaviors of teachers in Bedouin schools in Israel. *School Psychology International, 18* (3), 201–215.

Ellinger, R., & Beckham, G. M. (1997). South Korea: Placing education on top of the family agenda. *Phi Delta Kappan, 78,* 624–625.

Everett, S. A., & Price, J. H. (1995). Students' perceptions of violence in the public schools: The MetLife Survey. *Journal of Adolescent Health, 17* (6), 345–352.

Farrington, D. P. (1989). Early predictors of adolescent aggression and adult violence. *Violence and Victims, 4,* 79–100.

Farrington, D. P. (1993). Understanding and preventing bullying. In M. Tonry & N. Norris (Eds.), *Crime and justice* (Vol. 17, pp. 381–458). Chicago: University of Chicago Press.

Feldman, O. (1998). Materialism and individualism: Social attitudes of youth in Japan. In M. W. Watts (Ed.), *Cross-cultural perspective on youth and violence* (pp. 9–38). London: JAI Press.

Fineran, S., & Bennett, L. (1998). Teenage peer sexual harassment: Implications for social work practice and research. *Social Work, 43* (1), 55–64.

Fizpatrick, K. M. (1997). Aggression and environmental risk among low-income African-American youth. *Journal of Adolescent Health, 21,* 172–178.

Flannery, D. J. (1997). *School violence: Risk, prevention and policy* (Urban Diversity Series No. 109). New York: Institute for Urban and Minority Education. (ERIC Document Reproduction Service No. ED416272)

Fraser, M. W. (1996). Aggressive behavior in childhood and early adolescence: An ecological-developmental perspective on youth violence. *Social Work, 41* (4), 347–361.

Furlong, M. J. (1996). Tools for assessing school violence. In S. Miller, J. Bordine, & T. Miller (Eds.), *Safe by design: Planning for peaceful school communities.* (pp. 71–84). Seattle, WA: Committee for Children.

Furlong, M. J., Bates, M. P., & Smith, D. C. (2001). Predicting school weapon possession: A secondary analysis of the Youth Risk Behavior Surveillance Survey. *Psychology in the Schools, 38* (2), 127–139.

Furlong, M. J., Casas, J. M., Corral, C., Chung, A., & Bates, M. P. (1997). Drugs and school violence. *Education and Treatment of Children, 20* (3), 263–280.

Furlong, M. J., Chung, A., Bates, M. P., & Morrison, R. L. (1995). Profiles of non-victims and multiple-victims of school violence. *Education and Treatment of Children, 18* (3), 282–298.

Furlong, M. J., Greif, J. L., Bates, M. P., Whipple, A. D., Jimenez, T. C., & Morrison, R. L. (2004). *Development of the California School Climate and Safety Survey–Short Form.* Under review.

Furlong, M. J., & Morrison, G. (2000). The school in school violence: Definitions and facts. *Journal of Emotional and Behavioral Disorders, 8* (2), 71–82.

Furlong, M. J., Morrison, R. L., Bates, M. P., & Chung, A. (1998). School violence victimization among secondary students in California. *California School Psychologist, 3,* 71–78.

Garbarino, J. (1995). The American war zone: What children can tell us about living with violence. *Journal of Developmental and Behavioral Pediatrics, 16* (6), 431–435.

Garbarino, J., & Kostelny, K. (1997). Coping with the consequences of community violence. In A. P. Goldstein, B. Harootunian, & J. C. Conoley (Eds.), *School violence intervention: A practical handbook* (pp. 3–22). New York: Guilford Press.

Garrity, C., Jens, K., Porter, W. W., Sager, N., & Short-Camilli, C. (1997). Bully proofing your school: Creating a positive climate. *Intervention in School and Clinic, 32* (4), 235–243.

Gladden, R. M. (2002). Reducing school violence: Strengthening student programs and addressing the role of school organizations. *Review of Research on Education, 26*, 263–299.

Gofin, R., Palti, H., & Gordon, L. (2002). Bullying in Jerusalem schools: Victims and perpetrators. *Public Health, 116*, 173–178.

Goldstein, A. (1994). *The ecology of aggression.* New York: Plenum Press.

Goldstein, A. (1996). *The psychology of vandalism.* New York: Plenum Press.

Gottfredson, D. C. (1990). Changing school structures to benefit high-risk youths. In P. E. Leone (Ed.), *Understanding troubled and troubling youth* (pp. 246–271). Newbury Park, CA: Sage.

Gottfredson, G. D., & Gottfredson, D. C. (1985). The community context. In G. D. Gottfredson & D. C. Gottfredson (Eds.), *Victimization in schools* (pp. 61–74). New York: Plenum Press.

Greene, J., & Caracelli, V. (1997). Defining and describing the paradigm issue in mixed-method evaluation. In J. Greene & V. Caracelli (Eds.), *Advances in mixed-methods evaluation: The challenges and benefits of integrating diverse paradigms. New directions for program evaluation* (pp. 5–17). San Francisco: Jossey Bass.

Gregory, J. F. (1995). The crime of punishment: Racial and gender disparities in the use of corporal punishment in U.S. public schools. *Journal of Negro Education, 64* (4), 454–462.

Greydanus, D. E., Pratt, H. D., Spates, C. R., Blake-Dreher, A. E., Greydanus-Gearhart, M. A., & Patel, D. R. (2003). Corporal punishment in schools: Position paper of the Society for Adolescent Medicine. *Journal of Adolescent Health, 32* (5), 385–393.

Griffith, J. (1995). An empirical examination of a model of school climate in elementary schools. *Basic and Applied Social Psychology, 17*, 97–117.

Grossman, D., Rauh, M. J., & Rivera, F. P. (1995). Prevalence of corporal punishment among students in Washington State schools. *Archives of Pediatrics and Adolescent Medicine, 149* (5), 529–532.

Groves, B. M. (1997). Growing up in a violent world: The impact of family and community violence on young children and their families. *Topics in Early Childhood Special Education, 17*, 74–102.

Guerra, N. G., & Tolan, P. H. (1994). *What works in reducing adolescent violence: An empirical review of the field.* (Report #F-888). Boulder: University of Colorado, Center for the Study and Prevention of Violence.

Guerra, N. G., Huesmann, L. R., Tolan, P. H., Van Acker, R., & Eron, L. D. (1995). Stressful events and individual beliefs as correlates of economic disadvantage and aggression among urban children. *Journal of Consulting and Clinical Psychology, 63* (4), 518–528.

Haapasalo, J., & Tremblay, R. E. (1994). Physically aggressive boys from ages 6 to 12: Family background, parenting behavior, and prediction of delinquency. *Journal of Consulting and Clinical Psychology, 62* (5), 1044–1052.

Haj-Yahia, M. (1997). Predicting beliefs about wife beating among engaged Arab men in Israel. *Journal of Interpersonal Violence, 12* (4), 530–545.

Hamburg, M. A. (1998). Youth violence is a public health concern. In D. S. Elliot, B. A. Hamburg, & K. R. Williams (Eds.), *Violence in American schools: A new perspective* (pp. 31–54). New York: Cambridge University Press.

Hand, J. Z., & Sanchez, L. (2000). Badgering or bantering? Gender differences in experience of, and reactions to, sexual harassment among U.S. high school students. *Gender & Society, 14* (6), 718–746.

Harel, Y., Ellenbogen-Frankovits, S. Molcho, M., Abu-Asbah, K., & Habib, J. (2002). *Youth in Israel: Social well-being, health and risk behaviors from an international perspective* (in Hebrew). Jerusalem: Joint Distribution Committee.

Harel, Y., Kenny, D., & Rahav, G. (1997). *Youth in Israel: Social welfare, health and risk behaviors from international perspectives* (in Hebrew). Jerusalem: Joint Distribution Committee.

Hareven, A. (1998). *Retrospect and prospect: Full and equal citizenship?* Jerusalem: Sikkuy.

Hawkins, J. D., Catalano, R. F., Morrison, D., O'Donnell, J., Abbott, R., & Day, E. (1992). The Seattle Social Development Project: Effects of the first four years on protective factors and problem behaviors. In J. McCord & R. E. Tremblay (Eds.), *Preventing antisocial behavior: Interventions from birth through adolescence* (pp. 139–161). New York: Guilford Press.

Hays, K. (1998, April 26). Boy held in teacher's killing. *Detroit News & Free Press*, p. 5A.

Hellman, D. A., & Beaton, S. (1986). The pattern of violence in urban public schools: The influence of school and community. *Journal of Research in Crime and Delinquency, 23*, 102–127.

Herrenkohl, T. I., Chung, I., & Catalano, R. F. (2004). Review of research on the predictors of youth violence and school-based and community-based prevention approaches. In P. Allen-Mears & M. W. Fraser (Eds.), *Intervention with children and adolescents: An interdisciplinary perspective* (pp. 449–476). Boston: Pearson.

Hoffman, J. P., & Johnson, R. A. (2000). Multilevel influences on school disorder: A comment on Welsh, Green, and Jenkins. *Criminology, 38* (4), 1275–1288.

Hu, L., & Bentler, P. M. (1999). Cutoff criteria for fit indexes in covariance structure analysis: Conventional criteria versus new alternatives. *Structural Equation Modeling, 6*, 1–55.

Hyman, I. A. (1990). *Reading, writing, and the hickory stick.* Lexington, MA: Lexington Books.

Hyman, I. A., & McDowell, E. (1979). An overview. In I. A. Hyman and J. I. Wise (Eds.), *Corporal punishment in American education* (pp. 3–22). Philadelphia: Temple University Press.

Hyman, I. A., & Perone, D. C. (1998). The other side of school violence: Educator policies and practices that may contribute to student misbehavior. *Journal of School Psychology, 36*, 7–27.

Hyman, I. A., & Snook, P. A. (1999). *Dangerous schools: What we can do about the physical and emotional abuse of our children.* San Francisco: Jossey-Bass.

Hyman, I. A., & Snook, P. A. (2000). Dangerous schools and what you can do about them. *Phi Delta Kappan, 81*(7), 488–501.

Hyman, I. A., Stefkovich, J., & Taich, S. (2002). Paddling and pro-paddling polemics: Refuting nineteenth century's pedagogy. *Journal of Law and Education, 31* (1), 74–84.

Hyman, I. A., & Wise, J. I. (1979). *Corporal punishment in American schools.* Philadelphia: Temple University Press.

Hyman, I. A., Zelikoff, W., & Clarke, J. (1988). Psychological and physical abuse in schools: A paradigm for understanding posttraumatic stress disorder in children. *Journal of Traumatic Stress, 1*, 243–267.

Imbrogno, A. R. (2000). Corporal punishment in America's public schools and the U.N. Convention on the Rights of the Child: A case for nonratification. *Journal of Law and Education, 29* (2), 125–147.

Israel Central Bureau of Statistics. (2001). *Annual report 2001.* Jerusalem: Author.

Jackson, J. F. (1999). What are the real risk factors for African American children? *Phi Delta Kappan, 81* (4), 308–312.

Kann, L., Warren, C. W., Harris, W. A., Collins, J. L., Douglas, K. A., Collins, M. E., et al. (1995). Youth risk behavior surveillance: United States. *Morbidity and Mortality, 44* (ss-1), 1–55.

Kaufman, P., Chen, X., Choy, S. P., Peter, K., Ruddy, S. A., Miller, A. K., et al. (2001). *Indicators of school crime and safety: 2001.* U.S. Department of Education and Justice. NCES 2002–113/NCJ-190075. Washington, DC.

Kenny, D. A., Kashy, D. A., & Bolger, N. (1998). Data analysis in social psychology. In D. T. Gilbert, S. T. Fiske, & G. Lindzey (Eds.), *The handbook of social psychology* (4th ed., vol. 1, pp. 233–265). Boston: McGraw-Hill.

Khoury-Kassabri, M. (2002). *The relationship between school ecology and student victimization* (in Hebrew). Unpublished doctoral dissertation, The Hebrew University, Jerusalem.

Kikkawa, M. (1987). Teacher's opinions and treatments for bully/victim problems among students in junior and senior high schools: Results of a fact-finding survey. *Journal of Human Development, 23*, 25–40.

Kim, D. H., Kim, K. I., Park, Y. C., Zhang, L. D., Lu, M. K., & Li, D. G. (2000). Children's experience of violence in China and Korea: A transcultural study. *Child Abuse and Neglect, 24* (9), 1163–1173.

Kingery, P. M., Coggeshall, M. B., & Alford, A. A. (1998). Violence at school: Recent evidence from four national surveys. *Psychology in the Schools, 35* (3), 247–258.

Kingery, P. M., Coggeshall, M. B., & Alford, A. A. (1999). Weapon carrying by youth: Risk factors and prevention. *Education and Urban Society, 31* (3), 309–333.

Klipp, G. (2001). *Resallying quids: Resilience of queer youth in school.* Unpublished doctoral dissertation, University of Michigan, Ann Arbor.

Klonsky, M. (2002). How smaller schools prevent school violence. *Educational Leadership, 59* (5), 65–69.

Knight, G. P., Guthrie, I. K., Page, M. C., & Fabes, R. A. (2002). Emotional arousal and gender differences in aggression: A meta-analysis. *Aggressive behavior, 28*, 366–393.

Kodjo, C. M., Auinger, P., & Ryan, S. A. (2003). Demographic, intrinsic, and extrinsic factors associated with weapon carrying at school. *Archives of Pediatrics and Adolescent Medicine, 157* (1), 96–103.

Kodluboy, D. (1997). Gang-oriented interventions. In A. Goldstein (Ed.), *School violence intervention: A practical handbook* (pp. 189–214). New York: Guilford Press.

Kop, J. (1999). *Israel's social services 1999.* Jerusalem: Center for Social Studies in Israel.

Kupersmidt, J. B., Griesler, P. C., DeRosier, M. E., Patterson, C. J., & Davis, P. W. (1995). Childhood aggression and peer relations in the context of family and neighborhood factors. *Child Development, 66*, 360–375.

Landau, S. F. (1988). Violent crime and its relation to subjective social stress indicators: The case of Israel. *Aggressive Behavior, 14*, 337–362.

Landau, S. F. (1998). Crime, subjective stress and support indicators, and ethnic origin: The Israeli experience. *Justice Quarterly, 15* (2), 243–272.

Landau, S. F., & Beit-Hallachmi, B. (1983). Aggression in Israel: A socio-historical perspective. In A. P. Goldstein & M. Segall (Eds.), *Aggression in global perspective* (pp. 261–281). New York: Pergamon.

Laub, J. H., & Lauritsen, J. L. (1998). The interdependence of school violence with neighborhood and family conditions. In D. S. Elliot, B. A. Hamburg, & K. R. Williams (Eds.), *Violence in American schools: A new perspective* (pp. 127–155). New York: Cambridge University Press.

Lee, V. E. (2000). Using hierarchical linear modeling to study social contexts: The case of school effects. *Educational Psychologist, 35* (2), 125–141.

Lee, V. E., & Croninger, R. G. (1995). *The social organization of safe high schools.* Paper presented at the Goals 2000 Conference, Reauthorization of the Elementary and Secondary Education Act and the School-to-Work Opportunities Act, Palm Beach, FL.

Lee, V. E., Croninger, R. G., Linn, E., & Chen, X. (1996). The culture of sexual harassment in secondary schools. *American Educational Research Journal, 33* (2), 383–417.

Lewin, K. (1935). *Dynamic theory of personality: Selected papers.* New York: McGraw-Hill.

Limper, R. (2000). Cooperation between parents, teachers, and school boards to prevent bullying in education: An overview of work done in the Netherlands. *Aggressive Behavior, 26,* 125–134.

Lockwood, D. (1997). *Violence among middle school and high school students: An analysis of implications for prevention.* Washington, DC: U.S. Department of Justice, Office of Justice Programs, National Institute for Justice.

Loeber, R., & Stouthamer-Loeber, M. (1998). Juvenile aggression at home and at school. In D. S. Elliott, B. A. Hamburg, & K. R. Williams (Eds.), *Violence in American schools: A new perspective* (pp. 94–126). New York: Cambridge University Press.

Lorion, R. (1998). Exposure to urban violence: Contamination of the school environment. In D. S. Elliott, B. A. Hamburg, & K. R. Williams (Eds.), *Violence in American schools: A new perspective* (pp. 293–311). New York: Cambridge University Press.

Lowry, R., Sleet, D., Duncan, C., Powell, K., & Kolbe, L. (1995). Adolescents at risk for violence. *Educational Psychology Review, 7* (1), 7–39.

Maccoby, E. E. (1998). *The two sexes: Growing up apart, coming together.* Cambridge, MA: Harvard University Press.

Martin, S., Sadowski, L. S., Cotten, N. U., & McCarraher, D. R. (1996). Response of African-American adolescents in North Carolina to gun carrying by school mates. *Journal of School Health, 66,* 23–26.

May, D. C. (1999). Scared kids, unattached kids, or peer pressure: Why do students carry firearms to school? *Youth & Society, 31* (1), 100–127.

Mayer, M. J., & Leone, P. E. (1999). A structural analysis of school violence and disruption: Implications for creating safer schools. *Education & Treatment of Children, 22,* 333–356.

McEvoy, A., & Welker, R. (2000). Antisocial behavior, academic failure, and school climate: A critical review. *Journal of Emotional and Behavioral Disorders, 8* (3), 130–140.

McKeganey, N., & Norrie, J. (2000). Association between illegal drugs and weapon carrying in young people in Scotland: Schools' survey. *British Medical Journal, 320* (7240), 982–984.

Meier, K. J., Stewart, J., & England, R. E. (1989). *Race, class, and education: The politics of second generation discrimination.* Madison: University of Wisconsin Press.

Mercy, J. A., & Rosenberg, M. L. (1998). Preventing firearm violence in and around schools. In D. S. Elliott, B. A. Hamburg, & K. R. Williams (Eds.), *Violence in American schools: A new perspective* (pp. 159–187). New York: Cambridge University Press.

Meyer, H. A., Astor, R. A., & Behre, W. J. (2002) Teachers' reasoning about school violence: The role of gender and location. *Contemporary Educational Psychology, 27,* 499–528.

Meyer, H. A., Astor, R. A., & Behre, W. J. (in press). Teachers' reasoning about school fights: An expanded cognitive developmental domain approach. *Aggression and Violent Behavior.*

Molidor, C., & Tolman, R. M. (1998). Gender and contextual factors in adolescent dating violence. *Violence Against Women, 4* (2), 180–194.

Morrison, G. M., & Skiba, R. (2001). Predicting violence from school misbehavior: Promises and perils. *Psychology in the Schools, 38,* 173–184.

Mulvey, E. P., & Cauffman, E. (2001). The inherent limits of predicting school violence. *American Psychologist, 56,* 797–802.

Murnen, S. K., & Smolak, L. (2000). The experience of sexual harassment among grade-school students: Early socialization of female subordination? *Sex Roles, 43* (1–2), 1–17.

Nansel, T., Overpeck, M., Pilla, R., Ruan, W., Simons-Morton, B., & Scheidt, P. (2001). Bullying behaviors among U.S. youth: Prevalence and association with psychosocial adjustment. *JAMA: Journal of the American Medical Association, 285,* 2094–2100.

Nirel, R., & Saltzman, P. (1999). *The structure of the sample and sampling weights in the "Israel National Study of School Violence"* (in Hebrew). Jerusalem: Laboratory of Statistics, Hebrew University.

Noguera, P. A. (1995). Preventing and producing violence: A critical analysis of responses to school violence. *Harvard Educational Review, 65* (2), 189–212.

Olweus, D. (1991). Bully/victim problems among schoolchildren: Basic facts and effects of a school-based intervention problem. In D. J. Pepler & K. H. Rubin (Eds.), *The development and treatment of childhood aggression* (pp. 411–448). Hillsdale, NJ: Lawrence Erlbaum.

Olweus, D. (1993). *Bullying at school.* Cambridge, MA: Blackwell.

Olweus, D. (1999). Norway. In P. K. Smith, Y. Morita, J. Junger-Tas, D. Olweus, R. F. Catalano, & P. Slee (Eds.), *The nature of school bullying: A cross-national perspective* (pp. 28–48). London: Routledge.

Olweus, D., Limber, S., & Mihalic, S. F. (1999). *Blueprints for violence prevention, book nine: Bullying prevention program.* Boulder, CO: Center for the Study and Prevention of Violence.

Omer, H. (2000). *Rehabilitation of parental authority* (in Hebrew). Tel Aviv: Modan.

Orpinas, P., Murray, N., & Kelder, S. (1999). Parental influences on students' aggressive behaviors and weapon carrying. *Health Education & Behavior 26* (6), 774–787.

Owens, L., & MacMullin, C. (1995). Gender differences in aggression in children and adolescents in South Australian schools. *International Journal of Adolescence and Youth, 6,* 21–35.

Owens, L., Slee, P., & Shute, R. (2000). "It hurts a hell of a lot . . .": The effects of indirect aggression on teenage girls. *School Psychology International, 21,* 359–376.

Paetsch, J. J., & Bertrand, L. D. (1999). Victimization and delinquency among Canadian youth. *Adolescence, 34* (134), 351–367.

Page, R. M. (1997). Helping adolescents avoid date rape: The role of secondary education. *High School Journal, 80,* 75–80.

Page, R. M., & Hammermeister, J. (1997). Weapon-carrying and youth violence. *Adolescence, 32* (127), 505–513.

Parks, C. (1995). Gang behavior in the schools: Reality or myth? *Educational Psychology Review, 7,* 41–68.

Pellegrini, A. D. (2001). A longitudinal study of heterosexual relationships, aggression, and sexual harassment during the transition from primary school through middle school. *Applied Developmental Psychology, 22,* 119–133.

Pellegrini, A. D., & Bartini, M. (2000). A longitudinal study of bullying, victimization, and peer affiliation during the transition from primary school to middle school. *American Educational Research Journal, 37,* 699–725.

Pellegrini, A. D., & Long, J. D. (2002). A longitudinal study of bullying, dominance, and victimization during the transition from primary school through secondary school. *British Journal of Developmental Psychology, 20,* 259–280.

Rapp-Paglicci, L. A., Roberts, A., & Wodarski, J. (Eds.). (2002). *Handbook of violence.* New York: Wiley.

Reinke, W. M., & Herman, K. C. (2002). Creating school environments that deter antisocial behaviors in youth. *Psychology in Schools, 39* (5), 549–559.

Rigby, K. (1996). *Bullying in schools: And what to do about it.* London: Jessica Kingsley.

Rigby, K., & Slee, P. (1999). Suicidal ideation among adolescent school children, involvement in bully-victim problems, and perceived social support. *Suicide and Life Threatening Behavior, 29,* 119–130.

Rose, L., & Gallup, A. (2000). The 32nd annual Phi Delta Kappa/Gallup poll of the public's attitudes toward the public schools. *Phi Delta Kappan, 82,* 41–66.

Rosenblatt, J. A., & Furlong, M. J. (1997). Assessing the reliability and validity of student self-reports of campus violence. *Journal of Youth and Adolescence, 26* (2), 187–202.

Sabba, L. (2003). "Saving the rod" by court order: Reflections following legal resolution. In M. Hovav, L. Sabba, & M. Amir (Eds.). *Trends in criminology: Theory, policy and application* (pp. 425–462). Jerusalem: Criminology Institute, Faculty of Law, The Hebrew University of Jerusalem.

Satorra, A., & Bentler, P. M. (1994). Corrections to test statistics and standard errors in covariance structure analysis. In A. von Eye & C. C. Clogg (Eds.), *Latent variable analysis: Applications to developmental research* (pp. 399–419). Newbury Park: Sage.

Satorra, A., & Bentler, P. M. (1999). A scaled difference chi-square test statistic for moment structure analysis (UCLA Statistics Series No. 260). Los Angeles: UCLA.

Schafer, M., & Smith, P. K. (1996). Teachers' perceptions of play fighting and real fighting in primary school. *Educational Research, 38,* 173–181.

Schreiber-Dill, V., & Haberman, M. (1995). Building a gentler school. *Educational Leadership, 52* (5), 69–72.

Shakeshaft, C., & Cohan, A. (1995). Sexual abuse of students by school personnel. *Phi Delta Kappan, 76* (7), 513–520.

Sharp, S., & Smith, P. K. (Eds.). (1994). *Tackling bullying in your school.* London: Routledge.

Shaw, S. R., & Braden, J. P. (1990). Race and gender bias in the administration of corporal punishment. *School Psychology Review, 19,* 378–383.

Sherer, M. (1991). Peer group norms among Jewish and Arab juveniles in Israel. *Criminal Justice and Behavior, 18,* 267–286.

Simon, T. R., Crosby, A. E., & Dahlberg, L. L. (1999). Students who carry weapons to high school. *Journal of Adolescent Health, 24* (5), 340–348.

Slaby, R. G., Barham, J. E., Eron, L. D., & Wilcox, B. L. (1994). Policy recommendations: Prevention and treatment of youth violence. In L. D. Eron, J. H. Gentry, & P. Schlegel (Eds.), *Reason to hope: A psychosocial perspective on violence and youth* (pp. 447–456). Washington, DC: American Psychological Association.

Smith, P. K. (Ed.). (2003). *Violence in schools: The response in Europe.* London: Routledge Falmer.

Smith, P. K., Cowie, H., Olafsson, R. F., & Liefooghe, A. P. (2002). Definitions of bullying: A comparison of terms used, and age and gender differences, in a fourteen-country international comparison, *Child Development, 73* (4), 1119–1133.

Smith, P. K., Madsen, K. C., & Moody, J. C. (1999). What causes the age decline in reports of being bullied at school? Towards a developmental analysis of risks of being bullied. *Educational Research, 41* (3), 267–285.

Smith, P. K., Morita, Y., Junger-Tas, J., Olweus, D., Catalano, R. F., & Slee, P. (1999). *The nature of school bullying: A cross-national perspective.* New York: Routledge.

Smith, P. K., & Sharp, S. (1994). The problem of school bullying. In P. K. Smith & S. Sharp (Eds.), *School bullying: Insights and perspectives* (pp. 1–19). London: Routledge.

Soriano, M., Soriano, F., & Jimenez, E. (1994). School violence among culturally diverse populations: Sociocultural and institutional consideration. *School Psychology Review, 23* (2), 216–235.

Stacy, A. W., Bentler, P. M., & Flay, B. R. (1994). Attitudes and health behavior in diverse populations: Drunk driving, alcohol use, binge-eating, marijuana use, and cigarette use. *Health Psychology, 13* (1), 73–85.

Stein, N. (1995). Sexual harassment in school: The public performance of gendered violence. *Harvard Educational Review, 65* (2), 145–162.

Stein, N., Marshall, N., & Tropp, L. (1993). *Secrets in public: Sexual harassment in our schools. A report on the results of the* Seventeen *magazine survey.* Wellesley, MA: Wellesley College Center for Research on Women.

Stephens, R. D. (1994). Planning for safer and better schools: School violence prevention and intervention strategies. *School Psychology Review, 23* (2), 204–215.

Sullivan, K. (2000). *The anti-bullying handbook.* New York: Oxford University Press.

Thompkins, D. E. (2000). School violence: Gangs and a culture of fear. *Annals of the American Academy of Political and Social Science, 567,* 54–71.

Tolan, P. H., Guerra, N. G., & Kendall, P. C. (1995). A developmental-ecological perspective on antisocial behavior in children and adolescents: Toward a unified risk and intervention framework. *Journal of Consulting and Clinical Psychology, 63* (4), 579–584.

Turiel, E. (1987). Potential relationships between the development of social reasoning and childhood aggression. In D. H. Crowell, I. M. Evens, & C. R. O'Donnell (Eds.), *Childhood aggression and violence: Sources of influence, prevention and control* (pp. 95–114). New York: Plenum Press.

Turiel, E. (1998). The development of morality. In W. Damon (Series Ed.) & N. Eisenberg (Vol. Ed.), *Handbook of child psychology: Social, emotional, and personality development* (5th ed., Vol. 3, pp. 863–932). New York: Wiley.

Voss, L. D., & Mulligan, J. (2000). Bullying in school: Are short pupils at risk? Questionnaire study in a cohort. *British Medical Journal, 320* (7235), 612–613.

Vossekuil, B., Reddy, M., Fein, R., Borum, R., & Modzeleski, W. (2000). *U.S.S.S. Safe School Initiative: An interim report on the prevention of targeted violence in schools.* Washington, DC: U.S. Secret Service, National Threat Assessment Center.

Walker, H. M., & Gresham, F. M. (1997). Making schools safer and violence-free. *Intervention in School and Clinic, 32,* 199–204.

Warner, B. S., Weist, M. D., & Krulak, A. (1999). Risk factors for school violence. *Urban Education, 34* (1), 52–68.

Watts, M. W. (1998). Introduction. In M. W. Watts (Ed.), *Cross-cultural perspective on youth and violence* (pp. 55–63). London: JAI Press.

Welsh, W. N. (2000). The effects of school climate on school disorder. *Annals of the American Academy of Political and Social Science, 567,* 88–107.

Welsh, W. N., Greene, J. R., & Jenkins, P. H. (1999). School disorder: The influence of individual, institutional and community factors. *Criminology, 37* (1), 73–115.

Whitney, I., & Smith, P. K. (1993). A survey of the nature and extent of bullying in junior/middle and secondary schools. *Educational Research, 35* (1), 3–25.

Wicker, A. W. (1968). Undermanning, performances, and students' subjective experiences in behavior settings of large and small high schools. *Journal of Personality and Social Psychology, 10* (3), 255–261.

Wiist, W. H., Jackson, R. H., & Jackson, K. W. (1996). Peer and community leader education to prevent youth violence. *American Journal of Preventive Medicine, 12,* 56–64.

Wilcox, P., & Clayton, R. R. (2001). A multilevel analysis of school-based weapon possession. *Justice Quarterly, 18* (3), 509–541.

Williams, G. J. (1979). Social sanctions for violence against children: Historical perspectives. In I. E. Hyman & J. I. Wise (Eds.), *Corporal punishment in American education* (pp. 25–40). Philadelphia: Temple University Press.

Wilson, H. (1980). Parental supervision: A neglected aspect of delinquency. *British Journal of Criminology, 20,* 203–235.

Wishnietsky, D. H. (1991). Reported and unreported teacher-student sexual harassment. *Journal of Educational Research, 84* (3), 164–169.

Youssef, R., Attia, M., & Kamel, M. (1998). Children experiencing violence II: Prevalence and determinants of corporal punishment in schools. *Child Abuse & Neglect, 22,* 975–985.

Zeira, A., Astor, R. A., & Benbenishty, R. (2002). Sexual harassment in Jewish and Arab public schools in Israel. *Child Abuse & Neglect, 26,* 149–166.

Index